GRAND OLD PARTY

Political Structure in the Gilded Age,

1880-1896

A politician should be like a football coach: smart enough to understand the game but not smart enough to lose interest.

Eugene McCarthy, 1968

Inasmuch as it is possible for us to obtain more and better information about things here on earth, our knowledge of them has the advantage over the philosophy which contemplates the things that are divine. So far as in us lies, we will not leave out any one of them, be it never so mean; for though there are animals which have no attractiveness for the senses, yet for the eye of science, for the student who is naturally of a philosophic spirit and can discern the causes of things, Nature which fashioned them provides joys which cannot be measured. Wherefore we must not betake ourselves to the consideration of the meaner animals with a bad grace, as though we were children; since in all natural things there is somewhat of the marvellous. We ought not to hesitate nor to be abashed, but boldly to enter upon our researches concerning animals of every sort and kind, knowing that in not one of them is Nature or Beauty lacking.

Aristotle, *De Partibus Animalium*, I,v

GRAND
OLD
PARTY

Political Structure
in the Gilded Age
1880-1896

ROBERT D. MARCUS, *1936-*

NEW YORK : OXFORD UNIVERSITY PRESS : 1971

FOR GRANIA

who saved me from

the greatest poverty

Preface

Under the impact of large-scale industrialism, organizations national in scope and bureaucratic in management increasingly dominated American life in the post-Civil War era. Samuel P. Hays has described the "evolution from smaller to larger and larger systems, accompanied by a persistent upward flow of the location of decision making" that marked the late nineteenth and early twentieth centuries. Robert H. Wiebe has noted the breakdown of "island communities" and the growth of "bureaucratic thought." The present study began in a search for these trends in national party organization. I chose the Republicans for several reasons. They were the more successful party; material on them was more readily available; their story led to Mark Hanna's legendary feats in 1896. The presidential election seemed the logical place to look for unambiguous signs of national direction and control. If no central organs or groups could dominate this process, it was hard to imagine where the American political system of the nineteenth century would overcome the fragmentation built into federalism and long institutionalized in Congress. Thus, in examining the evolution of instruments of national control in the Republican party, I expected my main theme to be the rise of the national committee to a position of power over the state organizations, at least in presidential campaigns. My story, I thought, would be one of emerging bureaucracy, organization, and system. Henry Adams had described the politics of the Gilded Age as "poor in purpose and barren in results." Behind the apparent sterility, however, might lurk important developments in party organization to forge the political instruments of the twentieth-century Age of Reform. It was this evolution that I sought—and failed to find.

Instead of increasing centralization and steady growth in power of the national committee organs, I found decentralization, an amazing lack of continuity between campaigns, weak national administrations, and even weaker national committees. Rather than a developing hierarchy of power in the party, I discovered a fundamental contradiction between state power and success in nominating a President. In place of increasing professionalism, political adventurers—businessmen without firm state party bases—invariably beat the pros in presidential politics. There was no evolution from Garfield's humiliations of 1880 to Hanna's dominance in 1896, but a quite sudden revolution between the campaigns of 1892 and 1896. This was not the product of managers and organizers or of any superhuman genius on the part of Mark Hanna, but of the emergence of a Republican majority and the mass conversion of large corporations to Republicanism as a result of the triumph of silver in the Democratic party.

My results raised many more questions than they answered. Indeed, since politics is usually such a small part of the life of a people, no study of political organization could answer the basic questions about the era. Nevertheless, an overview of the practice of politics in the Gilded Age seemed a useful introduction to this study of national coalition formation in one party. And I could not resist concluding with some speculation on the role of presidential elections in the American political system and on the implications of the result of 1896 for twentieth-century politics. More interesting questions about the great gulf between the way Americans view parties and the way these organizations actually operate must be the subject for future study.

Many people contributed to this book: some with useful suggestions or acute criticism, others with aid and encouragement at crucial moments. My thanks to Ruth Schwartz Cowan, Ari Hoogenboom, Gloria and Jackson Turner Main, Walter T. K. Nugent, Martin Ridge, Jerome Sternstein, Grania Bolton Thistlethwaite, David F. Trask, Clarence L. Ver Steeg, and Allen Weinstein. Special thanks to Charles Cohen who led me over the hurdles of work and life at the magnificent but undercapitalized New York Public Library. Deborah Zwecher improved the manuscript considerably in her capacity as copy editor. My gratitude to the Honorable William Henry Harrison for permission to examine the papers of his father, Russell B. Harrison. Although I have not quoted from this collection, it provided valuable background information and is occasionally cited in the footnotes. The librarians who helped me and made the work pleasant are too many to name, but the staffs of the Library of Congress Stack and Reader Service and Manuscript Room and the unfailingly helpful people of the New York Public Library deserve special accolades.

The Department of History of Northwestern University gave me some of their own research funds to tide me over my first summer's work on this project, a gesture which seems more and more worthy of notice the longer I live in the academic world. The Inland Steel-Ryerson Foundation financed a year of research. The Penrose Fund of the

American Philosophical Society gave me two grants to visit libraries. The Graduate School of the State University of New York at Stony Brook and the State University of New York Research Foundation provided generous and indispensable financing. Nor can I forget the generosity of Mr. and Mrs. Leonard R. Marcus.

My deepest gratitude, however, is reserved for two superb scholars who have left their mark on every good page of this book. Robert H. Wiebe was a model dissertation supervisor, a penetrating critic of my arguments at every stage of the work, and a friend and support throughout. He set me on the road toward becoming a historian. David Burner read the manuscript over and over, making shrewd suggestions, uncoiling tangled sentences, and performing major surgery on my involuted prose. As E. B. White once wrote, it is not often that someone comes along who is a true friend and a good writer. David is both.

R. M.
Stony Brook, New York
April 1970

Contents

GRAND OLD PARTY

Political Structure in the Gilded Age,

1880-1896

I

〜

National Party Structure in the Gilded Age

American political parties are what Maurice Duverger calls "cadre parties." They have no official roster of supporters. There are no dues to pay or cards to carry and no rigid membership requirements. Before the twentieth century, the parties had no definable legal status, nor was there any official listing of who had a right to participate in their nominating procedures. They were simply, as Lord Bryce observed, "extra-legal groupings of men." The concept of party membership had "no meaning at all" in the American system, Duverger correctly notes. Rather one could only enumerate in the order of their importance the political roles men played: "the militants who are part of the 'machine,' the supporters who reinforce it during election campaigns, the people who take part in 'primaries,' and the citizens who vote for the party's candidates at election." The politician, not the party member, had the central role.[1]

In the Gilded Age, the men we would call professional politicians did not form a distinct interest group, as reformers then and historians since have often supposed.

The professional politician did not necessarily earn his living directly from politics (although there were many who did). He was simply the man from whatever walk of life who made a continuous identification between his own political interests and that of an ongoing organization, which in American politics has always meant a state or local organization, a "machine."

These political leaders included a large number of businessmen. The great political boss of Michigan, Zachariah Chandler, was a wealthy lumber merchant; Pennsylvania's Simon Cameron a banker and railroad director; and New Yorker Tom Platt a banker, president of a lumber company, and director of an express company. Theodore Roosevelt conceded that Boss Platt's political lieutenants throughout New York State included "the leading and substantial citizens"—bankers, railroad and traction executives, and manufacturers. Most railroad company presidents engaged actively in politics in this era; and in fields facing public regulation, such as banking and insurance, some executives like John A. McCall, insurance company president and prominent Democrat, or Chauncey Depew, railroad counsel and important Republican, held positions that depended on their political activities.[2]

The parties also included the actors kept alive in the textbooks: the letter carriers and veterans, the customshouse tide waiters and the ward heelers, the "shoulder-hitters" and thugs, as well as the ambitious lawyers, the butchers, the barbers, and the saloon keepers. Politics was a national pastime to a far greater degree than it would be in the twentieth century, and the personnel of the parties—although one could find spectacular local exceptions—constituted a fair cross-section of the population. The same social class would not provide both letter carriers and Senators, but the parties, in sharp contrast

4

to twentieth-century experience, reached all the way across the social spectrum.

When the politician, however wide or narrow his gaze, viewed his electorate, what he counted on most was an overwhelming party regularity. From the seventies until 1889, national elections were close, voters tended to vote straight tickets—supporting the party generally, not just particular candidates—and voting turnout was very high. Walter Dean Burnham in a careful statistical study found that between 1876 and 1896, 78.5 per cent of the eligible voters turned out for presidential elections and 62.8 per cent for off-year elections, figures remarkably high by twentieth-century standards.[3] He also found that about two-thirds of the voters habitually voted straight tickets, with about an additional 10 per cent voting with a relatively high frequency for one party's candidates. Moreover, this electorate constituted a genuine national cross-section: poor people, rural Americans, and (with numerous and shocking local exceptions) Negroes voted along with their more affluent and socially favored compeers in a way that is no longer typical of the American electorate.[4]

The parties of the Gilded Age continued the political system that had matured before the Civil War. Political fervor remained high for a forty-year period after the log cabin campaign of 1840: campaigns were major events offering entertainment, information, and emotional satisfaction. Then in the 1880s politicians noted a slackening of enthusiasm as "the brass band, the red light, and the mass meeting seemed suddenly to have lost their power." This mood deepened until 1892, when politicians complained that it was "difficult to tell from the manners of the people that this [was] a presidential campaign." The decline in political enthusiasm and participation gave way momentarily to a new and intense interest in the battle of the standards, but in the twentieth century American voters have failed to show the level of interest in political contests which they manifested in the past.[5]

The closeness of elections, high turnout, and party regularity of the period seemed to be mutually reinforcing phenomena. The voters who identified with a party were —then as now—those who cared enough about the election to vote, while the expectation that an election will be close spurred both the voter to make his franchise count and the political organization to get to the polls everyone likely to vote its way. Close elections also supported party regularity by raising the cost of expressing one's dissatisfaction with the party above what most voters were willing to pay. When Tom Platt during the depression year of 1894 hoped to get New York Democrats to vote for a Republican congressional candidate, he instructed his canvassers to remind voters that they were not threatening the Democratic majority in Congress, but only serving "a warning to the Democrats that they must go slow in the passage for laws that interfere with industry." In short, Platt did not think that voters ordinarily were willing to sacrifice a possible party victory to express their dissident opinions.[6]

These three factors—close party balances, high turnout, and party regularity—gave a particular form to presidential contests of the Gilded Age. In the twentieth century, these elections have been marked by periodic "surges" of voter participation—the result of a charismatic and prominent candidate who could bring out the potential voters not in the habit of exercising their franchise, not bound by party ties, and needed to break the stranglehold of a majority party. The election of Dwight Eisenhower in 1952 and 1956 is, of course, the best example. Gilded Age presidential contests did not and indeed could not show such a trend. Since most eligible people voted, the possibility of a radical surge of otherwise non-participatory citizens was not the usual expectation and statistics clearly indicate that it did not occur. Also, the "independent" voters who might be swayed by an especially attractive candidate were not a huge statistical quantity as at present, but a small number of usually well-to-do and college-educated men whose role as publicists far outshadowed their size as a voting group. Moreover, neither party felt the need for a presidential candidate with the independent and individual strength of the charismatic leader when they could very well hope to win with some regular party member so long as he was "available." [7]

After 1880, when Republican politicians began to worry about the waning of the old-time enthusiasm of the Civil War era, the party turned for the first time to a "prominent" rather than an "available" leader. James G. Blaine, with a long, colorful, and controversial national record, was a man whom we would call charismatic and whom contemporaries described as "magnetic." He had a personal following, especially among Irish nationalists, in addition to normal Republican support, and he seemed capable of re-arousing the traditional dedication among party workers.

Modern students of voting behavior have discovered that Blaine's 1884 campaign was reasonably successful in retrieving significant losses suffered two years previously in the off-year elections. But his contemporaries saw only the more obvious results: that the new strategy of appealing to voters not normally Republican led to dangerous incidents upsetting the loyalties of both new and old Republicans, and most of all that Blaine had been the first unsuccessful Republican candidate since Frémont in 1856. And as Blaine's magnetism had seemed to fail in 1884, so did Grover Cleveland's issue-oriented tariff campaign four years later. These incidents of the eighties slowed the tendency to put prominence over party, postponing for several years longer the era of the charismatic, issue-oriented national leader that Theodore Roosevelt was to inaugurate.[8]

There is a more sophisticated explanation of Blaine's and Cleveland's failure to inaugurate the era of presidential leadership and charisma. For the nineteenth-century analogue to the "surge" election was what we might call the "decline" election. One could expect the normal party vote for virtually any reasonable candidate. But someone of national prominence was liable to have made a few enemies in his political career. He was unlikely to gain opposition votes in an age of straight-ticket voting, there were few independent surge votes to pick up, and he might keep a few of the otherwise faithful who disliked his past record away from the polls. This in fact was the only kind of swing election the era saw: 1872, when Democrats stayed home rather than vote for Greeley; and probably 1892, when a few hundred thousand Republicans must have neglected to support Benjamin Harrison, who as President had committed enough sins of omission or commission to alienate many party members. Blaine in 1884 probably suffered this "decline" effect among Republicans, but apparently compensated for it by picking up normally Democratic support from Irish-Americans. Throughout the period, Presidents found it hard to win a second term for just this reason: they had become too prominent. The unpopular Lincoln had had to create a new "Union" party and needed the good fortune of major military victories to win re-election; Grant had been equally unpopular and had had to withstand a party split, triumphing only because the opposition party split even more completely. For the remainder of the era no other

8

leader could do it until the fundamental facts of voting behavior had changed.[9]

The leaders of the Gilded Age have long been excoriated for their colorlessness and their failure to confront significant issues. But this accusation—which is wholly just—must be understood in terms of the voting public the politicians represented. Recent students of voting behavior have demonstrated that the questions that voters of the Gilded Age found salient revolved almost exclusively about local cultural conflicts: native versus immigrant, Protestant versus Catholic, evangelical temperance-oriented church groups versus liturgical tradition-oriented Lutherans. National politicians avoided these explosive cultural issues, capitalized on immediate circumstances such as economic downturns, and depended on close party organization. Blaine's perennial problem as a presidential candidate was his facility for reflecting the deep-seated cultural issues, especially the overriding one of anti-Catholic prejudice among the Protestant electorate. His early advocacy of national campaigns based on the tariff was not—as many have interpreted it—an effort to rearrange the politics of the age, but an attempt to move personally to a more neutral national position.[10]

The national political results of the era show clearly that anything which detracted from the overt appeal of partisanship, such as issues or personalities, brought a decline in support. Even the third parties, the era's characteristic expression of political dissatisfaction, bear this out. They not only withheld votes from the major parties, their presence actually was a sign of shrinking political participation. They flourished in off-year elections when fewer voters turned out; in the two presidential years of the Gilded Age in which third-party movements were serious forces, 1872 and 1892, voting turnout dipped significantly. The third-party issues of reform and economic regulation by which twentieth-century historians have judged the era apparently frightened and confused the electorate of the Gilded Age, who probably were either baffled into political impotence or sent scurrying back into the comfortable and familiar world of the old parties.[11]

The major parties rapidly moved into a modern personality and issue-oriented style in the twentieth century. But the world in which McKinley could easily win re-election and in which Teddy Roosevelt became so outstanding a national leader that he dared create a party in his own image, was one in which the electorate had wholly changed: the Republicans were the clear majority party, voter turnout had mysteriously shrunk, and "insurgency" became a major political style. It was, in Burnham's image, a newly shaped political universe, stressing well-defined issues, much independent voting, active national leadership, and the confinement of the national political family to those with a stake in society. This last came about in part by systematic exclusion, as in the case of the Negro, and in part by the elaboration of electoral machinery that made the political system more accessible to, and more controlled by, educated issue-oriented elites, and also better buffered against the vagaries of a lower class that—under the new dispensation—became increasingly depoliticized.[12]

II

The late nineteenth century was preoccupied, in Robert Wiebe's phrase, with a "search for order." Men grasped for elements of predictability and continuity amid furious social and physical change. Politics was one area where men sought a link with the past. This theme was especially prominent in the seventies and eighties when the events of the Civil War and Reconstruction continued to provide the main topics of national debate. These issues, in stabilizing political loyalties by keeping eyes focused on a past full of familiar friends and enemies, fulfilled some of the need for order, even if this psychological advantage came at the cost of any meaningful attempt to control the world of early industrialism.

The men actively engaged in party politics welcomed and encouraged the electorate's disposition to re-live and relieve the traumas of the sixties: it helped them maintain their own order in the world of politics by keeping the behavior of voters generally predictable. Politicians could usually tell how various groups would vote. They talked, as politicians usually do, about the "Germans" or the "wheat farmers" or the "wool-growing counties." They knew roughly where there were Democrats and where Republicans. They could predict with considerable accuracy sure victories, certain defeats, and which contests would be close and require attention. This was not because they possessed insight superior to that of the politicians of other eras, but because of three related factors: the predictable party voting of the electorate, the party structure which provided them with a range and level of information that the modern politician with all his computers and survey data clearly does not have, and the forms of political indoctrination to which their electorate was exposed.

Although the men of the nineteenth century knew about sampling the close counties where minor changes would mirror what a larger voting public was doing, it was not the main prop of their information structure. Instead they relied on virtually total polling. When they wanted information about the "condition" of an electorate, in some cases over as large an area as an entire state, they got it through an attempt at a full poll of the state. The state committee chairman would request the information from his county chairmen, who would enlist all available workers to visit every voter. These workers included the postmasters in the little villages, the editors of the party paper—and rare was the small town outside the South without its Republican and its Democratic newspapers—every federal official wherever he held a post, as well as men engaged in work for the state, county, or town governments, and any of a number of businesses (street cars, railroads, banks, utilities) having extensive dealings with these governments. In short, with politics a hobby to hundreds of thousands and a livelihood or part of one to hundreds of thousands more, there was usually enough labor to conduct a full survey.[13]

The results were impressive. The "inside polls"—those for party use, not for scare tactics—often were amazingly accurate. Politicians complained that 1892 was a particularly hard year to tell in advance how the "silent vote" tended. Yet the Indiana Democratic poll showed a state-wide margin of 6000 votes against an actual victory by 6482 votes. Similarly, the chairman of the Republican state committee of Maine figured a 12,000 vote victory against a final margin of 12,531 votes. Not all polls were so accurate, but they suggest the capability of the politicians to get accurate information when they required it.[14]

Politicians calculated their chances by handfuls of votes. They pinpointed the areas where a few votes would make the difference, and sought means to gain them. Their principal method was to stir up "enthusiasm" to bring their potential voters to the polls, or, less frequently, to demoralize the opposition into staying home. They knew what students of voting behavior have since confirmed, that campaigns rarely change voters' minds, that "a candidate's major resources should go into getting out his supporters and latent supporters and only peripherally attempting to convert the opposition." Only in very special circumstances when voter allegiances seemed to be shifting did they actually expect to convert waverers.[15]

Their other mainstay in making up votes which their polls told them were lacking was a set of hoary but not hallowed methods, which included buying up purchasable voters, intimidating fearful ones into staying away from the polls, voting "repeaters," stuffing ballot boxes, falsifying returns, and creating imaginary voters on the rolls and producing them from out of town on election day. Some of these techniques, such as intimidation and repeating, were apparently most common in the cities; others, such as outright vote-buying, seem to have been practiced most often in the small towns and rural areas.[16]

There is far too much evidence to dismiss these techniques as folklore, and sensible and successful politicians were too frank about their use to discount them as factors in overall results. Surely many an election on every level was determined by who was in the best position for perpetrating frauds. One source of political stability must have been the built-in advantage a majority party had in any given area in being able to control the election machinery, or often simply the balance of physical force at a polling place. Its importance in the South was too overwhelming to question. But in many northern localities it was crucial as well, and "election-day expenses and operations" were a large item in the party managers' organization and expenditures.

Corruption was a real factor in political calculations. Nevertheless two major qualifications must be entered to place this force into a proper perspective. As charges and counter-charges during each campaign bear witness, both parties practiced it, so that in national politics over the long run much of the impact must have canceled out. And most important of all, the widespread fraud in this era must be understood as far more a product than a cause of the close elections. No one would pay as much as $15 per vote (as Indiana politicians did in 1888) in a runaway contest. Only because the parties were so closely balanced did chicanery have this importance in the calculations of the professionals. Historians today tend to underestimate this factor in response to the fantastic overestimation of it by the Progressives, but an image of clean politics in the Gilded Age would be much like Sophocles's *Philoctetes* without the wound.[17]

The electorate itself helped mightily in the politicians' efforts to keep track of it. Crucial to party regularity in the era's voting patterns was the delimited body of political information available to most of the electorate. Charles Sellers has argued that the flow of political information in the ante-bellum period was probably greater than at present, even if far less varied.[18] This appears true of the post-Civil War period as well. Rather than a mass of relatively independent media in competition for the attention of voters, most political information came in the direct party form: newspapers were party newspapers, and political conversations, which were clearly innumerable, were among committed party members. In short, the party in each area had a far larger degree of control of the political information flow than at present, and this in turn reinforced party loyalty.

Survey data has confirmed that voters without a clear party commitment are more easily swayed by propaganda during a campaign than those who are more party-oriented.[19] In the nineteenth century few people would be greatly influenced by outside, independent sources of political information. This naturally discouraged the production of such material. The era sported independent political journalism of a high order in periodicals such as *Harper's Weekly* and *The Nation,* but their clientele was extremely restricted and their indirect political influence through that small but select readership seems also to have been slight. The world of the magazines was the world of sensibility which, as cultural historians have repeatedly observed, was ruled by women in the late nineteenth century. Roscoe Conkling scored a direct hit when he stigmatized George William Curtis, the editor of *Harper's Weekly* and a leading civil service reformer, as a "man-milliner." Men, the politicians shouted, had party labels. The caustic Kansas Republican Senator, John J. Ingalls, berated the "new school of political philosophers who announce that nonpartisanship is the panacea for all the evils that afflict the Republican party" as "the neuter gender not popular either in nature or society." They were "a third sex." [20]

Politics, the Gilded Age believed, was masculine, and culture feminine. Men got their information from the stump speech, the party paper, and the smoke-filled tavern and meeting room, while women read magazines and novels and attended lectures and sermons. Judging from their rhetoric, practical politicians worked hard to maintain the artificial separation between these two realms. They attacked political independence with its attendant interest in civil service, women's rights, prohibition, and general efforts to raise the tone of politics, with a vehemence that suggests they knew their real enemy. Politics was that generation's moral equivalent of war, and politicians did not welcome a middle ground between friend and foe. The party faithful were inured against enemy propaganda, but politicians knew from experience that an independent appeal could be seductive. In 1884, for example, an Iowa Republican reported to a party leader on the "Edmunds feeling . . . at Stanwood," caused, he explained, by *The Nation,* "which has a small circulation there." Politicians rejoiced that the audience for independent political attitudes remained small and its influence limited either by standards of literacy or by the official cultural dichotomy reinforced by the ridicule of politicians. Thus did these small men make their contribution to the great bifurcation between the masculine life of business and politics and the feminine genteel culture of the age.[21]

Everything about this picture: the party regularity, the well-coordinated information structure of both parties, and the general party control of political information started to fade in the late eighties as voting habits began to shift in one of those mysterious cycles which have come once a generation throughout the history of the republic.[22] Politicians worried all during the eighties over slackening enthusiasm and the weakening of old means of campaigning. They experimented unsuccessfully with new forms of political organization designed to appeal to more genteel citizens. They tried one makeshift after another to catch the changing moods of restless workingmen and immigrants. As the decade advanced the old moorings began to slip everywhere. The rise of the Knights of Labor, the Haymarket affair, and Henry George's strong showing in the New York mayoralty race of 1886 sent tremors throughout middle-class America. Agricultural depression shook the countryside. People expressed their fear of the "trusts," unhappiness over the railroads rose to a crescendo, and a new concern over the dangers of unlimited immigration settled upon the land. Even the Negroes, the most loyal of Republican groups, manifested discontent by forming a short-lived "Afro-American National League" hoping to organize the entire black community independent of the Republican party.[23]

The off-year election of 1889 showed that this discontent had reached the parties, as long-held voting patterns gave way, especially in the Midwest, revealing a significant trend away from the Republican party.[24] In the cycle of fluctuation into which the parties plunged thereafter, the politician found himself no longer certain of his electorate. The degree of predictability had abruptly shrunk. Previously only a limited part of the electorate had eluded the politicians' estimates. Workingmen in times of economic hardship and restive Irish voters in periods of intense agitation of the "Irish question" in the British Isles were the outstanding examples. Other groups, such as the harder-pressed farmers, had gone through various third-party romances, but in most cases this had been a measurable quantity in political calculations and Republican party managers could closely gauge the size of such movements and the probabilities of arranging fusions with them or avoiding fusions with the Democrats. But after 1889 politicians were never sure of their votes. The congressional election of 1890 showed a massive defection from the Republicans, a revitalization of the Democratic party, and the growth of the Populists. On the other hand, four years later, the Republicans scored the greatest congressional victory in their party's history. The changeability of the electorate became as much a byword among politicians as its predictability had been years before. The most astute politicians shared the general feeling of crisis that so clearly marked the nineties.[25]

The parties' control of the flow of political information was seriously diminished as well. Suddenly a spate of utopian and muckraking books appeared and commanded wide audiences. William Allen White recalled years later the "tremendous thrill" of "the books from the late Eighties and early Nineties" that broke down the conservatism of his upbringing. The most influential of these, and the one most indicative of their place in the political changes of the nineties, was Edward Bellamy's *Looking Backward, 2000–1887*, published in 1888. The first and most successful of some fifty utopias committed to paper in the few years after its publication, this pleasant—if somewhat static—utopian romance not only sold half a million copies, it also gave rise to a network of Nationalist clubs which Bellamy and many of his supporters hoped would become "a party aiming at a national control of industry with its resulting social changes." [26]

That never happened, but many erstwhile Nationalists found their way into the People's party and then into various socialist or progressive movements in the ensuing years. An incipient American socialist movement which, Howard H. Quint has argued, "owed more for its inspiration to Edward Bellamy's *Looking Backward* than it did to Karl Marx's *Das Kapital*" began to show the first signs of what many expected would be a massive political future. Leading Americans voiced hysterical fears of social revolution, and some of the most sober politicians quietly calculated the probabilities. [27]

The gap between culture and politics, which, artificial as it was, men like Henry Adams despaired of bridging, slowly gave way of itself in the nineties. The older magazines suddenly confronted competition from newer, cheaper, and more topical journals such as *Munsey's, McClure's,* and *Cosmopolitan.* These magazines aimed at capturing the middle-class family audiences of the age by appealing to the father of the household, not the mother. Under pressure of this competition, the older magazines became increasingly political as well. Ministers started to become far more vocal in their comments on the political order while reformers in numerous localities challenged the parties and their methods in ways similar to the more successful challenges of the progressive era. [28]

Beneath all of this was the obvious and palpable fact that the voters' long-ingrained habits were changing, that some kind of vast generational shift was occurring whose end no man could see and no man—not even Mark

Hanna—could hope to guide. Politicians could only guess at the direction in which the electorate was moving and wonder if the party system they knew was capable of containing the new populations, the new pressures, and the new demands that all parts of an increasingly interconnected society made on the political system.

National leaders had their first glimmering of this changing electorate in 1888. The old world of hard, recognizable factions had become blurred and indefinite, and the landmarks of sure Republican or Democratic states with but a few marked "doubtful" had eroded to a grey mass of marginally doubtful states stretching across the country. Yet the older mold was strained rather than broken, and party leaders, puzzled but still basically confident, pushed on in the old way, discounting the alarms of local politicians, and concentrating their resources where they had in years past. In the end, 1888 proved an Indian Summer for the Gilded Age, the last moment before the optimism of the eighties gave way to the insecurities of the next decade.

Four years later there could be no doubt of the changed world that the politicians faced. The Republican party seemed in a continuing crisis with its traditional support threatened all over the country, its national structure chaotic, and its personnel demoralized. The rise of the Populists, the growth of the Democratic party, and the unpopularity of the administration suggested an unhappy future for the Grand Old Party. Its national leadership, confused by change and riddled with discontent, seemed at a loss to adjust to the equally confused discontent of the electorate.

Yet within two years, the whole political scene had been transformed. Instead of the Republican demise which many had feared, the Democrats collapsed under the pressure of a grinding depression, exacerbated ethnic tensions, and a national administration even more unpopular than its predecessor. In 1896, both parties had to make a major attempt to accommodate the new and mysterious electorate of this period of fluctuation, although neither effort disrupted the traditional forms of national party politics.

On the surface, the Democrats made the most radical attempt to reform their party within the old identity. Behind William Jennings Bryan, the silverite, anti-administration Democracy made the old machinery labor for a new western-based coalition. With few experienced engineers to move the levers and practically no money to lubricate the gears, the clanking and grinding reverberated across the plains and the engine never reached the farms of the Midwest and the cities of the East, where new fuel might be located. The Republicans, on the other hand, found nothing but pleasant surprises when they brought out the old engine for its quadrennial journey. Massive shifts in voter preference offered unprecedented majorities in many areas; a frightened business community turned its financial support almost exclusively to the Republican candidate; local party politicians rushed to aid the national cause that promised campaign funds and electoral success. It was still the old machine, but fresh fuel and oil had radically improved its performance, preparing it to lumber on into the twentieth century.

The 1896 campaign was the first clear test of the ability of an amorphous national party system to absorb massive changes in political demands without great structural alterations. For certainly the Civil War had pointed ambiguous political lessons to the next generation. Then, new demands had seemed to fracture the parties, although in retrospect, one is impressed with how the party system continued unchanged despite the replacement of the Whigs by the Republicans. The men of the nineties could not see that this would happen again—and this time without a war or a new party. They did not know whether the parties and the whole national system would metamorphize into some strange new form, or if its evolution was to be brief but final, like the ganoid fish, *Pteraspis,* which (along with the progress in Presidents from Washington to Grant) had cost Henry Adams his belief in evolution.[29]

II

〰

1880: Faction

Decentralization was fundamental to American political life in the nineteenth century. The Republican party, arising less than two decades after the American party system had reached maturity in the Jackson era, became deeply rooted in local organization and the loyalty of voters. Yet it ruled the nation for nearly a quarter of a century without creating any elaborate, continuous, or powerful institutions for national party cooperation. The party was a congeries of state and local organizations each of which named candidates, raised funds, conducted campaigns, distributed patronage and favors, and governed or sniped at the opposition scarcely disturbed from outside their immediate jurisdictions.

This was true from the party's inception. Its first national organ had been the "Republican Association of Washington, D.C.," founded in 1855 as an informal clearing house for state party cooperation. The meeting of the thirty-fourth Congress in December 1855, which threw together anti-Nebraska politicians, suggested the need for a firmer national organization. But five Republican state party chairmen rather than the Association itself or the Republican congressmen issued the call in January 1856 for a convention to organize a national party. The convention, which met in Pittsburgh on February 22, 1856, created the Republican National Committee consisting of one member from each state and assigned it the tasks of calling a convention to nominate presidential and vice-presidential candidates and of completing the organization of the party in the states.[1]

The chairman of the New York state committee, Edwin D. Morgan, became national chairman. His activities in the 1856 campaign, and his repeated performances in 1860 and 1864, defined the role of the national committee. He wrote as broad and inclusive a call as possible, and moved cautiously to complete organization in the states. On the crucial question of how and by whom delegates were to be selected, Morgan wisely declined to lay down specifications, instructing correspondents that "each State should decide the manner of choosing its Delegates to the Republican convention." This decision, inevitable for a new party that had to attract as many people as possible, marked out the future configuration of power within the party, fixing the dominance of the state parties and the relative weakness of the national committee in party counsels.[2]

Under Morgan, the national committee settled into its role as the servant of the state parties during presidential campaigns, coordinating where necessary but chiefly raising money, hiring speakers, and publishing literature. Its principal activities were in the states holding early elections—considered to be of psychological importance to the November presidential contest—and especially the doubtful states. Between campaigns the committee served no function until the chairman called it together in the December before the next presidential year to issue a call and make convention arrangements.[3]

The national chairman's main job was raising money.

In 1856 and 1860, Morgan collected funds from New York, Boston, and Philadelphia businessmen, as well as from wealthy prospective office holders. Starting in 1864, assessments of government employees and contractors became an important source of Republican party funds. This gave new power to congressional Republicans who controlled appointments. While an informal Republican congressional committee had existed since 1855, in the past the national committee had had to support it. But in 1864 Morgan, now a United States Senator, headed the "Union Executive Committee" of three Senators and three Congressmen, which dominated the campaign.[4]

Andrew Johnson's administration further strengthened the position of these leaders as the party completely rejected the President's policies. The legislators dominated the national campaign of 1868, and prepared for revolutionary activity in case Grant was not elected. Zachariah Chandler, Senator from Michigan, made his debut as chairman of the newly re-organized Republican Congressional Committee, while William E. Chandler of New Hampshire, a leading Washington lobbyist, became secretary of the national committee and in effect succeeded Morgan as the neutral campaign manager. The result of the Johnson administration had been to concentrate national direction in Congress to an extent perhaps never surpassed in American history, a condition that few thought likely to continue once the silent man from Galena took office.[5]

Instead, the Grant administration enthroned a directory of Senators and Congressmen, while the President, unequipped to rule from the White House, gradually allowed still more power to flow by default into the hands of such men as Roscoe Conkling, John A. Logan, Zachariah Chandler, Oliver P. Morton, Simon Cameron, and Benjamin Butler. This group, called the "stalwarts," used its role in the administration to create loose alliances in presidential politics, which in the decentralized party of the seventies, made it the pivot of Republican national politics. As the best coordinated center of power in a slack political system, it became the focus of all other counter-organization, defining the well-known factional structure of the decade's politics.[6]

This congressional clique easily triumphed in 1872 over an odd coalition of all its enemies: the Democrats, anti-administration factionalists, and "sadly honest-looking gentlemen." The Republican National and Congressional Committees neatly divided the work of the campaign; the one raised funds by donations from businessmen and assessments on the diplomatic corps while the other assessed federal and occasionally state office holders. The national committee raised approximately $200,000 as it had in 1868. But the congressional committee played the larger role in the election. In addition to collecting money, it put federal office holders to work speaking, raising funds, forming clubs, and editing newspapers.[7]

With the re-election of Grant, the congressional committee seemed a possible source of power, while the national committee, again chaired by the neutral Morgan, lacked influence with the administration. But the question was whether any committee could effectively exercise power when it ceased to be an arm of the national administration with federal patronage and contracts at its disposal. Whether the party's national structure had any vitality apart from a party administration firmly tied to a majority of the Republican representation in Congress remained unproven and unprovable until the Grant administration finished distributing its favors. The men who had enjoyed these favors feared that they could not continue their hold on the national party under a new administration. To them, it was a genuine succession crisis.

With 1876 approaching, the men around Grant prepared to keep control of the party regardless of what might happen. Predictably, the congressional committee—where the secretary, Zach Chandler's lieutenant, James M. Edmunds, remained as sole administrative officer—made the first concerted effort to turn a national organ into a power over the state parties. In June 1875, Edmunds informed postmasters all over the country that "in view of the approaching presidential campaign and the State elections which are to occur the coming autumn, this committee has been directed to provide for the immediate and thorough reorganization of the Republican party." To carry out this work, he asked for an assessment from each of the office holders.

In trying to collect funds for the state elections of 1875, Edmunds had taken a bold stride toward centralization that was both resented and resisted. Elisha W. Keyes, postmaster of Madison, Wisconsin, and chairman of the Wisconsin state committee, answered Edmunds with a protest against "this squeezing out of our Federal officials in this state, that little which we so much need in our own campaign." Keyes warned the secretary that he would "advise all our officials . . . not to respond." [8]

Both state politicians and reformers objected. During the 1876 campaign, even the secretary of the national committee denied that assessments were being made with his knowledge. Some people, like the candidate Rutherford B. Hayes, opposed them altogether. More commonly, office holders wanted to "contribute direct to their location," rather than to a national committee. Throughout this period, Presidents and cabinet members complained that patronage created loyalties to the man who recommends, not the administration that appoints. [9] The state party and the Senator or Congressman who recommended for appointments to federal jobs had a common interest and tended to join together. To tie the state parties to a national administration seemed to require the senatorial leadership of the Grant era, a lesson not wasted on men like Zach Chandler, Conkling, Cameron, and Logan. They wanted another administration which they could dominate.

But the senatorial leaders failed to control the national convention. With the general out of the race, the men who had held power under Grant could not agree on a candidate, and in response to a rising demand for reform, the nomination went to Hayes. The old leaders then moved to take command of the national party machinery in hopes of controlling the candidate. Zach Chandler, against the candidate's wishes, became chairman of the national committee and ran the campaign virtually without consulting Hayes. The disputed outcome of the election thrust the Republican National Committee and its chairman into special prominence. Until March 1877, the committee raised money, pressed Republican claims, and hired legal representation for the party, bringing new prestige to the chairmanship.[10]

Yet Chandler's performance did not lead to the power he sought. Hayes, like Grant before him, did not lean on the committee for advice. The congressional committee, chastened into a mutual-aid society for Congressmen rather than a threat to the state parties, showed more activity in the late seventies than did Chandler's organization. In August 1879, to one informed observer, the national committee was "practically defunct, its only remaining function being to call the next National Convention." Even in doing this, its power was subject to amazingly petty limitations. In organizing matters at the convention site, for example, it had to bow to the authority of the local committee on arrangements. It could not even fill its own vacancies between conventions, surrendering this elementary power to the state committees. It was a most unpromising political weapon. No wonder knowledgeable politicians were surprised at the rumors that J. Donald Cameron, Simon's son and political heir, wanted to succeed Zach Chandler after his death in 1879.[11]

If the chairmanship lacked power, it did have prestige, and that could be an ingredient of power. Controlling the available patronage of the federal government was important to a state politician, but the kind of prestige that national politics could confer on a man was sometimes even more important. This, in fact, was one major ingredient in the significance of having patronage to dispense. Followers had to believe in the leader's power. The first suggestion that a leader had lost power was, if believed, soon likely to become a reality. This necessity to bluff, endemic among professional politicians, has always made it difficult to understand them with any precision and has often been the only explanation of many an incredible incident in which a professional "boss" appeared to surrender substance for form. Cameron had become a Senator through his father's machinations after Hayes had refused to retain him as Secretary of War. This was probably why he was willing to accept the chairmanship of the Republican National Committee on the vote of a small majority of its members—a majority made up largely of southerners.[12]

Running through all the stalwarts' dealings in national politics in 1880 was a desperate effort to build up their prestige, and the national committee, however weak it might be, was the one national organization they could hope to control. The lesson of 1876 had been that they needed Grant. Without his candidacy, there would be, as Zach Chandler wrote just before he died, "a trial of strength between the friends and supporters of a few stalwart radicals." Unless they found a way to make Grant the candidate "without a contest" their own disagreements would give the nomination to an "unknown man of luke-warm sentiments or obscure antecedents." In a rare display of cooperation among state parties, the most important remaining stalwart leaders committed themselves to a desperate attempt at nominating Grant on the first ballot.[13]

Both their cooperation and their desperation were unusual in the annals of nineteenth-century American politics. But these men were in a particularly difficult position. Not only were they at war with a President of their own party, but their main strength—control of three large states, New York, Pennsylvania, and Illinois—was seriously threatened. National prestige would aid in controlling the three state parties, and controlling the parties in these three large states would thereby influence the parties of the smaller states and the South. The state and national situations ran parallel: they would use the last ounce of strength on the state level to shore up their national position, while the last ounce of strength on the national committee had to be used in the states.

II

In Illinois, John A. Logan was struggling to regain political power. His control of the state party had always been uncertain. Beginning as a southern Illinois Douglas Democrat, he had gained fame in the Civil War and capitalized on it afterward as a founder of the Grand Army of the Republic and instigator of Memorial Day. Radical on Southern policy, savage in his opposition to civil service reform, unsound on financial policy, and uncertain in his grammar, by the seventies he had a reputation among his enemies as "the embodiment of the worst phase of machine politics." Defeated for re-election to the Senate in 1877 he had with difficulty re-entered that body two years later. By 1880, he faced open opposition from Chicago Republicans as well as downstate supporters of James G. Blaine. Even Grant's "discoverer," Elihu B. Washburne, who nursed presidential hopes himself, abandoned his old ally. In May the anti-Grant Republicans succeeded in capturing the Cook County Republican Convention and electing a slate of Washburne and Blaine delegates, which forced Grant's men to withdraw and choose their own delegates.

At the state convention, Green B. Raum, the Commissioner of Internal Revenue, whom John Sherman later described as "the most active and efficient agent of Gen. Grant in the National Convention," chaired the meeting with an iron hand. The convention seated Grant's Chicago supporters and shattered Illinois precedent by selecting its state delegation through a special committee instead of by district caucuses. The chairman refused to recognize Blaine's supporters when they tried to protest. The convention proceeded to instruct for Grant. Logan's enemies secured their revenge later when the contesting Blaine delegates gained their seats at Chicago in the first significant test of Grant's strength on the convention floor.[14]

Roscoe Conkling had controlled the New York state party through the early seventies. Behind the Conkling trademarks—the stage eloquence, the colossal vanity, and the "finest torso" in public life—had lurked a brilliant legal mind and a shrewd politician. After the abysmal failure of the liberal movement, his control of the customs house, with its thousand-man political army and its influence on the politics of important merchants and their employees, had enabled him to retain his hold on the party despite his organization's indifferent success in winning elections.

By the late seventies, however, the political suppleness had been completely buried under his mountainous ego and the legal genius had not yet been liberated from the theatricalities of national politics. And after 1877, he was in a state of siege. Hayes on entering the White House immediately launched an attack on his control of the customs house. Conkling fought a long losing battle, ending in February 1879 with the confirmation of a collector and naval officer committed to removing the customs house from politics.[15]

This in itself Conkling could endure, but the nearly two-year battle had cost him much of his prestige within the state, destroyed his hold on reform-minded Republicans, and stirred the hopes of all the New York Republicans who had been political casualties of the Grant era. Although he was unanimously re-elected to the Senate in 1876, this was due largely to the Greenback movement, which forced the party to close ranks. Otherwise, his control of the party was by a thin majority. His choice for the speaker of the New York House passed the Republican caucus by only 9 votes. His candidate for governor the following year squeaked through the state convention with 234 out of 450 votes. A public scandal diminished his prestige still further when in August 1879 ex-Senator Sprague in a jealous rage drove Conkling out of his house.[16]

Conkling's response to danger was arrogance. When his control was challenged in 1879, he gambled on crushing the opposition. Conceding nothing, he nominated for governor a man Hayes had removed from a lower post in the customs house. Then despite his paper-thin majority in the state convention, he proceeded to complete the slate with his own followers. Ex-Collector Arthur became chairman of the state committee. While the New York convention was in session, Grant was on his way back to America from his triumphal world tour; and well before his arrival in San Francisco, Conkling's enemies correctly connected the Senator's action in New York with an attempted revival of "Grantism" in 1880.[17]

As Conkling's enemies grew in power, his control over his own organization slipped badly. Governor Alonzo B. Cornell's loyalty seemed up for grabs. Arthur would accept the vice-presidential nomination over the Senator's objections; and Tom Platt was actively making the alliances with Blaine's New York supporters which would put him in the Senate the next year under onerous and embarrassing obligations to them. Conkling's lieutenants, increasingly independent, would force him "by main strength" to campaign for Garfield in 1880.[18]

His organization attacked from without and his leadership undermined from within, Conkling was a desperate man in 1880. In the state convention which he called for the unusually early date of February 25, before opposition could form, he maintained only a small majority, 216 delegates to 183. Compelling instructions for Grant and the unit rule on the delegation to Chicago appeared a desperate move, given the size of the minority and the lack of Republican precedent for enforcing unit voting in a national convention. Conkling, unsure of himself, exacted a pledge from each delegate to abide by his instructions—a pledge which nineteen members of the delegation broke.[19]

In Pennsylvania, Don Cameron had been in an increasingly uneasy position since the beginning of Hayes's administration. After his rejection by the incoming President, his father had stepped down from the Senate in his favor. While possessing a potent name, the younger man had no reputation for political success when he took control of the organization, and he faced a hostile Republican President who might become a rallying point for his enemies.

Greenbackism was a particularly great threat in soft-money conscious Pennsylvania, but Cameron had been fortunate in finding in Matthew Stanley Quay the man who could, through adroit maneuvering with the Green-backers and a liberal use of money, forestall a Democratic-Greenback coalition and carry the state in 1878 by a comfortable majority. Behind the majority, however, was a divided party, and the Cameron organization lost control of the state legislature of 1879. The Pittsburgh riots of 1877 had caused $2.5 million damage to property of the Pennsylvania Railroad for which Allegheny County was liable. The railroad and the Republican leadership concocted a plan to have the state legislature appropriate $4 million to pay the damages. It was rumored that the extra $1.5 million would be put to political uses. Companion to the Pittsburgh riot bill was a measure to tax oil at fifty cents a barrel to cover the expenditure.

The Cameron organization underestimated the power of the Pennsylvania oil producers. About twenty-five members of the legislature representing oil-producing areas held the balance of power between the parties and refused to follow the Republican leadership. Cameron lieutenants offered several of them bribes, which were refused, leading to a public scandal and the trial and conviction of several important organization Republicans. The Pennsylvania Pardon Board, of which Quay was a member, instantly pardoned the conspirators, an action which received national attention. The New York *Tribune* called it the "most insolent defiance of public sentiment that has been seen since Tweed asked the tax-payers of New York what they were going to do about it." Thereafter opposition to Quay and Cameron was open. An Independent movement prevented Cameron from naming his senatorial candidate in 1881, and eventuated in an Independent Republican candidate for governor in 1882 who cost the Republicans the statehouse for the first time in a generation.[20]

This is the context of Cameron's strategy in national politics. Desperate for a national success to put down rising opposition in his state, Cameron was willing to take the chairmanship of the national committee by a narrow margin (a post which by its nature is inoperative unless reflecting broad support). He had the Pennsylvania state committee call a very early state convention in the first week of February, and forced through instructions for Grant by a slim majority of 133 to 113—instructions to delegates, again, being effective only if reflecting an overwhelming consensus. Many observers thought that had Blaine or his managers put up a fight, they might have prevented instructions at Harrisburg. But Blaine's supporters lacked leadership, and the Grant managers, moving before there was counter-organization, made enough deals for minor offices to squeeze through. Cameron had completed a not entirely successful first step on the way to a national reputation.[21]

The stalwart leaders hoped that pledged delegations from Pennsylvania, New York, and Illinois would create new strength all over the country. The early New York and Pennsylvania conventions did have some effect in other states. But the furor over stalwart methods made politicians wary. An important Iowa Republican argued against instructing conventions for anybody on the grounds that he did not want "to introduce New York or Pennsylvania politics into Iowa." The revolts in New York and Illinois, and the size of the anti-Grant vote in Harrisburg, limited the effect of the three conventions. When the national party met, the stalwarts lacked strength for a first-ballot victory unless the majorities they controlled in the three states could be turned into unit votes for Grant—a move without precedent in Republican party history.[22]

To accomplish this they devised a simple but revolutionary scheme. Knowing the weakness of the national committee in the party's loose structure, they planned to take advantage of that very weakness by having Cameron as chairman refuse to entertain any motions related to questions of convention representation—such as the unit rule—on the grounds that the committee had no power to decide substantive issues. Then, since the chairman had the ceremonial function of calling the convention to order, he could apply the unit rule to any contest over the temporary chairman, insuring this office to a Grant man, who could in turn apply the unit rule to the reports of the committees that passed on rules and credentials. Thus the convention would be denied the opportunity to vote on the unit rule except under that very rule.

This clever plan, doubtless far too clever to succeed, attempted to turn the national committee's weakness in substantive matters and its ceremonial functions into control of the convention by three states. Considering that Grant's supporters lacked a majority on the committee itself, the scheme was quite incredible. Obviously, it would oblige the friends of every other candidate to coalesce against Grant. At a meeting of the committee on June 1, these scattered groups, apparently led by Blaine's manager W. E. Chandler, forced the selection of a neutral temporary chairman, Senator George F. Hoar of Massachusetts, who was supporting the token candidacy of George F. Edmunds of Vermont.[23]

This ended the danger of forcing the unit rule on the convention, but did not eliminate the stalwart threat. Even after the crucial minorities in New York, Pennsylvania, and Illinois went over to the opposition, Conkling, Cameron, and Logan held the remainder of their lines through all of the 36 ballots. The group that would later be known as the "Old Guard" or the "306" "went down with their colors nailed to the mast," Tom Platt recalled. "They participated in a display of devotion unprecedented in American Politics." Perhaps not devotion, but it was surely unprecedented for southern Republicans to stand aloof from the winner. Apparently they regarded all but Grant as their enemies; in short, they shared their leaders' political desperation.

Facing desperate men, the opponents of Grant were equally well-disciplined. Few conventions have had such a clearly factional structuring. W. E. Chandler described the Chicago meeting as a contest between the Grant forces and a Blaine-Sherman-Washburne coalition, which took its shape from the battle over the unit rule. But it is indicative of the state of party organization that despite the obvious stalwart threat, such a logical alliance had not materialized before the convention.[24]

Of the other candidates, Blaine was clearly the front-runner. In every Republican National Convention between 1876 and 1892 large numbers of delegates were ready to support him. Blaine was the consummate politician of his age: a man of genuine intellect and culture, supple and ever-willing to accept political counsel, and most of all, a man of extraordinary charisma—what his age called "magnetism." "It was not possible," claimed a long-time observer of the Washington scene, "for an unprejudiced person to meet the man from Maine without being attracted to him." With uncanny precision he had for a generation fallen into the public mood on every major question from the time of his entry into politics as an original Republican of 1854. He supported Lincoln, stayed a shade behind the Radicals, satisfied both the Liberals and the GAR in the early seventies, played with civil service reform, and found the precise eye of every storm over the currency. But from the late seventies through the years when he reached for the presidency, he seemed to lose the magic touch. Blaine fell behind the demand for reform of the government service and forged too far ahead of his party's commitment to tariff protection and to an adventurous foreign policy. Worst of all he became enmeshed in a conflict-of-interest scandal that has permanently blotted his historical reputation. However, his personal magnetism, oratorical skill, and consistent partisan regularity made him the logical rallying point in the eighties for those regular Republicans who were either hostile to the dominant machine in their locality or jealous of the power of the largest states. His was a candidacy that hardly required organizing—or, one might say, *only* required organizing—to win.[25]

Yet virtually nothing that can be described as a Blaine organization existed in 1876 and 1880. William P. Frye and Eugene Hale, Congressmen from Maine, represented his interests at the convention of 1876. These men were local political associates who struggled to coordinate Blaine's supporters in the midst of the convention. In no sense had they constituted a national organization working beforehand to gather delegates. Nor had the situation changed four years later. Prominent state politicians pleaded for aid, but none came. Joseph H. Manley, Blaine's associate from Maine, complained that his candidate had "plenty of soldiers and captains but no generals." [26]

The other leading candidate was John Sherman. If Blaine spoke to the hearts of Republicans, Sherman aimed at their heads. The "Ohio Icicle" lacked all Blaine's warmth and popularity. His oratory was abstruse and his private conversation formal. He was magnificent with figures but poor at remembering names. Yet Sherman was by far the most important public figure of the seventies and eighties. More than any other single individual, he was the architect of the major economic policies of the period. A master of administration and technical detail, he assiduously arranged compromises for his party's benefit. Perhaps most valuable of all, Sherman took public responsibility for the results: he was the great political target of the age. After such services, he thought he was entitled to his party's nomination. More extraordinary, he believed he could get it.[27]

Sherman thought that if he exercised tact, some of Grant's strength would eventually come to him. Cameron and Conkling had given insincere promises that he would be their second choice. As a result he had cooperated in making Cameron chairman in 1879, and this alliance had prevented his Pennsylvania supporters from combining with Blaine's men to stop Grant in 1880. W. E. Chandler had pleaded for a Sherman-Blaine coalition against Grant. But with both factions fearful that the other was bargaining with the stalwarts, the opposition had lost its shaky majority giving Cameron his narrow victory.[28]

Another deterrent to cooperation before the convention was that some of Grant's enemies also opposed Blaine. After a moment of hope that the anti-third-term movement led by General John B. Henderson of Missouri would benefit his cause, Blaine was soon denouncing it as a "Bowles-Adams, 'young Republican,' sentimental-civil service-jackass concern, resulting with equal fervor against Grant and Blaine." Its convention in May, while predominantly anti-Grant, took care to insert a resolution clearly aimed against Blaine: "As Republicans, we cannot be hero-worshippers, and we demand from a party without a master the nomination of a candidate without a stain." [29]

Just as many of Grant's opponents distrusted Blaine, so did Blaine distrust the men with whom he had to cooperate. He and Chandler had been anxious to end Sherman's candidacy even in Ohio. Had Sherman "cleared the track," Blaine was convinced, "I would have beaten Grant ten to one in Ohio and then ploughed him under in Illinois with ease." Similarly, he urged Whitelaw Reid to use his newspaper to undermine Washburne's candidacy. Perhaps Blaine himself tried to deal with the stalwarts, only entering total opposition when he could not come to an agreement. Such, at least, was the impression that Chandler conveyed during the fight is Pennsylvania. Blaine was convinced throughout the pre-convention period that he could reach an understanding with Conkling.[30]

In short, while competing factions made the battles of 1880 unusually intense, all were members of the same party and they were far from absolute enemies. Only the desperate measures of the stalwarts created a firm though temporary organization of the other factions. When the convention was finally "Garfielded" (a verb that had some currency among politicians for about a decade thereafter), it was the work of the anti-Grant forces organized at the convention. The candidate, although not a major protagonist in the struggle, still carried the incubus of being the anti-Grant candidate. Unlike Hayes, he faced, from the outset, a fixed factional opposition within the party.

III

The day after the convention, the stalwarts, in yet another incredible maneuver, called an impromptu meeting of the national committee where Grant's supporters planned to elect officers who would force Garfield to terms before the campaign began. Chandler and William P. Frye heard of the attempt and blocked it. With Cameron thoroughly discredited, the candidate and his supporters now had to select their own chairman. In this accidental way, Garfield established an important precedent as the first Republican candidate to pick his own national officers.[31]

No one was quite sure how to do this. Although the candidate would make the real choice, the national committee itself had to elect the officers. Chandler advised naming someone already on the committee so as not to slight the wishes of the state parties that selected the national committeemen. Garfield, on the other hand, favored someone not on the committee, Governor Charles Foster of Ohio. John Murray Forbes, the wealthy and influential committeeman from Massachusetts, also thought that someone from outside the committee could be selected, and volunteered to resign his position in favor of whomever Garfield chose for chairman. But he learned to his chagrin that the Massachusetts party refused to surrender its choice of national committeeman—especially to a man from another state. Forbes's surprise suggests how vague ideas of national party organization were even in the minds of the men most concerned.[32]

Garfield's range of choices was narrowly circumscribed by the political realities of the forthcoming campaign. Governor Foster was not a real possibility. He was a talented political organizer, but his duties as governor would have made him a part-time chairman, and his appointment, as one correspondent emphatically stated, *"would mortally offend Mr. Sherman"*—who felt betrayed by Ohio's turning to Garfield at the convention. No other faction would countenance a stalwart as chairman, yet a follower of Blaine might alienate the New York, Illinois, and Pennsylvania leaders whose cooperation was indispensable. Chandler seemed the logical choice, and was Garfield's pick after Foster. Although a Blaine man, he had worked hard for Grant and for Hayes, and remained on good terms with stalwarts and reformers alike. But despite heavy pressure, Chandler refused the office. "Mr. Blaine's friends," he explained, "should not be forward to decide or direct." [33]

Chandler opposed any strong man in the office. A powerful chairman would only invite more plotting such as the stalwarts had just attempted. His choice was Marshall Jewell of Connecticut, a wealthy manufacturer whose reputation as an honest Postmaster General under Grant would help in raising campaign funds. Chandler convinced Forbes that the chairman had to be a figurehead. While accepting Chandler's logic, Forbes had one serious reservation: who, he asked Chandler, was going to do the work of the committee. From Forbes, as we shall see, the question was prophetic. Chandler's reply was equally prophetic: Stephen B. Elkins, he wrote "would employ good help and would do well." Elkins would have been a good choice to serve as the neutral party functionary Chandler sought. He was astute, not yet forty, and although loyal to Blaine, not prominently identified with him. Representing New Mexico, a politically indifferent base, he had sufficient wealth, executive ability, and connections in New York to run a good committee organization. He would be a logical successor as secretary to McCormick, who had given Elkins his start in politics in the territory.[34]

Garfield, on the other hand, suggested some friend of Blaine's as chairman and Thomas C. Platt, Conkling's representative on the national committee, as secretary. Rather than a technical or clerical committee of neutral political operators, Garfield now sought one that would represent—and balance—the major factions. Both types of organization would have a long history in Republican politics, producing powerful national chairmen from large states such as Quay of Pennsylvania and Hanna of Ohio and at other times virtually powerless servants, such as Thomas Henry Carter of Montana. In 1880, however, circumstances quickly passed beyond anyone's capacity to impose a clear solution. When the national committee met on July 1, the Grant forces had selected Platt as their candidate and intended through him to "exact concessions from Garfield before opening any vigorous campaign." To avoid open conflict, the committee referred the choice to a subcommittee of three—the stalwart Logan, Chandler, and the neutral Forbes. The result was a compromise. Chandler and Forbes selected Jewell as chairman, but reluctantly allowed Logan to choose as secretary the able but suspect Stephen W. Dorsey, soon to be notorious in the star route frauds.[35]

As a device for unifying the party, Chandler had correctly insisted upon a figurehead chairman. Only as an impartial agency could the committee solve factional disputes. Yet Chandler had still failed in his task, for while Jewell was in fact a figurehead, Dorsey was certainly not a neutral technician. Jewell was a "careful and slow" man: fussy, pessimistic, suspicious, endlessly writing lengthy but insignificant jeremiads. At one crucial juncture, he promised Garfield that he would "within a week have an opinion and perhaps a definite one." Visitors to headquarters throughout the campaign complained of his inadequacy, sympathized with his self-pity at the abuse he took, and worried about the sums he laid out from his personal fortune for the committee's expenses.[36]

Dorsey, on the other hand, was "nothing if not extravagant." A flamboyant political operator with many shadowy connections, he offered the party "the inconveniences as well as the advantages of a strong willed man who thoroughly knows what he wants and tries to get it every time." Nearly everyone distrusted him, but no one—not even Jewell who immediately clashed with him—doubted that he was, as Reid described him, "a man of admirable executive qualities and great force." [37]

The new secretary also had an enormous capacity for attracting publicity. In the eyes of the nation he was the leader of the Republican campaign: its director and treasurer, the man responsible for bringing Garfield to New York, and finally, the savior of Indiana and the presidency. Dorsey climaxed his campaign for personal aggrandizement with a self-arranged testimonial dinner at Delmonico's designed to apply pressure to the new President by assigning the secretary all credit for Garfield's success. Grant presided, Henry Ward Beecher said Grace, and leading stalwarts made speeches. The Vice-President-elect scandalized the nation with a particularly unfortunate reference to purchased votes. Dorsey modestly took credit for carrying Indiana.[38]

Garfield was perplexed by the Dorsey dinner, that "curious affair, whose whole significance I do not yet understand." But Chandler was quite sure he understood. Beside himself with rage, he protested to Garfield "against the gross want of sense, propriety and taste which prepared a public celebration and glorification of the use of money to carry elections." The dinner, Chandler claimed, was an attempt "to degrade and injure the party and the new administration by public proclamation that they hold power through the corrupt acts of corrupt men," and would lead to a demand of rewards for Dorsey. Blaine was even more specific, predicting that Dorsey's request would "in the end modestly center in the second assistant Postmaster-Generalship, through which channel there are cunning preparations being made by a small cabal to steal half a million a year during your administration." [39]

By puffing Dorsey, the stalwarts attempted to maintain the prestige of having elected a President after they had lost the fight to nominate one. But, making a hero out of Dorsey was a tall order. They could only praise him for things that usually did not bear mentioning. In order to make claims on the new administration they trumpeted forth and perhaps exaggerated facts usually kept silent.

Although some historians, notably Matthew Josephson, have considered Dorsey's claims as the cat let out of the bag, Dorsey may not have revealed the magnitude of campaign expenditure and the nature of national organization but simply inflated his own role.[40]

Dorsey's role was far more equivocal than he and his prestige-hungry friends pretended. Rather than directing the entire campaign, he was rarely at the national headquarters. He and Jewell took an instinctive dislike to each other, and, shortly after the great meeting in early August, which Garfield attended, their open conflict sent Dorsey west for the remainder of the campaign. He even wanted to resign his official duties at headquarters but no one would assume the onus of replacing him.[41]

Dorsey's one great service in New York was to bring the reluctant Garfield east for the famous Fifth Avenue Hotel Conference. Nearly every nationally prominent Republican attended this meeting, which was arranged to bring Conkling and his forces into the campaign. Its earliest and most constant advocate, however, was not Dorsey, but vice-presidential candidate Arthur, who urged such a conference even before Dorsey was appointed secretary. Garfield had countered by inviting Jewell, Dorsey, and Arthur to visit him at Mentor. But the stalwarts thought a meeting in Ohio without Conkling would be useless, and Garfield feared that any trip east to placate the New Yorkers would cost him both his dignity and the support of civil service reformers.[42]

Matters remained at a standstill with "no money . . . raised, no general organization effected, . . . little or nothing accomplished" at the New York headquarters through most of July. Finally, the impatient Dorsey, taking advantage of Jewell's absence, peremptorily organized an enormous meeting of the congressional com-

44

mittee, the national committee, the chairmen of all the state committees, and virtually every leading Republican, including the candidate, whose itinerary and travel party he arranged with but the most cursory consultation. *"I am going ahead in this matter,"* he notified Garfield, "upon the assumption that you will consent to be here." He hinted that if the candidate refused, he would resign from the committee. While Garfield decided and Jewell equivocated, Dorsey had already invited "one or two hundred people" to meet the candidate in New York.[43]

The resulting conference on August 5, which, to Garfield's chagrin, Conkling neglected to attend, is one of the famous incidents of Gilded Age politics frequently recounted, and just as frequently misunderstood. Historians have naturally followed the one first-person account of the crucial meeting, that of Tom Platt's autobiography, questioning only Platt's interpretation of what was agreed between Garfield and the New York stalwarts. But even his facts are largely false. Throughout his memoirs, Platt never hesitates to falsify his history in order to preserve his political reputation for "promisekeeping and truthtelling." The story of the Fifth Avenue Conference is not the one Platt depicts of Garfield versus the tight-knit and loyal New York stalwarts. Rather the tale has two parts: campaign finances, and conflicts within the New York organization.[44]

The rhetoric of loyalty to the organization has always been important to professional politicians, and never more so than in the late nineteenth century when civil service reformers attacked the whole concept of organization politics. People, however, cry for loyalty not when they have a smooth-running machine, but when it is functioning badly. In 515 pages of turgid prose, Platt recites over and over the legend of the loyal organization's battles with the "malcontents" who thought themselves "greater than the organization." "During an experience of over fifty years in politics," he confesses, "I have learned that obedience to instructions and gratitude are about as scarce as snow in the dog-days." But of course Platt never dreamed of using his own rise to power in New York as an example of the truth of this maxim.[45]

"Up to the 1st of August, 1880," Platt writes, "no steps had been taken by the State committee to do any work or perfect any plans, so thoroughly were they disheartened and demoralized." This was only the stalwarts' public posture of following their leader, Conkling. In fact they behaved quite differently. By the end of July, Platt as chairman of the New York State executive committee was engaged in exactly the kind of "close organized work that must be done by the State Committee" which the stalwarts claimed would not begin until Garfield came east. Platt was doing "a tremendous job," Jewell reported to the candidate, in drawing up block-by-block lists of 350,000 voters in New York City. Arthur as well was eager to make peace and get the campaign moving. Dorsey was in "an embarrassing position" because of Conkling's "ugly" mood. Banker Levi P. Morton, crucial to the campaign's finances, feared to take any official position on the committee without Conkling's assent, but in the meantime cautiously cooperated with Jewell on fund raising.[46]

The conference's primary aim, then, was not so much to placate the stalwarts as to aid them in forcing Conkling into the campaign. Although one would never know it from his memoirs, Platt was furious with Conkling when he failed to attend the meeting. There was no united faction making demands: it was the New Yorkers' need for unity that precipitated the conference. Conkling's restive lieutenants were eager to begin work, not because they cared about Garfield, but because they were in competition for control of the state party. The great prize was the upcoming senatorship and the activities of the state committees especially would determine who would get it. Arthur, despite his presence on the national ticket, still considered that "a point worth looking after," Reid noted. Platt, Governor Cornell, and other important stalwarts were determined that Arthur would "not get the Senatorship in any event." Conkling, fearing to take sides, had already begun to withdraw from active leadership. He was "in the hands of his friends" he confessed, and would "do whatever they ask[ed]." [47]

They asked that he publicly campaign for the ticket, in part because the facade of unity was important to them, but principally because it was even more important to the men who might finance the campaign. In a closely divided electorate choosing between two conservative candidates, businessmen saw little purpose in supporting a loser, and the division between Conkling and Garfield made the Republicans look as if they would lose. Dorsey had found that the large railroadmen and bankers "whether their sympathies [were] with Conkling or not, . . . [saw] no reason for throwing away their money." This argument convinced Reid as it did the reluctant Garfield, who rationalized his trip on the grounds that the national committee considered it "vitally important to their financial success independent of the personal questions connected with Mr. C." [48]

Thus the success or failure of Dorsey's conference did not rest on Conkling's attendance. The real test was its contribution to the financing of the campaign. But here again Dorsey's record is curious and equivocal. The facade of unity which the meeting created undoubtedly helped in fund raising. Morton, to Garfield's relief, finally consented to serve as chairman of the finance committee. But Dorsey's presence as secretary was itself a hindrance in raising money. Conkling's hesitation was not the only thing troubling potential contributors. They did not trust Dorsey.[49]

Forbes regretted his role in picking the secretary as soon as he heard of the "good many scandals" that surrounded the man. Morton, partly because of Conkling's attitude but also because of Dorsey's notoriety, made very peculiar arrangements for raising the funds. When Garfield came to New York, he met with a group of New York Republican businessmen and bankers at Reid's home. At this meeting, they agreed that Morton would take charge of a special fund that would be kept secret and that would be entirely apart from the regular finances of the Republican National Committee—which Morton would also raise as chairman of the finance committee. Amazingly, this arrangement—certain as it was to breed confusion and mistrust—persisted throughout the campaign.[50]

Morton intended his secret and separate fund for use in the two main doubtful states of New York and Indiana. However, once Dorsey and Jewell openly quarreled, the secretary went west and ostensibly took charge of Indiana, which raised the hackles of Morton's prospective contributors. Dorsey, short of money, hinted to Garfield that because of Conkling's dissatisfaction, Morton had slackened his efforts. Reid investigated this allegation and found that Morton was eager enough to raise funds, but that his friends were suspicious that Dorsey was "not absolutely trustworthy in the matter of money." Morton wondered how to overcome this problem. Reid suggested that "if the people who furnished the money were unwilling to put it solely into Dorsey's hands, they could send out their own agent who should act in cooperation with him, and be able to report to them in detail." Dorsey's statement, in a post-election interview which became notorious, that of the "about $400,000" which Republicans spent in Indiana, "not a nickel . . . came into my hands," suggests that some such system as Reid advised must have been followed.[51]

Nor was Dorsey's reputation the only problem Morton

faced. He and Jewell were in an uneasy, sometimes hostile, competition for funds. Jewell tried to raise money for some of the Southern states, and when this plan met with the committee's hostility, he "farmed out" individual states for wealthy Republicans such as Forbes to finance, thereby absorbing money which might have gone to Morton.[52]

In addition, the Republicans collected funds through the congressional committee that assessed office holders. However, the reforms of the Hayes administration sharply reduced the sums that could be raised from this source. Its collections would not in any case have been used for Dorsey's purposes. Although this group cooperated with the national committee, especially in printing documents, it raised money to re-elect Congressmen and Senators, thereby contributing directly to the support of the state parties. The national committee, on the other hand, was often a rival to the state parties for funds. That committee's most acceptable function would be to tap those sources that a state party could not reach—notably businessmen with national interests. Until it learned that role, the committee would be the enemy of all but those who controlled it.[53]

Not surprisingly, individual Republicans in some areas raised funds outside the committee's control, seeking direct influence with the candidate. Cleveland Republicans, under Governor Foster's direction, raised funds for the candidate's personal use. A Philadelphia businessmen's committee raised a large sum as well. Yet independence could be dangerous. Blaine, careful to avoid alienating the committee or the candidate, made sure that contributions offered to him privately were channeled through the committee once the donor had specified that they be sent to Maine.[54]

IV

Of course, the roughest competition for funds came from the Democrats. Even after Conkling and Garfield made peace, the potentially large contributors had no deep commitment to the Republicans. Railroadmen such as Collis P. Huntington, Cyrus M. Field, and Jay Gould, and bankers like John A. Stewart of the United States Trust Company were dominated by one major interest in the campaign of 1880:

> The real anxiety of these people [Reid explained to Garfield] is with reference to the Supreme Court. All monied men, and especially all corporations, regarded the course of the Supreme Court in the Granger cases and in the Pacific R.R. case as bad law and bad faith. . . . These people hesitate [to contribute] because they say they are unwilling to elect a President unless they are sure that he disapproves what they call the revolutionary course of the majority of the court. If they could be satisfied on this point, I know we could make a big demonstration at once, and probably settle things beyond a peradventure.[55]

In these two sets of decisions to which Reid alluded, the Court had upheld in the one case state laws regulating railroad and warehousing rates, and in the other a federal statute of 1878 establishing a sinking fund in the United States Treasury to insure the repayment of the federal loans that subsidized the construction of the Union Pacific Railroad. The Court's decisions were legally conservative ones, in keeping with lengthy precedents regarding the power of legislatures to exercise police powers over corporations. But in the tense depression era of the seventies, this legal traditionalism appeared to Reid and other men with money to spend on a presidential election to be a "revolutionary course." Legal and social conservatism had parted company. Men of wealth found the radical jurisprudence of Stephen J. Field better suited to their needs than the old-fashioned legal conservatism of the Court's decisions which now seemed to play into the hands of angry farmers and disgruntled workers.[56]

The dissent of Field in the Granger cases and of Field, William Strong, and Joseph P. Bradley in the Sinking-Fund cases were early landmarks in the evolution of the doctrine of substantive due process as a guard against legislative control over corporate property. While Chief Justice Morrison R. Waite, speaking for the Court, judged that "the people must resort to the polls, not the courts" to correct legislative abuses, Field was arguing that corporation charters "constituted contracts between the States creating them and the corporators," making any issue between them "a judicial question, and not a matter for legislative determination." In the Sinking-Fund cases, he extended this argument to the federal government which, he claimed, should be held to the constitutional provision forbidding states from passing laws impairing contracts. The lines were being drawn on the crucial question, which in this era was not so much laissez-faire versus regulation as it was judicial versus legislative control of regulation.[57]

The railroadmen and bankers were resorting both to the courts and to the polls, or rather to their point of intersection: the elected official who appointed federal judges. Jewell had heard from the businessmen as well. He urged the candidate to send "privately, for my own personal use . . . your general views on this question of the rights of corporations so that I could show it to Gould and perhaps Huntington." Reid too demanded a "prompt and careful answer" from Garfield.[58]

Handling such political dynamite, Garfield—as always—proceeded cautiously.

> I note carefully, [he wrote to Reid] what you say in reference to the danger to vested rights from impending changes in the Supreme Court. On the suggestion of two or three friends, I left out a paragraph from the letter of acceptance, touching that very subject, and this was its purport, that, while in every just way we should promote

cheap transportation yet the Government should not only sacredly respect vested rights, but should refrain from adopting any policy which would prevent capitalists from extending our great railroad system. I did not leave this out because of any doubt as to the justice of the sentiment itself, but from motives of campaign discretion.

Even this reply, Reid notified him, was too discreet: Garfield's statement was "scarcely so precise on the point of the decision of Judge Field as wd. be desired by some of the gentlemen concerned," who insisted on assurances that Garfield "as a lawyer concur[red] in the views of the minority in those cases." If he did that, these men would "give to Indiana all you want." [59]

But Garfield continued his cagey course, insisting that he must first reread Field's decision in the Sinking-Fund cases before committing himself. Meanwhile, he had Foster write a letter for Senator Plumb in New York to show "our friends," impressing on them "the very great importance of carrying Indiana for the Republicans at the October election" and assuring them that rather than being in sympathy with "what is popularly known as Grangerism," Garfield had "the highest possible regard for the sacredness of vested rights and . . . [would] not do or permit to be done any act to impair their sacredness." In proof of this, Foster directly quoted the politically indiscreet sentence on the sacred character of vested rights that the candidate had excised from his letter of acceptance. [60]

This still was not enough, for Garfield had made speeches in the past that gave at least qualified support to railroad regulation. He remonstrated in another letter to Reid that although he believed "in protecting the interests of the U.S. and the rights of the people," he was against "repudiation" or "violating the plain terms of a contract." More important, he pointed out that he had opposed the

1878 Sinking-Fund Act in the House and that he concurred in Judge Strong's dissenting opinion (which stated Field's position a bit less forcefully).[61]

Again Garfield had halted too soon. Reid's friends wanted the right actually to name his appointments to the Court. The Ohioan rejected the "proposition" on the grounds that "any agreement that should be or appear to be a delegation of the power vested in the Chief Executive implies such distrust of his faithfulness to his own convictions of duty, as I cannot tolerate with self respect." Apparently, Presidents had vested rights as well. Still, he promised to appoint only men "entirely sound on these questions" and made a further pledge to Reid that his selections would be based "upon evidence . . . satisfactory to you as well as to me." In short, he offered Reid and his friends at least a veto over appointments to the high court.[62]

This must have sufficed to allay their fears, for by the end of September even Jewell reported in his usual negative way that "Morton's Committee has raised, and is raising, so much money for Indiana that we can not do anything for Ohio." The necessary money—although certainly not the $400,000 of which Dorsey boasted—went west on October 1 for the successful effort in the October election. Its use there suggests why there was so much difficulty in raising it.[63]

Garfield, in soliciting funds for Indiana, admonished Reid that the "friends of good order and public faith" had good reason to support the Republicans when "the Democracy has been rapidly drifting in the wake of the Greenback party, toward communism and a general assault on the public faith and vested rights." While Garfield mouthed this conservative rhetoric, Dorsey was keeping him informed of his efforts to "make some arrangement with the Greenbackers in Indiana." Nor was he alone in pursuing this strategy. The chairman of the Indiana state central committee, John C. New, used his newspaper to attack Indiana Democrats who voted against the re-monetization of silver, and he dealt gently with the Greenbackers as well. The Republican Congressional Committee lent its aid by circulating Greenbacker literature in areas of strong soft-money sentiment.[64]

On other matters, however, the various Republican groups working in Indiana found it difficult to cooperate. "It seems impossible," men at the New York headquarters complained, "to find out the precise relations of Dorsey and New." There were "two committees" in Indiana, Jewell noted, that lacked "confidential relations" between them. New's group did the normal campaign work of co-ordinating the local committees, canvassing, distributing documents, and organizing election-day procedures. Dorsey's work, on the other hand, was "of a secret kind," his "plan of operations . . . mapped in mystery." Jewell, in the end, had to dispatch investigators to find out what was happening.[65]

These complexities went back to President Hayes's famous Civil Service Order No. 1, which, by limiting the political activities of federal employees, had left the state committee with largely inexperienced men. Its real director was William Wade Dudley, the United States Marshal at Indianapolis, who, because of the President's order, was only "an honorary member of the State Committee." A war hero who had lost a leg at Gettysburg, Dudley was equally intrepid on the political battlefields of the Gilded Age, and just as dedicated to the principle of victory at any price. From first to last—which is to say from the first careful poll of the state to directing election-day activities—he ran the state committee's campaign.[66]

It was for this kind of close organizational work that

Dudley, working through Garfield, sought to enlist John D. Rockefeller's aid. Standard Oil's Indiana supervisor was "a live Republican and would like to bring all his men into line if Mr. Rockafeller [sic] would stand by him at home." The corporation, Dudley had pointed out to Garfield, employed 1500 to 2000 men to cut wood for staves and barrel heads *"in our close counties."* Their votes and the political activities of other Standard Oil men in Indiana would "accomplish much toward redeeming the State." Garfield approached Rockefeller through an intermediary and received assurances that the oil man was *"all right"* and would lend his aid.[67]

This episode is hardly the example of Garfield's "pursuing the large capitalists more systematically, more directly than party leaders had ever attempted before," which Josephson supposed. The initiative for this venture came from Dudley, who maintained pressure for its accomplishment throughout. Moreover, Dudley was working with Rockefeller's ardently Republican supervisor in Nashville, Indiana, who directed whatever political work Standard Oil did there. All that Dudley asked of Rockefeller was that he not interfere with his local agent's activities. He was not being asked to act positively through the corporation to serve national Republican ends—something which under his cautious political management he would doubtless have refused. In fact, Dudley cared most about electing state legislators who would be choosing a United States Senator from Indiana. He worried about the *"close counties"* which some woodcutters' votes might carry, and used the national contest to enlist Garfield's aid in his endeavours.[68]

Dudley and the state committee firmly resisted Dorsey's attempts to impinge on its traditional roles. By mid-September, Dorsey and Dudley had to arrange a formal division of labor in which Dudley took charge of "the appointment of supervisors and Deputy Marshals, and the selection of judges and clerks of election" while Dorsey continued the mysterious "work inaugurated at Chicago." The nature of this work, if it cannot be precisely stated, is not difficult to infer.

Dorsey's main job was to meet the challenge posed by "the inroads of the enemy." Dudley had a spy on the Democratic state committee who informed him of enemy plans to import "professional repeaters & bulldozers from large cities & the South," and to intimidate Negro voters. Jewell in New York collected detailed reports about the movements of New York, Philadelphia, and Baltimore gangs, and telegraphed Dorsey the names of the "well-known roughs" who led them. Chairman John C. New published exaggerated reports of the "Killers," "Desperados," and "notorious ruffians" collecting in Indiana.[69]

Defensive operations against these Democratic tactics were in Dudley's hands, as Dorsey himself testified. The secretary's role was confined to conducting a good offense. The "great vigilance and watchfulness" of Dudley's men would stop some Democratic mischief, Dorsey explained, but "in large Democratic counties and precincts where they [had] entire control, it [would] be impossible to prevent it." Dorsey's job was to "prevent the Democrats from counting us out" by matching their frauds. In doing this, he was carrying on that most viable—however ignoble—tradition of "venal Indiana" which James N. Tyner's activities had exemplified in 1876 and which Dudley was to make famous in 1888.[70]

Dorsey financed about eighty men in forty to fifty counties, probably to lead blocks of "floaters." This however, required nothing like the $400,000 which he later claimed to have spent. On September 27, he wrote to Garfield that "there has not been spent over $40,000 in the entire state" and that he required "not less than $25,000 or $30,000" more by no later than October 5. Even if these election-day expenses had to be repeated in November, Dorsey seems to have gotten by on a great deal less than he claimed.[71]

V

Of course, precise details about the organization of the campaign can never be known—if only because even people in the thick of things at the time did not know what was happening. Richard C. McCormick's description of how the national committee's money went to Indiana vividly evokes the confusion surrounding the entire campaign:

> Indiana delegations have been here in force—all clamorous for money. They have gone, some satisfied and some dissatisfied. Jewell has been kept in the dark concerning the Morton Committee. He thinks the whole fund raised by that committee went to Indiana on Friday night and to Dorsey. It seems impossible to find out the precise relations of Dorsey and New. In all the conflicting elements seem to have patched up at once within a few days, and to be hard at work. I tremble, however, for the result. Where there has been so much confusion and jealousy there can hardly be real harmony and efficiency. Moreover some of our worst men are in the lead, and God only knows what they will do. If they do not cover the party with disgrace, I shall be thankful. Jewell had been badly used, and is a model of patience to submit without making a row. If we lose Indiana I shall have some very plain words for utterance at our committee meeting on the 14th. . . .

With success in Indiana, the "very plain words" were probably never spoken, and the record remained obscure, allowing people to take credit as they would.[72]

Obviously neither Dorsey nor anyone else on the national committee dominated the conduct of the campaign. Rather they all reflected the pressures put upon them by the state committees and the various factional leaders. The committee was reluctant even to send speakers without authorization. "We place no speakers upon the stump," the assistant secretary of the committee explained, "except upon the demands of the Committees of the States." [73]

Thus, despite the attempts of Zach Chandler, Don Cameron, Dorsey, and others of the "old guard," the Republican National Committee remained through 1880 an ancillary to the state committees, with no power over the action of the national convention, little central direction, scant control of the way the funds it raised were spent, and hardly any organizational continuity. The more active role of the candidate himself in naming the chairman and attempting to guide the use of funds, and the establishment of *ad hoc* financial committees diffused rather than concentrated power. The necessities of the state committees, especially in doubtful states, remained determinative. The stalwart attempt at national organization had been flawed from the start. Lacking national goals, it had tried to make national means serve the ends of a few state parties. A desperate venture, it failed to alter the historic decentralization of the party and only succeeded in completing the demolition of the factional structure by which the men of the seventies had responded to that decentralization.

III

❦

1884: Confusion

Conflicts between a stalwart faction and its various opponents no longer defined Republican national politics after 1880. The catastrophic events of Garfield's short, stormy administration fatally weakened the old factional structure. What Roscoe Conkling called the "United States of Ohio" suffered a temporary division when Garfield's death left the Ohio party badly split on presidential candidates for the first time in its history.[1] Blaine became a private citizen writing *Twenty Years of Congress* and anonymous letters to the press. Conkling actually retired from politics, leaving the stalwarts of 1880 to seek new alliances and leaders.

The new party situation confused even experienced politicians. Accustomed to the more rigid factionalism of the past, even men like Blaine and Sherman did not fully adjust to the more amorphous political world emerging in the eighties. They easily slipped into facile assumptions about who were friends and who enemies in a world in which the main requirement for organizing a presidential coalition was to erase old enmities, not to draw fresh battle lines. While some leaders were still laboring to rouse the faithful and cast out the wicked, others, more attuned to the subtleties of a changing national party, quietly worked out informal means of bringing together old opponents. The two pursuits could even go on together in the same cause: Blaine worked to maintain the old factions even as his chief manager, Stephen B. Elkins, artfully arranged tenuous alliances among enough Republican leaders to nominate Blaine. Yet the two functions could complement each other. For the only available ground on which to hold together even temporarily a community of interest among old enemies was a common hostility, and its most likely object was the new and accidental President.

Chester Alan Arthur by virture of an assassin's bullet occupied center stage. Tall, handsome, well dressed, a member of good New York clubs, Arthur was a model gentleman and very much looked the part of a president. His scrupulous honesty was well-known: who else had been quartermaster-general for a rich state in the Civil War and had left service with empty pockets and a reputation for efficiency? Yet his sudden elevation aroused anguished cries of "My God, Chet Arthur in the White House!" For Arthur was thoroughly identified with the factionalism and machine politics of the Grant era. Knowledgeable politicians prophesied a return of the "machine methods" of 1880. Blaine ranted that "Arthur means death and political destruction to every Garfield man." But the President knew he could not revive a dead faction. Instead he retained many of Garfield's appointments and continued the Hayes-Garfield Southern policy rather than returning to power the Negro Republicans who had supported Grant so faithfully in 1880.[2]

Blaine, on the other hand, had not learned that his war with the stalwarts had ended. While he was Garfield's Secretary of State, he had pressed the President's attack on the Conkling machine in New York. After the assassination, he returned to his traditional strategy, hoping to lead an anti-stalwart coalition against the President. Blaine attacked Arthur both publicly and surreptitiously for his Latin American policy, his Southern policy, and especially his tariff policy, while Arthur struggled—although less and less as time went on—to maintain friendly relations with Blaine. Even before anti-Blaine newspapers began to attack the ex-Secretary of State openly, Blaine was planting items denouncing the President and his cabinet in Reid's New York *Tribune*. For two years Blaine poured his energy into a vain attempt to establish a party platform for 1884 that could support Blaine or a candidate of his choosing, but not Arthur.[3]

The attempt had to fail. A politician needs the most emotion-laden issues for successful ideological warfare with a President of his own party. The year 1884 was not 1896, nor was Blaine a William Jennings Bryan. He was arguing minor policy differences in a particularly slack political climate. In the South, the argument was simply over which white factions to support; on the tariff, over what gestures to make toward reform. Only in foreign policy was there any real difference between Arthur and Blaine, and this was hardly the issue to stir voters or party politicians in the early eighties.[4] In fact, very little stirred voters in those years. James S. Clarkson recalled the politicians' surprise in 1884 when "the brass band, the red light, and the mass meeting seemed suddenly to have lost their power." John Sherman was upset by the "lassitude" he found in 1884. "Clubs are formed," he complained, "but do not meet and but little is said about politics." Even the lead-off speaker of the Republican convention of that year, instead of rousing the faithful, noted "the comparative lull of party strife which distinguishes the present condition of National politics."[5]

Blaine had realized none of this. Despite his reputation for political shrewdness, he seemed out of touch with the confused and sluggish currents of the era's politics. This is true not only of his sense of issues, but also of the organizational basis of the party's politics—no longer divided into identifiable factions. Blaine's main success was simply in keeping his name before the public and maintaining enthusiasm for him among party workers. Fortunately for him, publicity and enthusiasm were a partial substitute for political organization in 1884. Reputation and popularity were more useful in gaining strength among active party workers than had been true in other years when clear lines forced politicians into one of two mutually antagonistic factions. When other Republicans would come to reckon up their interests in the presidential nomination, Blaine's popularity among their constituents would encourage them to turn toward him in alliance against the President rather than to Arthur against the popular man from Maine. Blaine's strength in many areas waxed unhampered by the abrasions of faction and very little encouraged by any organized effort of his friends.

Blaine's supporters did little to organize their forces. His political managers were a small but influential group of prominent New York Republicans who had opposed Conkling and identified politically with Blaine. Of these men, derisively called "half-breeds" by the stalwart politicians, Whitelaw Reid was the logical clearing house for information about any Blaine organization. His newspaper had been a national organ for the faction since the seventies and Reid was close to almost all the prominent New York Blaine men both in the party organization and in the business community. Politicians in other states who favored Blaine naturally turned to him.[6]

One such man was James S. Clarkson, editor of the *Iowa State Register,* and one of the most powerful Iowa Republican leaders. From 1876 to 1884, he had led solid Blaine delegations to the Republican National Convention. By

1884 he was tired of seeing his hard work wasted for lack of convention organization. Early in May, with the convention scarcely two weeks away, Clarkson heard only of organization in the President's interest and still had no idea what to do when he reached Chicago.[7]

Anxious to avoid a repetition of past failures, he wrote letters to William Walter Phelps and Reid—both of whom he knew only by reputation. His letter offers a remarkable overview of management for Blaine.

> We are getting a little bit anxious out in Iowa to know if there is going to be any Blaine wigwam at Chicago. We also want to know when we should be there, to go to work, and to whom we are to report and under whom we are to work. . . .
>
> In 1876 there was but the poorest of organization for Blaine at Cincinnati. In 1880 there was practically no organization, and many of our best men were frozen to death in the Blaine ante-rooms. We do not want to repeat these mistakes this year. . . .
>
> Have you any information to give us—or any suggestions to make? We are anxious to be at work, and uneasy at seeing the other side so active.
>
> We would all be glad to hear from you, or from somebody. We want to be put to work.[8]

Reid meanwhile had received a similar message from Judge William H. West, the one open Blaine man among the Ohio delegates-at-large, and therefore marked as the leader of that state's Blaine forces.

Since no national organization yet existed, Reid was at a loss for a reply to either man. He could only promise that Elkins and the other New York Blaine men would "doubtless have consultations on the subject, and may communicate further with you." He urged West to "get the Blaine forces in Ohio thoroughly organized," but made clear that the New York Blaine men would supply neither money nor any serious help. Ohio and the other states would have to take care of their own.[9]

One important point, however, was finally settled: Elkins was "the man to organize the forces." By May 21, Reid could notify Clarkson that "the Hon. S. B. Elkins formerly of New Mexico, who is very familiar with the Blaine strength, is likely to be on the field early and to act efficiently in bringing the Blaine delegates together." Obviously, arrangements were still tentative. The vaguely apologetic tone of Reid's letter was typical of the whole Blaine drive toward a national organization of its forces.[10]

Stephen Benton Elkins who emerged as Blaine's manager in 1884 was then forty-three years old. In a career that had led him from Missouri to New Mexico, to Washington, to West Virginia, and finally to New York, he had amassed a fortune from law, lobbying, land and mineral speculations in New Mexico; and railroad, timber, and coal development in West Virginia. He had been a member of the Republican National Committee as well as territorial representative to Congress from New Mexico since 1875, and he had made himself into the man of the hour in 1884 by a series of strategic political liaisons growing out of his multifarious business involvements.

Elkins had gotten his start in politics under the patronage of McCormick, secretary, territorial delegate, and governor of Arizona, and secretary of the Republican National Committee. Another important association going back nearly to the Civil War was with Jerome B. Chaffee. They were both territorial delegates in the mid-seventies, had combined forces to push bills for Colorado and New Mexico statehood, and had become partners in land, mining, and railroad interests in New Mexico, West Virginia, Colorado and elsewhere. Probably through Chaffee, Elkins became involved in land speculations with John A. Logan. In addition, his friendship with Blaine, which went back to Elkins's term as territorial delegate to Congress, blossomed forth both politically and in business dealings until, as Blaine's biographer notes, "Elkins was his most constant financial adviser." [11]

Thus, by 1884 Elkins was in a position to influence events. He had close political and financial connections with prominent Republicans of all persuasions. Although he had worked for Blaine's nomination in two previous conventions and directly represented his interests on the national committee, he remained friendly with prominent stalwarts, and was not widely identified with Blaine's interests. Dorsey knew him well enough to seek his aid when the star route scandal broke. He was friendly with Senator Edmunds of Vermont, another presidential hopeful, and through his father-in-law, Henry Gassaway Davis, had numerous contacts in the Democratic party.[12]

Elkins had increased his political flexibility enormously when he left his profitable Washington lobbying and law practice and moved to New York City in 1878. Starting with "$100,000 and . . . many thousand acres of land," he sold land and mining shares, while building a great industrial empire in West Virginia in partnership with his father-in-law. He was fortunate to avoid the factional strife and prominent identification with Blaine that would surely have been the result of his remaining in Washington during the Garfield administration. In New York, he kept clear of the political spotlight, avoiding with Blaine's approval any public involvement in the battle against Conkling. He seemed out of anyone's immediate competition for political preferment.[13]

Thus, if the situation in 1884 were to lead Blaine's former opponents into his camp, there would be few roads less painful to travel in that direction than to be guided by so astute, so businesslike, and so apparently even-handed a manager as Stephen B. Elkins. Undoubtedly Blaine made a wise move in sending him to Chicago with a letter that gave Elkins "entire and absolute discretion" to represent the candidate's interests and even to commit Blaine to any agreement Elkins chose to make.[14]

II

Elkins made his most important contribution to Blaine's nomination not as convention manager, but in a much more informal role in the early eighties. He and Chaffee were extraordinarily well placed to bridge the gap between Blaine and the old stalwarts. Chaffee had been close to Logan and Grant since the seventies, and his connection with Grant became even more intimate in 1879 when his daughter married Grant's son. Elkins, we have seen, was a major figure in Blaine's entourage. As the asperities of 1880 faded, the two partners' potential for influencing presidential politics waxed enormously. Both were rich and involved in exciting speculative enterprises. Grant, Blaine, and Logan, all relatively poor men, were tempted by prospects of easy money. Logan speculated in New Mexican land with Chaffee and Elkins. Grant invested everything he had in a banking house that Chaffee apparently financed. Blaine had pinned his financial hopes on the West Virginia and Pittsburgh Railroad (popularly known as "Blaine's Railroad"), which Elkins and his father-in-law were building.[15]

All of this is not to say that Chaffee and Elkins were manipulating these politicians any more than Reid was manipulating Tom Platt politically because Platt was receiving a salary from him. The political connections were not dependent upon business connections any more than the business interests in question were seriously dependent on national politics. (State politics in many instances would be a different matter.) Rather, political contacts could be an effective opportunity for partnership in business, or business relations a contact that could be turned to political advantage. What Elkins and Chaffee offered Grant, Logan, and Blaine was the *opportunity* for political alliance. When these men's political interests were in conflict as in 1880, such an opportunity did not exist any more than Elkins's business and family connections with Henry Gassaway Davis provided an avenue for uniting with him on national politics.

Chaffee and Elkins served rather than commanded the politicians whom they were trying to enrich and to project into high office. They sought public honors: a reputation as president-maker or a position in the cabinet. They enjoyed the game and the company of politicians, were politicians themselves, and did not distinguish too sharply their political from their economic activities. Each called for similar talents and was justified by a similar rhetoric. They might show more talent than a Logan or a Blaine in making money, but these men had achieved more politically: each could respect the other in his striving for the goods and glories of life.

The usual ground for coalition in American presidential politics is not a common policy, but a common enemy. What joined Blaine, Grant, and Logan—indeed Elkins and Chaffee as well—was opposition to the Arthur administration. Blaine considered Arthur an old enemy. Grant, initially friendly, became increasingly hostile as his advice on patronage was ignored. Logan, whose greatest political capital was his friendship with Grant and his popularity with the GAR, followed Grant into opposition.

Logan became the President's first open competitor. Grant was no longer a serious presidential possibility. Blaine, probably as a result of the election of 1882, which had gone badly for the Republicans, believed that "the tides [would] run irresistibly for a Western man for President," and claimed that his own ambition was to be Secretary of State again. By October 1882 newspaper rumors had Logan and Blaine agreeing that whichever man developed the most strength against Arthur would receive the support of the other. If Blaine were the candidate, Logan would be on the ticket, and if Logan were the candidate, he would make Blaine his Secretary of State.[16]

Like most rumors, this one was partly true and partly false. Blaine had several western candidates in mind. The election was far off and Blaine's mind would change with his own prospects. But the efforts of Chaffee, now Logan's manager, to combine almost all elements opposing the administration behind Logan's candidacy supplied the kernel of truth in this rumor. Chaffee expected Grant's support, approached Roscoe Conkling as well, and for a time had hopes of reaching Don Cameron until it became obvious that Cameron was moving close to the administration. Chaffee had some vague arrangement with Blaine, but remained suspicious. "Sometimes I fear Blaine is not sincere in saying he is not going to try," he wrote to Logan in June 1883, "or not let his name be used by his friends." [17]

Chaffee, to boost Logan's candidacy, tried to become chairman of the Republican National Committee in December 1883. Because of his wide reputation as an able political manager, his outspoken hostility to the President, and the novelty of someone from outside the committee campaigning for the chairmanship, Washington buzzed with rumors and excitement. But most Republicans, and most national committeemen, remembering the incidents of 1880, insisted on a neutral chairman. A long night of lobbying produced a compromise in which Chaffee withdrew his candidacy in return for being named temporary chairman of the committee. A neutral—in fact obscure—figure, D. M. Sabin of Minnesota, became chairman until the meeting of the 1884 convention.[18]

For all Chaffee's efforts, Logan's candidacy failed from

the first, while Blaine, despite all disclaimers, gained support in such Republican states as Iowa, California, and Pennsylvania. Logan continued to have strength only in Illinois, and even there he needed Blaine's cooperation to keep control of the party. But the agreement that had been rumored since 1882 apparently was still in force. Blaine newspapers in the spring of 1884 began to smooth the way for Logan to throw his support to their candidate by defending those who had worked back and forth between the two men from the charge that they had throughout been working for Blaine. The Philadelphia *Press* justified Chaffee's connection with both candidates by arguing that his activities were not so much "pro-Blaine" as "anti-Arthur." His goal all along had been "to keep intact the alliance of elements that oppose the President." [19]

In mid-May, Chaffee and the Blaine leaders finally made the inevitable decision to push Blaine's candidacy. Naturally some of Logan's friends were upset over his relegation to the second place. One wrote bitterly to him of the New York meeting "to determine whether you must pull off the track and give all to Blaine." [20] Chaffee and Elkins cajoled Logan into accepting this outcome. Chaffee still claimed to prefer Logan's nomination, but "How," he asked, "can it be done?" This is hardly the question a manager asks his candidate, but Chaffee was more interested in keeping the convention geared against the administration than in nominating Logan. In any case, as Elkins pointed out to his reluctant vice-presidential prospect, he and Blaine now had the same enemies: "[T]hey say beating Blaine beats Logan." The old general understood this well enough to cooperate and the Blaine-Logan combination succeeded at the convention.[21]

III

Arthur was obviously Blaine's most dangerous opponent in 1884. His control of the southern delegations neatly balanced Blaine's dominance in the smaller Republican and doubtful states.[22] As in the past, the contest for the nomination would be fought out in the large states. With both Illinois and Ohio presenting candidates, the direct contests between the President and his popular rival came in Pennsylvania and New York. Events in these two states strikingly demonstrated Arthur's political weakness.

In Pennsylvania, the President made the first move by appointing a Cameron supporter, Benjamin Harrison Brewster, as Attorney General. Blaine in turn cautiously identified himself with an anti-Cameron Independent Republican reform movement. Hostility to the organization, encouraged by the stalwarts' defeat at the national convention of 1880, came to fruition in 1882. Pittsburgh's wealthy ironmen led an attack on Christopher L. Magee's Allegheny County machine, demanding conventions in each state senatorial and representative district rather than a single county convention. In Philadelphia, reformers and local anti-Cameron politicians ran Independent Republican candidates in the state election, winning enough votes to give the Democrats victory.[23]

The result pleased Blaine, who had himself anonymously attacked Cameron's candidate for governor in the newspapers, but it terrified everyone in Pennsylvania politics except the Cameron organization and the Democrats. Politicians who had encouraged the Independents saw themselves on the edge of an abyss. With the loss of state officers, federal patronage grew more vital. James McManes of the Philadelphia "city" machine, who had dallied with the independents, was begging for help within weeks. He needed the city's federal patronage to prevent it from going Democratic the next year, a result which could make the state permanently Democratic by transforming the 13,000 to 15,000 men in the city government, the utilities companies, and comparable agencies, into Democratic voters. Cameron had the upper hand. His opponents were *"abject* in their offers of submission." The Independents seemed to have become dependents of the machine.[24]

But just as the opponents of 1882 needed Cameron, neither could he, even with administration backing, do without them. Before the 1882 elections, Quay, Cameron, and the Attorney General had planned to retake control of Philadelphia by appointing Quay naval officer of the port at the head of a slate of organization men who would control the city's port, post office, and mint. But even while Quay prepared to gather delegates pledged to Arthur for 1884, he feared any overt effort to crush—or even to arouse—the Independents. He and the President awaited the moment when he could safely be named naval officer, but that moment never came and Quay never got his federal appointment.[25]

The entire party desired peace above all else. The Blaine newspapers called for a united state party in 1884. Leaders of the Independent Republican movement, unlike similar groups in New York and Massachusetts, cared too much about the protective tariff to risk Republican defeat nationally in order to achieve reform, and made their peace with Cameron before the 1883 elections. The President labored to satisfy all the state's factions in his appointments. Yet even after victory in that year, Don Cameron still feared that Pennsylvania might be "none too sure for the Republicans" in 1884.[26]

Arthur's relationship with Quay and the organization became increasingly difficult. Fearful of the reformers' hostility, the President could not give Cameron all the appointments he expected. Nor could the organization totally commit itself to the President's ambitions unless he was sure of success. The Pennsylvania leaders' national interests had changed completely since 1880. They planned no desperate coup; rather the presidential contest was a potential embarrassment that might stir up the opposition—over which they were only now regaining control. Because of their need for the "over-ripe patronage" which the President doled out to them ever so slowly, they would not back an anti-administration candidate. But neither would they commit their prestige to Arthur unless he could be nominated without renewing the old battles.[27]

Early in 1884, Quay carefully began to move away from Arthur. In the interest of harmony, Quay conceded Philadelphia's share of the delegates-at-large to the Blaine men. McManes could boast of a "very complete" victory in the closely fought primaries in March, but Cameron and Quay had only lost what they had already conceded, and had gone a long way towards dissociating themselves from the fortunes of the President. Blaine clearly had more popular support in the state than Arthur, and Quay had no intention of gratuitously pitting the Cameron interest against the Blaine sentiment. A few days after the Philadelphia primaries, as a graceful concession, state committee chairman Thomas V. Cooper's newspaper came out for Blaine after having steadily supported the President.[28]

But the organization could not avoid all conflict. In Pittsburgh, a citizens committee, led by Congressman Thomas M. Bayne and Benjamin Franklin Jones, president of the American Iron and Steel Works and soon to be chairman of the Republican National Committee, renewed the attack on Magee's leadership in a call for procedural reform and the election of delegates pledged to Blaine. Bayne, an able politician, avoided the tactics of the Philadelphia Independents of 1882. Having no intention of bolting the organization, he instructed the citizens' committee to "go to the primaries and . . . beat them at their own game." This combination of support for Blaine and reform did not seen incongruous in Pennsylvania. Bayne hoped to use it to capture control of the Pittsburgh organization.[29]

With conventions meeting all over the state and instructing for Blaine and the state convention certain to instruct the delegates-at-large for him, Quay's only concern became that of saving Magee. This was the Pennsylvania boss's metier. Quay was not the type to operate smoothly and quietly behind the scenes: he was a pathological gambler who loved an open political battle, preferably rough, dirty, and with the odds slightly in his favor.[30] But in 1884, tied to an unpopular president, he had to move cautiously. "While he is quite willing that the Convention should hurrah itself hoarse for Blaine," the Philadelphia *Press* explained with grudging admiration, "he is desirous that it should also perpetuate the power of former recognized leaders." [31]

Quay's skill in doing this in a convention overwhelmingly in favor of Blaine, ranks with his finest feats of political legerdemain. He managed on the night before the convention to round up a majority of delegates who, in the language of the *Press,* "if not actually opposed to Blaine, would support any plausible programme looking to the maintenance of the old machine establishment." Using this rather uncertain strength, he made a deal with some of his opponents to insure that Blaine's victory did not split the party. He surrendered the first contest of the convention, the temporary chairmanship, without a fight. In return, Blaine men supported Thomas V. Cooper's re-election as chairman of the state committee, insuring the Cameron organization's continuing control of the state political machinery.

Quay failed, however, to get the competing Pittsburgh factions to agree on a compromise, and, when the convention met, Quay "was fighting Magee's battle as if it were his own." For six hours the credentials committee argued over which Allegheny County delegates to seat. Transferred to the convention floor, the contest provided the convention's sole drama. Under Quay's persuasion, enough Blaine delegates voted for Magee to give him a small majority. With Magee's delegation seated, the convention named the delegates-at-large and by an overwhelming majority instructed them for Blaine.

Blaine's triumph was complete. The President had been completely sacrificed to the exigencies of state politics. Two days later, Quay, asked for comments on the convention, blandly stated that he had controlled it throughout [32]—an assertion far less astonishing than the results of the convention for presidential politics suggest. In fact, this pattern of sacrificing national power for state control was typical of the great state bosses. Presidential coalitions were not created by state politicians out of state power blocs. Men like Elkins without local commitments and having neutral non-political avenues by which to seek coalitions were in a far better position to put over a presidential candidate. Politicians like Quay were glad to concede an honor they did not need—that of being the president-maker—for a power in their state that was their political lifeblood.

IV

Until Garfield's assassination, the principal theme of New York Republican politics had been the steady erosion of Conkling's power. The subsidiary theme was Tom Platt's quiet, careful rise to leadership. Unlike the grandiloquent Senator, Platt was a diffident, cautious man with infinite patience for the minutiae of state politics. To become Senator in 1881, he had made peace with the administration. Prodded by Reid, with whom he maintained business relations, he was moving further and further from Conkling. He "lent a willing ear," Reid wrote Garfield, "to my suggestion that he and Cornell could get along well enough with you, and that they must not consider themselves bound up for life with Conkling." [33]

Platt, under serious obligation both to Conkling and to the administration, was skating on thin ice, and when Garfield nominated the senior Senator's arch-enemy, Judge Robertson, as collector of the port of New York, the ice broke. Robertson, rejecting all of Platt's overtures, refused to withdraw. The administration rebuffed all pleas for cooperation. Platt was left only with the prospect of betraying one or another of his contradictory obligations and destroying at one blow his reputation for "promise-keeping and truthtelling," which, in the absence of either charisma or patronage, was at this point his only stock in trade.[34]

Platt escaped the dilemma by persuading Conkling to resign with him and seek vindication in the state legislature. But this cure was almost as bad as the disease, and when Platt withdrew from the re-election contest his political career seemed over. However, he was more resilient than anyone imagined. Garfield's death presented him with unique opportunities by throwing into disarray the forces that were working to replace Conkling, leaving a gaping power vacuum in New York such as had not existed since the early seventies.

Arthur faced enormous difficulties in becoming leader of the New York party. He understood New York politics too well to run the stalwart administration his enemies expected. Conkling was finished, Platt seemed so, and Arthur was on poor terms with Governor Cornell. Moreover, Blaine's friends had controlled the state convention of 1881, picked the slate of candidates, and almost succeeded in putting through a re-organization of the party in New York City that promised long-term power for them.[35]

Cornell, anxious for renomination, turned to the Blaine men. Blaine urged Reid to bring the *Tribune* to Cornell's support because "Conkling and Arthur [were] determined to kill him." He was virtually the Blaine gubernatorial candidate in the 1882 state convention. Conkling's old supporters split between Cornell and Secretary of the Treasury Charles J. Folger, whose candidacy the administration sponsored by methods that infuriated the opposition. In several cities, Arthur replaced treasury officials in the middle of their terms. Jay Gould's agents reputedly worked in Folger's behalf. Delegates received forged telegrams.

These distasteful methods produced Folger's nomination by the slimmest of margins. But they totally demoralized the party which suffered what was then the greatest state election defeat in American history. Everyone blamed the President. He had alienated Cornell and his followers, as well as the Blaine men and the Independents, and had pleased no one. Without question, had he allowed events to take their own course instead of resorting to such extraordinary means, Cornell would have been nominated and Blaine's adherents taken control of the party. But Arthur's gamble had lost as much as it won. It looked easier to wield power in New York as collector of the port than as President of the United States.[36]

Platt had supported Folger against Cornell. Because of the vast federal patronage in New York, especially important after the Democrats took control of the state government, he had tried to maintain good relations with the administration. But Arthur, desiring to maintain harmony with all factions while carrying out the new civil service legislation, could not satisfy Platt's innumerable demands for patronage, especially in the Brooklyn Navy Yard, where Platt's recommendations were more and more frequently rejected by Secretary of the Navy Chandler. By late 1883, he and Chandler reached an open break. Platt, "deserted" by Arthur and finding much anti-Blaine sentiment among the reformers, saw that his future in New York politics was tied to Blaine's. If he could put Blaine's New York supporters under obligation to him, he might discover the road back to power.[37]

Platt's advocacy of Blaine was a risky step. In his autobiography, he has Conkling "struck speechless" at the news. "When he finally found his breath he exclaimed: 'Well, Senator Platt, you are about to do what I could not bring myself to do. You know what Blaine did to us.' " Truly, he could not expect a warm welcome from Blaine's supporters after the events of the Garfield administration and the state election of 1882. They had even tried to block his election as delegate to the state convention from his home district. At Chicago, although he performed services for Blaine that were compared to those of Elkins, and advertised his support for Blaine in a seconding speech, he worked without the cooperation, and even with the hostility, of most of the Blaine leaders. Phelps described him as "a little hero, in a remote parlor upstairs, without any recognition or summons to caucus or council, [who] organized his forces, paid his own bills, and made victory possible." [38]

The Blaine men with their ex-stalwart allies achieved only a plurality of the state convention. A small group of Independent Republicans supporting Senator Edmunds held the balance of power between the major candidates. But by the eve of the convention after much confused negotiation among the factions, the Blaine men seemed on the brink of victory. Arthur's managers, desperate to avoid a defeat in the President's home state, held a midnight meeting with the Edmunds men in Theodore Roosevelt's rooms at Utica. After several hours of discussion, they surrendered everything to prevent a Blaine victory, agreeing to four Independents as delegates-at-large.[39]

The result was equivocal at best. The men selected were clearly hostile to Blaine. On the other hand, no one could claim victory for the President. Elkins's prediction proved accurate: "Whatever may be done," he wrote to Blaine the day of the convention, "will show Arthur's weakness in his own state." Blaine's position had improved since 1880; the seventeen New York delegates of that year had grown to twenty-eight on the first ballot. While New York was not quite Blaine territory, it could no longer be said to oppose him.

The President had fared badly in the two contests. In both states, a reform movement held the balance of power. The Pennsylvania organization sacrificed Arthur to the reformers when they took Blaine's presidential aspirations as a rallying cry, conceding the delegation in order to retain control of the state party. In New York, the reform movement was even more hostile to Blaine than it was to Arthur, and the continuity of political organization had been seriously disrupted by the events of the Garfield administration and the Folger campaign. A small group of political reformers wielded a disproportionate and very temporary power while the practical politicians were uncertain of their interests. Blaine's popularity among the party rank and file, his unpopularity among reformers, and Arthur's inability to be either stalwart or reformer had produced a delegation divided among three candidates and unlikely to exercise very much influence at the national convention.[40]

V

Blaine's strength in New York and Pennsylvania made Sherman's candidacy a forlorn hope. Unable to compete with the President for southern delegates, he had not declared himself a candidate, hoping for a convention dead-lock as in 1880 which might bring the party to him. But this depended upon Blaine being weak in the large East-ern states. "The known opposition of the Independents, the stalwarts and, generally, the money men of New York who fear *magnetic statesmanship*," might defeat him, Sher-man hoped.[41]

Sherman tried to negotiate with both Arthur and Blaine. He offered both candidates agreements on the Ohio delegation in return for cooperation at the conven-tion. Such agreements took one of two forms: a united state delegation for Sherman in return for a promise to switch to the major candidate if he appeared to be win-ning, or a united state delegation for Arthur or Blaine in exchange for a promise that if the major candidate's cause became hopeless, he would turn his forces to Sher-man. These bargains, which Sherman's managers offered in almost every possible variant, depended to a great ex-tent on the by now decadent factional structure. They assumed that the major factions would not tolerate the nomination of an enemy, and that the leaders had suffi-cient control over their delegations to "deliver" them to a pre-arranged second choice.

Neither assumption was true any longer in 1884. J. Don-ald Cameron considered entering an agreement with Sherman, but in the end preferred Blaine's nomination to a risky maneuver which would provoke his Pennsyl-vania opposition. Blaine agreed not to press his candidacy in Ohio in return for Sherman's promise to release his delegates when their votes would give Blaine the nomina-tion, but his managers turned down more elaborate pro-posals to solidify the Ohio delegation either for Sherman or for Blaine in return for agreements on convention strategy. Sherman in the end failed to prevent open divi-sions at the state convention which selected the strongly partisan Judge West as one of the delegates-at-large and produced a delegation about one-half for Blaine.[42]

Blaine entered the convention with a strong position. A majority of the Pennsylvania delegation, half of Ohio, and a sizeable minority from New York would support him on the first ballot and Illinois was ready to switch to him. He had, as in the past, a heavy majority in the solidly Republican states outside of New England, and in the states that were considered doubtful. His main rival, the President, had simply failed to gain strength beyond what he could create out of patronage in the Democratic states and New York.[43] Being so close to a majority from the start, Blaine required only reasonable management at the convention or the failure of the opposition to coalesce behind an alternative candidate.

Blaine's organization at Chicago, although much improved over those of previous conventions, was scarcely a well-oiled machine. Discipline and even communication among Blaine supporters was often highly amateurish. In Ohio, Judge West wrote to every delegate inviting those "chosen by constituencies favoring the nomination of Blaine" to an organizational meeting at the convention site. Such a letter, mailed a week in advance to friend and foe alike, was quickly in Sherman's hands. Another sign of confusion was C. A. Boutelle's old-fashioned attempt to round up delegates in his capacity as president of the "Maine Blaine Club." In mid-May he was writing to Clarkson offering the Maine delegation headquarters as the natural gathering place for his "Iowa friends." That this close friend and political associate of Blaine would create a pale reflection of the 1876 and 1880 organizations is striking testimony to the Blaine camp's disorder in 1884.[44]

Blaine's adherents controlled the national committee, giving them the opening gambit of the convention, the selection of temporary chairman. Like the stalwarts in 1880, they made too much of this minor opportunity. Seeking to publicize a break in Arthur's strength, they named Powell Clayton of Arkansas who had been supporting the President until shortly before the convention. But Clayton was a highly vulnerable figure, linked politically to the men who had perpetuated the star route swindle. His selection gave Blaine's opponents a perfect opportunity to lead off the convention with a test vote which stood an excellent chance of success. The Edmunds supporters, led by Henry Cabot Lodge, immediately moved to substitute the name of John R. Lynch, a Negro Republican from Mississippi. The test vote, which Lynch won 424 votes to 384, revealed an opposition large enough to defeat Blaine if it concentrated on a candidate.[45]

Clayton's loss was also Blaine's. A comparison of this vote with the first ballot shows that Clayton received the solid support of the Blaine forces. In addition, his status as the official candidate and his Civil War record—graphically symbolized by his "empty sleeve"—gave him additional votes from delegates who heeded his supporters' pleas not to "stigmatize a man placed before you by the national committee." His defeat suggested an even lower first ballot total for Blaine. With any fear of his nomination on the first ballot removed, it became certain that an opposing coalition could hold together at least for a time. Both friend and foe recognized that the Blaine managers had led off their efforts with a first-class blunder.[46]

The Blaine men suffered further setbacks on the second day. They were forced to withdraw a motion intended to force delegates either to pledge that they would support the nominee or to withdraw from the convention. Then their candidate for permanent chairman was defeated in committee. By the end of the second day, Blaine's cause seemed to stumble towards catastrophe. Despite strong enthusiasm among delegates and the crowd at the convention, the strategy of his supporters left an impression, as one reporter wrote, that "the managers [were] not skilled, and that Mr. Blaine's cause must suffer at their hands." [47]

But the opposition had its problems as well. The President's supporters, Sherman's following, and the Independents or Edmunds men had coalesced to dispute the temporary chairmanship, but were never able to fix on a compromise candidate. The President's following, largely southern Republicans and other office holders, formed the bulk of this coalition. They scarcely constituted a coherent or disciplined unit, and no one could tell how they would vote if released from their obligation to support Arthur. Probably they would go for whichever candidate appeared strongest—most likely Blaine. Because of this, all attempts at fixing on a candidate other than Arthur or Blaine possessed a somewhat unreal quality.

The President's managers were his old New York associates, James D. Warren, DeWitt Clinton Wheeler, and John J. O'Brien, with the addition of Postmaster General Frank Hatton. They impressed no one. One of Sherman's managers complained of the lack of "Conkling-Cameron leadership to solidify and hold the Southern Delegates to Arthur as they were . . . held to Grant." But it is difficult to see how even the best management could have overcome the weaknesses inherent in Arthur's candidacy, and a return to the kind of southern-based faction that existed in 1880 was now impossible. At best, the Arthur managers might have swung their votes to another candidate acceptable to the rest of the coalition. But, as one of Sherman's correspondents put it, "the administration men found that they could not unite upon any one in such a shape as to succeed." The most likely coalition candidates, Sherman or Benjamin Harrison, both suffered from the same liability: too strong a sentiment for Blaine in their own states.[48]

One of Sherman's managers had an alternate strategy. Mark Hanna was one of the great surprises of 1884. Only a few months before, one of Sherman's correspondents described him as "a quiet, intelligent businessman with no political acquaintance or political influence." When he was elected one of Ohio's delegates-at-large no one was sure which candidate he supported. "I think Hanna is for you," one politician wrote to Sherman after the state convention, "tho' he promised Blaine men right and left." But at Chicago he amazed everyone with the zeal and expertise he displayed in the Ohio man's cause.[49]

Hanna adopted the classic strategy of the second choice. Since he could not move the Arthur men as a group, he worked among the southern delegates and the purchasable or bargainable northern ones seeking agreements that if their first choice—usually Arthur—faded and Sherman showed a gain, they would switch to him. To show this gain for Sherman, Hanna worked out a loose agreement with the Edmunds men for them to come to Sherman when it became apparent that Edmunds had no chance and that Blaine's nomination was imminent. In return the Sherman men supported Lynch for temporary chairman —the one move by which the Independents intended to show their power.[50]

Although Blaine was gaining in the first three ballots, Hanna still nursed the hope that a movement to Sherman by the Edmunds men—almost 70 votes—would provoke a break in the South bringing with it the rest of Arthur's votes. Lodge and Roosevelt promised such a move if Hanna kept his delegates from going over to Blaine. "I felt," Hanna later explained to Sherman, "that I could not in justice to you neglect that chance."

But Sherman's candidacy was woefully weak. His vote even in his own state had shrunk from 25 to 23 to 21 on the three ballots, and the Edmunds men could see no purpose in switching to him. They did not believe that Arthur's delegates would follow. Roosevelt knew that Blaine was the second choice of most of the Arthur men, which, he later explained, "made it absolutely impossible to form a combination against him." The Sherman men, however, were angered by what they considered the broken promises of the Independents. One talked of "the absolute downright bad faith of Massachusetts people"; another telegraphed Sherman that "the failure of the Massachusetts delegation to come to us on the 2 and 3 ballots as arranged for results in the nomination of Blaine on this ballot." The coalition had not coalesced.[51]

Most observers agreed that both the Arthur and the Independent managers were inept. But this judgment must be tempered by the observation that both were in a situation where they were virtually unable to make a deal, however shrewd they might be. The Edmunds delegates did not want to abandon their candidate and the Arthur managers could not hope to transfer delegates who preferred Blaine to another candidate. Hanna's strategy, although worth the attempt, was doomed to fail. What he tried to do, another and at this point more successful political manager had already guessed would be tried. "I am inclined to think Sherman has some sort of understanding with the opposition," Elkins wrote to Logan shortly before the convention. "In the end I think Arthur and Edmunds will go to him to beat Blaine." Elkins had also diagnosed why it would fail: "I don't think they can transfer enough [votes]." [52]

Elkins was right. The last attempt to combine against Blaine came after the third ballot showed Blaine nearing the 411 votes he needed for the nomination. Still seeking their elusive compromise candidate, the opposition combined on a motion to recess. When Roosevelt, in response to the harangue of a Blaine supporter, rose to the point of order that "the motion to adjourn is not debatable nor amendable," Phelps snapped back, "We do not wish to debate it, but to vote it down." [53]

Voted down it was, by 458 votes to 356.[54] This was conclusive. First Ohio then Illinois moved Blaine's name by acclamation. When the Independents insisted on voting, Blaine easily triumphed on the fourth ballot. However unimpressive his convention managers seemed, they had been successful, and the candidate's gratitude bordered on incoherence. He wrote Elkins from Augusta:

> I want you to come here. I can write nothing. I must speak. I want to express to you now all the gratuitive admiration obligation [sic!] which the human heart can feel. For myself I want to speak of my hopes for us, perturbations, confidences and distrusts. It is idle to open the subject on papers, I must see you face to face.
>
> I postpone everything till I see you.[55]

For what it was worth, Blaine had the nomination and the national party.

VI

Unlike Garfield in 1880, Blaine had definite ideas on the organization of the campaign. The key to his plans was Elkins, the man who "will have to do the work in any event." Elkins, he hoped, would be chairman of a small executive committee, with another skilled manager as secretary of the national committee. These two would bear the brunt of the political work. Blaine, remembering Dorsey's role in 1880, thought that the secretary would be "the executive man" just as W. E. Chandler in 1880 had conceived the organization of the campaign in terms of the campaign of 1876 in which the chairman had been so powerful. Where there was so little continuity, everything seemed to set a precedent.

Blaine assumed that as in 1880 the chairman would be a figurehead whose main role would be fund raising. He hoped to tap the protected industries of the East to finance a campaign devoted to the tariff, and thought that B. F. Jones, the Pittsburgh steelman, was the key to his plans. The national committee duly followed his scheme, selecting Jones as chairman, making Samuel Fessenden, an experienced Connecticut politician, secretary, and naming an executive committee which, at Elkins's insistence, had Chaffee as its head and Elkins as simply a member. Jones also took charge of a finance committee, which he knew in advance would be his main field of activity.[56]

Blaine's organizational plans probably reflected the decreasing reliability of assessments as a means of raising funds. The rising sentiment for civil service reform which had produced the conviction of a treasury official in 1882 for collecting assessments and the passage of the Pendleton Act in 1883 made it doubtful that the Arthur administration, hostile to Blaine in any case, would cooperate in collecting from federal employees. The experience of 1880 suggested that someone like Jones as chairman of the national committee could open alternate sources of funds.[57]

Since it was now clearly illegal for an employee of the federal government to collect assessments, the Republican leadership appointed a committee called the "District of Columbia Finance Committee of the Republican National Committee" with five members, none of them currently federal employees. They were empowered to "receive such voluntary contributions as Government employees and others [might] desire to offer." The committee was by no means unskilled in the darker political arts. One of its members was Green B. Raum of Illinois who had only recently resigned after a lengthy term as United States Commissioner of Internal Revenue, one of the most powerful political positions of the so-called "minor cabinet." But lacking the possibilities of coercion and the wholehearted support of the Arthur administration, this group raised about a quarter to a half of what the party had formerly received from federal employees.[58]

This decrease in the importance of assessments, and the appointment of a new committee to collect them, made the role of the Republican Congressional Committee uncertain. Since it no longer collected assessments, the committee's secretary, Edward McPherson, assumed that the national committee would defray its expenses. But National Chairman Jones had no such intention. He expected the congressional committee to meet its own expenses by "what your committee could collect from people desiring to make contributions" (which is to say covert assessments), by a generous use of the franking privilege to distribute its literature, and by charging fees to the state committees and clubs that received the documents. But Jones's hopes were unrealistic. McPherson could not support his own operations, and the national committee was forced continually to divert funds to Washington, although always later and less than promised.[59]

Blaine and his manager Elkins had taken a far more extensive role in the organization of the national committee than any previous Republican presidential candidate. This annoyed some party leaders. Early in August, before the committee had done very much in the campaign, their dissatisfaction had already convinced Blaine of the need for "two or three more members of National Committee at Headquarters, . . . to take away the impression of the thing being run exclusively by my familiar friends." [60]

With Blaine firmly in control of the national organization, maintaining harmonious relations with the vice-presidential candidate was another sensitive matter. Amid rumors of conflict, Elkins immediately established himself as the go-between, and at least pretended to consult with Logan on the major decisions. As he went to confer with Blaine, he asked Logan to "drop . . . a line to Augusta making any suggestions that [might] occur to you." He sent Logan passes for the B. & O. Railroad to come to Deer Park "where we expect to see you often during the summer" for conferences. Most of all, he urged Logan to do what Blaine could not: "write Grant and Conkling you expect them to help." [61]

When problems arose in Illinois, Chaffee and Elkins were the men to deal with Logan. Party divisions were intense, and Chaffee went to make peace among Illinois Republicans early in August before any serious campaigning could begin. When the national committee wanted to raise funds in Chicago for the early election in Ohio, Elkins first had to smooth the way with Logan who was jealous of any attempt to take money out of the state. The Republican National Finance Committee's one member from the Midwest was a follower of Logan. Jones found him an unprofitable servant, eventually turning to the anti-Logan men for aid. [62]

Blaine and his managers had to set policy toward the minor parties: the Prohibitionists and the Greenback-Labor-Antimonopoly candidacy of Ben Butler. Completely independent third parties were rare in this era. They frequently arose in circumstances where they could hope to possess the balance of power between the large parties, and in such cases, were ready for fusion arrangements to gain minor offices in exchange for their crucial votes. When a small party resisted fusion, it was often because the party had won an outright subsidy from whichever major party stood to gain by keeping it in the field.

Republican managers underestimated the Prohibitionist

candidacy of John P. St. John, ex-governor of Kansas, until it was too late and then they could only exhort those interested in temperance to vote Republican rather than risk a Democratic victory. Republican newspapers published appeals from Republican temperance men asking St. John to quit the race while Elkins and others made unsuccessful attempts to negotiate his withdrawal. In all likelihood St. John found support from the Democratic party and therefore continued his campaign. After the campaign, Teddy Roosevelt charged that "if the Prohibitionists had been as honest as they claim, Blaine would have won." [63]

The old mountebank Ben Butler, preparing his final public performance, was easier to manage. The question was never whether he could be bought, but merely if he had anything to sell. "It was difficult to tell what the gains and losses would be by his staying out or his going in," Blaine wrote Elkins in July. When the Greenback and the Antimonopoly parties nominated Butler in May, he had written a noncommittal reply to the offer and waited for the actions of the major parties. Rejected by the Democrats, he was ready to turn to their enemies to defeat Cleveland and his Mugwump allies. Blaine at first did not want him in the race, arguing that a majority of the vote that might go to Butler would otherwise be Republican. Bu when it became clear that the Mugwumps were hopelessly gone, Butler looked like a means of making up the loss. Although the Greenbackers were primarily an agrarian party, if Butler could appeal to laboring men in the East who would vote for him but not for Blaine, he could offset the independent bolt. As a result, the national committee agreed to subsidize Butler's campaign to the extent of $5000 per week.[64]

Soon after his nomination, Blaine commissioned the respected John B. Henderson to persuade the reform leader Carl Schurz to support the ticket. Henderson did not reach very high ground in defending Blaine. "If he has been a Prince Hal in days gone by," Henderson wrote to Schurz, "when responsibility comes he will be a Henry V. The Falstaffs . . . will not . . . be suffered to bring odium upon his administration." Schurz was unimpressed by such reasoning, arguing that even were it true, "the mere fact of his election" would have a deleterious moral effect on the nation.[65]

The Mugwump revolt rapidly became one of the realities of political life about which the managers could do nothing. Exactly why some of the most respectable Republicans found Blaine the incarnation of political evil, while others became deeply involved in defending him, is a mystery of American ego politics that cannot be answered by studying political organizations. When the president of Yale and the president of Harvard disagreed on a moral issue, who could decide? Blaine could only try to limit the influence of the bolt by obscuring the motives behind it, ascribing it not to uneasiness over his political morality but to the tariff issue—of which he fervently believed he was on the politically correct side. Continually he urged the tariff issue. The *Tribune* must "agonize more and more on the Tariff"; "keep a steady flow in editorial columns on Tariff—protection—*wages*—especially *wages*." This would keep down the "howl about Mulligan and . . . that kind of hog-wash." [66]

Another question the national leadership had to consider was the party's stance toward the South. Blaine hoped to win Southern states by playing down the "bloody shirt" theme and stressing that section's interest in the tariff. As part of this campaign, the national committee opened a branch headquarters in Nashville and issued an "Appeal to the South," urging voters to place present economic interest over past prejudice. Blaine's policy met considerable opposition in the party. Logan, who never believed in the strategy, furiously waved the bloody shirt. The West Virginia October state elections, on which the managers had pinned their hopes, went against the Republicans, and a few days later Blaine was once again attacking the solid South.[67]

The practical politicians of the Gilded Age found the so-called "labor vote" one of the great mysteries of the American electorate. Sometimes they saw it simply as the "Irish vote" which would respond to "twisting the lion's tail" and speaking kindly of the Catholic Church. But that was not always a satisfactory approach. Political involvement serves the need for self-identity, and to make a successful appeal politicians must approach a group through the identity that the group wishes to assert. Whether to appeal to workers on economic issues or to ethnic groups on "sentimental" ones was never an easy choice. An incident of the 1888 campaign illustrates the problem. A delegation from one of the many short-lived labor parties of the era visited the national committee in search of a place in the campaign. Much to their disgust, they were referred to "a Capt. Delaney who declined our offer to cooperate in this canvass" advising them instead to join "the Irish-American League." "We regret," their secretary wrote to the Republican candidate, "that no effort is made by your committee to secure the aid of Workingmen as Workingmen."[68]

The Irish were sensitive both to events in Ireland and to their position in America. The slow movement of a portion of the Irish vote to the Republicans, which was of such importance in New York and Connecticut, could be checked by the least wrong move, the vaguest hint of a slight from their new allies. The association with the Democratic party was traditional by the eighties and hallowed by the numerous success stories of Irish Democratic politicians. But every dramatic event in the Anglo-Irish struggle produced a new outburst of factionalism among the American Irish, so that Irish nationalist organizations multiplied, and inevitably as some were connected with branches of the Democratic party, others turned for help to the Republicans. By the eighties there were a number of important Irish leaders such as Alexander Sullivan, Patrick Egan, John Devoy, Michael Breslin, Patrick Ford, and William Carroll who organized their following with Republican funds, serving both Irish nationalist and Republican party ends.[69]

Blaine had long been making appeals to Irish votes by emphasizing his hostility to Great Britain, his part-Irish background, his Roman Catholic relatives, his support for Irish freedom, and his opposition to "British free trade." His chances in New York rested heavily on making heavy inroads among Irish voters. Blaine planned to make both an ethnic and an economic appeal on the tariff issue, stressing both its assumed effect on wages and its hostility to British interests.[70]

Other labor issues were not so easy to handle. A bitter strike in the Hocking Valley coal fields of Ohio, which even John Sherman admitted was "justified by the unreasonable reduction in the price of mining coal," caused alarm when rumors spread that Blaine owned stock in the struck company. He denied this charge on the stump, the only personal accusation that he answered in a campaign filled with them.

The longstanding dispute between Reid's newspaper and the powerful New York Local No. 6 of the International Typographical Workers was another serious problem. Immediately after his nomination, a committee from the union pressured Blaine to mediate. "Is there any way," he asked Reid, "where I can properly interpose in the Typo Union matter to the advantage of the campaign?" Reid dismissed the unionists' opposition. "The men are mostly against us anyway," he assured the candidate, "and are a thoroughly treacherous and unscrupulous gang, who think they see a chance for political blackmail." Blaine, he advised, should "take a bath and undergo fumigation" after contact with such a "dirty, worthless, cowardly gang."

But Blaine continued to believe that a settlement "with a slight intimation that I labored to bring it about" would change 5000 votes in New York and might mean the election. Late in October the union did endorse Cleveland and Hendricks, although a faction broke off to form an anti-Cleveland club. When Reid himself ran for Vice-President in 1892, he finally risked infestation and came to an agreement with his printers.[71]

The tariff was the key to Blaine's entire campaign, the all-purpose expedient to explain away the Mugwump revolt and appeal to the workers economically, to the Irish as an anti-British policy, and to the "new South" as a "great national movement" in which present and future economic interests would bury past hostilities. And of course the protected industries would underwrite the campaign. As in so many other things, Blaine and his friends were thinking back to 1880 for their precedents, remembering the "tariff scare" occasioned by Hancock's foolish remarks.[72]

The tariff issue never became as important as Blaine hoped and expected. Instead, it was a one-man argument, with Cleveland silent on the issue and Democrats matching Republican promises where protection sentiment was strong. The electorate failed to take great interest in the tariff, being more concerned with vague but perhaps not insignificant—even if unanswerable—questions of moral standards in an age of rapid social and economic change. Identifying the tariff with prosperity and economic growth was simply not persuasive in an economy that had been depressed since 1882 and that had suffered a short but sharp panic in May 1884.

In addition to weakening the Republicans' arguments, the state of business destroyed their hopes for large contributions from the manufacturers. In listing the negative features of the campaign, Jones stressed "the extreme depression of trade especially in manufacturing and mining districts." The campaign was never adequately financed. By mid-summer, politicians feared that wealthy Republicans were not going to "put their shoulder to the wheel." In September and October, when collections usually increased sharply, the same gloom hovered about national headquarters. "Money is coming in *very* slowly," wrote Clarkson, and the party found itself as he later described it, "playing the mendicant upon manufacturers and corporations." The committee issued desperate appeals to the national banks, the railroads, and to individual businessmen such as Huntington and Gould.[73]

Finding money for the early state elections was a traditional function of the national committee since success in them brought out workers and money for the final weeks of the campaign. Ohio, always an important "October state," was a special problem in 1884. The opposition controlled the state government; the party was wracked with dissension; the state committee was desperate for funds; the state organization lacked "aggressive" leadership. The national committee turned to W. W. Dudley, now head of the pension bureau and the great campaign organizer of the era. Through August, complex negotiations, of which only traces remain in the documents, took place among Dudley, the Indiana state committee, the Republican National Committee, the Republican Senator from Indiana, and probably the Arthur administration. They resulted in Dudley resigning from the pension bureau effective November 10 (after election day) and going out to Ohio to organize the campaign and look after the soldiers' vote.[74]

As the October election neared, Clarkson and other members of the committee went west to look over Dudley's organization and decide on financial aid. Blaine had always intended to pour money into Ohio. He considered it good policy to leave the state on its own as long as possible and make no promises, but he never planned "to trust Ohio to its own resources." Having aided in the organization of the state, the committee needed money—estimated at $70,000 to $100,000—to man the polling places, check on Democratic bullies and repeaters, and, one assumes, purchase a few for the Republicans.

The money came hard. Early in October, facing daily pleas from Ohio, Elkins begged Reid to give all his time to fund raising. Clarkson in Cincinnati wrote a desperate plea to Jay Gould for money, describing the difficulties in Ohio. Gould concluding that "Ohio is lost," sent the note along to Reid (who had also been soliciting him) with an angry judgment that while the party had been "frittering away their money at other points the democrats [had] concentrated everything in Ohio." Gould finally promised $5000 but only on condition that the committee raise the full remaining amount needed, at this point $40,000. By October 8 the committee had amassed $36,500 enabling Reid to collect Gould's contribution.

It had been a close squeeze: most of the money had come not as Blaine had hoped from corporations supporting the party that protected and nurtured them, but from wealthy Republican party politicians such as Morton, Chaffee, and Reid. Clarkson raised about a quarter of the total, probably in Ohio. Apparently some of the money came from the far from wealthy candidate himself. Years later a Democratic politician would recall "the great campaign in Ohio in 1884, which bankrupted the Republican party." He was amazingly close to being correct.[75]

Even with victory in the Ohio state elections, the managers still had trouble organizing and financing the doubtful states. Hard pressed for funds and hoping that the Ohio result would be decisive for the West, the committee concentrated on New York, Connecticut, and New Jersey. Indiana, the remaining doubtful state, starved for lack of funds. The state committee had received only a token $5000 from New York late in October. Benjamin Harrison finally solicited funds from Wharton Barker, a Philadelphia banker and prominent reform Republican with ambitions as a president-maker. Barker raised $2250, $1500 of it his own money. If Clarkson's memory of four years later is correct, the national committee finally did send some money three days before the election, which he acknowledged was "scarcely better than no help at all." [76]

The managers' crucial concern for the last three weeks of the campaign was New York. Blaine and Logan were both expected to come east and spend the last weeks in New York and New Jersey, but Logan seems to have refused and continued in the West. Blaine met his commitments in Indiana, but his thoughts were elsewhere, as he wondered whether he should come east to finish the campaign.[77]

New York Republican managers wanted Blaine both for the canvass and to raise money. The state committee, manned by Arthur's organization, was concentrating in some areas on local candidates instead of the national ticket. With the national committee playing an uncertain and dangerous game of vote-trading with Butler, John Kelly of Tammany Hall, and other wavering Democrats, it was important to avoid counter-trades upstate for stalwart candidates. Men who had followed Conkling or who simply recalled the way Blaine's supporters had treated

Folger in 1882 might well feel that they too had license to trade. Blaine, by stirring up a positive enthusiasm upstate, could minimize such defections.[78]

With these questions in mind, Blaine corresponded with his friends in New York. Chaffee, worried about funds, urged him to attend an already scheduled fund-raising dinner. Elkins opposed the whole idea and refused to attend the dinner when it was held. Blaine's first reaction was also negative. "It would be the height of folly," he wrote, "for me to have a great dinner of 100—or to have any semi-public process of raising money. It would cause a panic in the West and make one in the East." Moreover, Blaine doubted its success in raising funds; men like Morton could do "more indeed than I. . . ." But Reid, whose "views in full touching situation in New York and New Jersey" Blaine had requested, presented the argument that convinced him.

In a long and careful reply Reid urged Blaine to come to New York. The state committee was out of funds and refused to spend in advance for collections. The "few people down town" who had provided funds for Ohio in addition to regular contributions, could not be "depended upon for a third supply." "The field of collections," Reid warned, "needs in some way to be greatly widened." Everyone was saying that "if you were here they could raise money. . . . Everyday I hear from them the same cry; money! money!" Reid also thought Blaine's presence upstate was essential: "In a word I suspect that the condition of the interior is still what that of Ohio was before you went into that State."

This extremely persuasive letter, reminiscent of some of Reid's best efforts at providing backbone for Garfield in his battle with Conkling, was neither panicky nor discouraging. Rather it suggested that New York was not yet sure but was ready to be *made* sure by Blaine's presence on the stump and in the conference room. With its constant comparison to Ohio, where Blaine had just won a signal victory after touring the state, it was well calculated to convince him that his magnetic presence would once again turn the tide. Blaine could not but respond to this call for heroics.[79]

Thus the trip east: across the state of New York, through his friend Phelps's district in New Jersey, and then to New York City to organize the final effort. The journey was a political disaster. In one of those incredible accidents that no one could possibly have foreseen, the tired, preoccupied candidate failed to note and correct the Reverend Burchard's stupid reference to "Rum, Romanism, and Rebellion." The effect of this incident, which all agreed was considerable, cost more votes than the Republicans could afford. Every presidential campaign in the eighties produced some symbolic incident—either by accident or plan—to affect the sensibility of the "Irish" or the "labor" vote. If not for the radical instability of this vote and the closeness of the state, the incident could not have had such significance. The Republican managers had important but tricky agreements with John Kelly, with Butler, with Charles A. Dana of the New York *Sun,* with an endless number of politicians controlling small pockets of votes among the highly politicized urban Irish of Manhattan and Brooklyn. While the results in the two cities suggest that these agreements were generally maintained, the Burchard insult meant that the men who had agreements with the national committee could deliver fewer votes than they had pledged and probably in some cases had to repudiate their agreements. The full story of such political dealings will never be known, but Blaine's excellent showing south of the Harlem River despite the independent revolt, and his very high vote in the Irish districts, suggests that the campaign strategy of depending on the Irish labor vote was no miscalculation. If not for Burchard, Blaine would have narrowly succeeded.[80]

The other catastrophe of Blaine's trip, the Delmonico dinner, was no accident. Blaine and Elkins had both opposed it, well aware of what lower class voters would think of a public meeting between Blaine and some two hundred millionaires. Perhaps the arrangements had gone too far and had implicated too many people, or perhaps the considerations that Reid had raised about funds forced Blaine to change his mind. The kind of politicians who had deals with Blaine's managers in Manhattan and Brooklyn demanded election-day funds. If the national committee reneged on its promises, this would not mean simply a decrease in the Republican vote, but undoubtedly a switch to the Democratic candidate as retribution for welching on promises. Blaine may have judged it worth risking the opprobrium that he knew the dinner would produce. Given the way third-party politics operated in the era, it is likely that the Antimonopoly votes which Blaine was said to have lost in New York State were the result no more of resentment over the dinner than they were of the sad fact that the dinner after all failed to raise the expected sum and the leaders of these splinter groups were never paid.[81] There is, unfortunately, scarcely any depth of cynicism to which the historian is not entitled in considering these short-lived creations of petty politicians who may well have been more corrupt than the men who ran the major parties.

Of course, in such a close election, there is no one factor that can be selected as having caused defeat, *any* one variable being enough to make the difference.[82] Yet the politicians were correct in evaluating their chances and performance in terms of such identifiable factors. Their job, especially in a closely divided electorate, was to do what they could and to avoid the avoidable. Shepherding votes

—even in the ten and hundreds—into the party was the core of their work. Clarkson, a consummate professional politician, regretted for years his last-minute decision to unpack his valise instead of going to Utica to assure Conkling's old followers that they would get a fair share of the loaves and fishes were Blaine elected. "I believe to this day," he wrote in 1887, "that if some one had gone there at that time Mr. Blaine's election would have been saved." [83]

Despite the recriminations against them, the Blaine managers had by no means disgraced themselves. In fact, the party had gained ground from the disastrous congressional elections of 1882. While they could not achieve the same importance they would have had in victory, what national organization there was under a Democratic administration centered about the men who had guided the campaign of 1884. By 1888, with the old factional structure completely gone, there would remain no other focus for national organization and counter-organization. About Blaine's amorphous following would revolve one of the least structured nomination contests in party history.

IV

1888: Expectancy

Republicans faced an unaccustomed situation in the approaching 1888 national election. They were now the "out" party, lacking an administration about which organization and counter-organization could revolve. The old factional structure that helped to define friends and enemies across state boundaries was thoroughly moribund. Moreover, the first faint signs of the impending shift in voter preferences which would dominate the politics of the 1890s had already become visible in 1888, leaving politicians increasingly more uncertain of their prospects. These developments pointed in two ways at once. They aroused fears of disorganization, defeat, and even of the collapse of the party if it could not find a way to come together successfully for the presidential campaign. At the same time, the lack of definite factions, the prospect of a wholly new administration, and the still viable hope that the old ways of campaigning and the old estimates of party strength might still hold well enough for one more victory, all created expectations of rewards commensurate with whatever efforts the party might call forth. Everyone could anticipate rewards if the party settled on a neutral candidate and elected him, while many feared political eclipse if they failed. Such an open party situation could lead to a candidate free from the factional hazards of the past, one able to capitalize on the amorphous expectations that such an outcome would create. With luck, the reasonably predictable political world of the eighties might survive a little longer, its outlines blurred but still recognizable, before the insecurities of the age forced new adjustments.

Arriving at a neutral candidate, however, was no easy task. The party had no organizational center. There was no administration to create a network of communications and mutual interests and the national committee under its timid chairman, B. F. Jones, was self-effacing and powerless. The only mechanisms for creating a national coalition —the various presidential "booms" and the national conventions—operated on the fuel of conflict. As Clarkson astutely noted early in 1887, in the "formal struggle" for the nomination, faction would "take its color, and men [would] not be able with self-respect to change positions." The fluid party situation, which held out such promise, would rapidly congeal into a new set of factions to tear apart a party that could hope to win only if it held tightly together.

Clarkson's solution was to use the neutral national committee to "unify and harmonize" the party behind its titular leader, Blaine. What he had in mind was nothing like the stalwart machinations of 1880. Rather, in the absence of any other locus of national organization, he saw the committee as an agency to lift the party above the factionalism of the past. Blaine had to use it well in advance of the convention to convince all the leaders that he would not "maintain a faction," that they would be "as near to Mr. Blaine" as his managers of 1884.[1]

This ingenious scheme to provide the party with both organization and a neutral candidate indicates the core of the party's problem in 1888. Blaine's name could hold together enough Republicans across the country to produce a nomination without new efforts at the creation of factions. But his nomination was useless unless he himself could be divested of the taint of the old factions. And this proved impossible. Blaine believed that his "friends" represented "the large end of the Republican party," and he never ceased to think of himself as the leader of an identifiable faction. Knowledgeable observers interpreted any sign of a candidacy on his part as a move "to keep his forces mobilized." His nomination was the one device that would bring the old quarrels back to life. Blaine's followers, however informally gathered, were a faction in spite of themselves. Less organized than the stalwarts of 1880, harder to define than Arthur's forces in 1884, these devotees of an unwilling candidate were nevertheless the only available focus for organization and counter-organization in the puzzled but still confident party that prepared to challenge Grover Cleveland in 1888.[2]

While the national committee met in December 1887 to select a convention site, issue a call, and delegate a committee on arrangements, Cleveland finally accepted the campaign issue that Blaine had tried to argue in 1884. Cleveland's famous tariff message instantly determined the course of the Republicans. Blaine immediately wired an interview from Paris answering it which was published in the New York *Tribune* on December 8. When the committee met on that day, Blaine's friends took control. Clarkson headed a subcommittee, staffed almost entirely by Blaine men, charged with making preparations for the convention. The convention call, issued the next day, was unique in its detailed enunciation of a party platform—following Blaine's Paris interview in its language on the tariff and treasury surplus, and stressing his foreign policy views of the early eighties.[3]

Many people thought Cleveland had settled the Republican nomination. But Blaine was reluctant to run again. In the fall of 1887, he began assuring his close friends that he would not be a candidate. A perennial hypochondriac, he argued that his health could not stand the campaign nor the office. Like Clarkson, he realized that "a general call of the party at least approaching unanimity" was requisite for his success after the defeat of 1884. Moreover, he disliked "the idea of becoming a chronic candidate." Therefore, he had resolved that "at the proper time . . . I will pull out . . . in a direct, open, and above board way." [4]

This straightforward declaration, however, did not convince Reid, Phelps, Elkins, or Manley—people who knew Blaine intimately. In fact, even his two sons worked vigorously at the convention to secure their father's nomination. They all knew that after his failure in 1876, Blaine had always talked this way, committing himself only after he had rationalized inclination into duty. Blaine's demand for "a general call of the party" seemed pregnant with possibilities. Were Blaine publicly to withdraw, a nomination *over his previous declination* would meet all his criteria for electoral success.

This is not to say that Blaine consciously schemed to create such an outcome—only his managers, especially Elkins, did that. Yet his letters to his friends tacitly asked for such a nomination. He had offered to run again if he were "called upon by an undivided and unanimous party, but not . . . if a contest were required to secure my nomination." The men who received such letters, not surprisingly, took them to mean that Blaine had not so much resigned from the race as delivered an ultimatum that if his friends wanted him as their candidate, they would have to get the entire party to turn to him as its savior.[5]

Blaine, writing to Elkins in March 1888, thought that

his friends should nominate Benjamin Harrison who was not identified with any of Blaine's enemies. Blaine's view of the campaign dictated his choice. He did not expect the Republicans to win in New York even after Cleveland's tariff message. The Democrats under Governor David Bennett Hill had "the national and state patronage and also complete control of the municipal machinery in New York City and Brooklyn." Blaine's hopes for a very thin electoral victory rested with Indiana and Connecticut. Harrison presumably could carry his home state, and the tariff argument would win in Connecticut as it had for Garfield in 1880.[6]

But the party generally refused to give up on New York. Blaine's friends thought that with him on the ticket, the Republicans might carry not only that state, but New Jersey and West Virginia. Politicians found it hard to conceive of a campaign in which New York was not the crucial battleground, and would not demoralize the party in the other doubtful states by openly planning such a strategy. For the first time, men favoring Blaine controlled the New York party. Therefore, his friends could hope to persuade the convention that it must turn to him as the one hope for carrying New York. If this move failed, they could still argue the need for a candidate acceptable to his supporters in New York. The Blaine element, Elkins and Reid cockily asserted, would "largely determine the result at Chicago" and would "elect the candidate, who ever he is," an assertion accepted by most of the other candidates.[7] Elkins's strategy in 1888 combined his candidate's expressed wishes and unstated hopes. He proceeded to play a difficult and slippery game aimed at Blaine's unanimous nomination, or—if that proved impossible—at maintaining control of the party by developing alternative candidates beholden to Blaine's friends for their nomination and election.

II

As Blaine had noted, Benjamin Harrison of Indiana was the most likely alternate candidate. His military career was distinguished, his demeanor glacial but dignified, and his voting record in the Senate unoffensive. Most of all his strength in Indiana had convinced many Republican leaders that he was their most available man for 1888. Elkins's problem was to bring him into the Blaine orbit so that his following could be used in Blaine's cause, or Harrison's nomination, if it came, would be at the hands of Blaine's friends.[8]

Elkins had already become a link between the two candidates, much as he had been for Blaine and Logan in 1884. His opportunity had come in 1886 when the Harrison family fell into financial difficulties due to an overoptimistic commitment in a Montana cattle enterprise undertaken to provide a career for Russell B. Harrison, the Senator's son. Through most of 1886, he teetered on the edge of a bankruptcy which threatened to carry off most of his father's savings as well as money invested in the business by some of Harrison's legal and political associates. Elkins, whose father-in-law Henry Gassaway Davis was a personal friend of the elder Harrison, appeared on the scene to take the young man under his wing. Both Russell and his father, over the objections of the other investors, turned to Elkins for help in selling off the Montana enterprise. Elkins labored for months to sell bonds in the Montana concern and afterward, remaining deeply involved in Russell's tangled finances, used his friendship to cement a political relationship with his father.[9]

Harrison moved closer to Blaine's friends when in the fall of 1887 he took his family for a vacation at Elkins's estate in western Maryland. In several conversations about presidential politics, Elkins made it clear that after Blaine, Harrison was his first choice, and that if Blaine chose not to run, he would work for his guest's nomination. In holding out this possibility, he sought to keep Harrison from following Sherman's lead and becoming an open candidate. Harrison was willing to be the Blaine candidate, with all the delegates that might mean, while from Elkins's perspective, Harrison was keeping the way clear for Blaine.[10]

It is hard to say exactly who was taking advantage of whom in these dealings. Harrison's strength in Indiana made his friendship crucial for any candidate. Elkins asked for and received "a kind word for Blaine" from Harrison's Indiana followers—which allowed him to argue for Blaine's ability to carry the Hoosier state. On the other hand, Harrison managers realized that they could not get a solid state delegation if they antagonized Blaine, and that their man would be much stronger at the convention with Blaine support in the doubtful Eastern states. Then too, Elkins and Harrison had a common interest in opposing the unmistakably anti-Blaine candidacy of Indiana-born Walter Q. Gresham, Arthur's Postmaster General and an advocate of reduced tariffs. In creating this community of interests, Elkins had turned Harrison's friendship into a major asset to Blaine's candidacy, neutralizing a formidable rival while remaining close to the throne if Blaine withdrew.[11]

Blaine's withdrawal complicated Elkins's task and and shifted his relationship with Harrison from ambiguity to duplicity. Since it was no longer possible to say that Harrison was his choice after Blaine, he began to prepare Harrison for the possibility that although "Blaine wants to be out of the canvass and does not desire the nomination . . . it is possible yet that the Convention may, if it finds a sharp division between the other candidates without result, go to Blaine by acclamation." He urged Harrison to get the Indiana delegation solidly behind him, but at the same time advised that "it will be good policy generally wherever a district wants to send a delegate who is, or has been, a Blaine man, uninstructed and untrammeled by pledges or promises, . . . to do so." Harrison, he advised, should stand on his Indiana strength, and wait for Elkins to advance his candidacy "at the proper time and when I think it will best serve your interest." [12]

Elkins was playing an extraordinary double game. He hoped to use Harrison's delegate strength as one of the obstacles blocking Sherman and freezing the convention into a stalemate. Then he envisioned Harrison's markedly pro-Blaine contingent leading a smooth and effortless switch to Blaine. Harrison appears to have understood this, but went along hoping to use rather than be used by Elkins when the moment arrived.

Through the spring of 1888, Elkins worked to build the convention stalemate which would lead to Blaine's nomination. Just as Harrison's delegates would be "for Blaine if necessary," so would those supporting Iowa Senator William Boyd Allison and Michigan Governor Russell A. Alger. Reid brought Alger into the Blaine orbit with a vague promise of the vice-presidency if Blaine were nominated. Elkins brought Allison into the combination through Clarkson, the Iowan's campaign manager.[13]

Clarkson's position was a peculiar one. Long an advocate of Blaine, he became convinced in the course of 1887 that Blaine would "avoid rather than seek the nomination," and worked actively for Allison. His background made it natural that he would try to ally his old friends behind the Iowa Senator. But Elkins's scheme for nominating Blaine was an intoxicant difficult for the old Blaine devotee to resist. In trying to sell Allison, he ended up buying Blaine.

Clarkson had worried all along that the old factional structure would emerge if Blaine became the candidate with anything less than "practically a unanimous vote." And he knew that such a result was impossible: Gresham's supporters would "stand out against him to the last," he reported to Elkins. Moreover, he took Blaine's word on his health. "If we should get him to reconsider and the contest should kill him what would we have to put between ourselves and our condemnation?" he asked. In the middle of a western trip in which he gathered Allison-Blaine delegates according to Elkins's plan, he stopped to agonize for five large typewritten pages on the moral and political impropriety of the scheme to which he had, in fact, become a party. What overcame these scruples emerged only on the sixth and final page: he found "our old line of friends everywhere ready to act together, and to unite at last. . . . The whole list [was] thoroughly formed and ready to respond." Only Blaine's name could keep together the amorphous group of "friends" who tenuously held the party. They found it humanly impossible to surrender the potential for power of their ability to "act together." Even after Blaine's second letter of withdrawal, Clarkson maintained that "holding the old line as nearly as possible" was "our life line." Even if Blaine did not wish to be a candidate, he could not help being an institution, a focus for the political behavior of a number of men.[14]

John Sherman was the great obstacle in the path of Blaine's managers. For two years, Sherman had carefully prepared his presidential bid, gathering an impressive number of able politicians to his banner. In Ohio, Mark Hanna, Charles Foster, Benjamin Butterworth, and John Sills Jones were working for him; in Pennsylvania, Quay and Cameron supported him; Warner Miller was his agent in upstate New York; Logan's old lieutenant, Green

B. Raum, gathered southern delegates for him with notable success; Frank Hatton, Arthur's manager in 1884, labored for him. Sherman, as Blaine noted, had inherited many of the old stalwart connections—and some of the attendant hostilities.[15]

Sherman had offered Blaine his support in 1887 if the latter wanted the nomination, and only announced his candidacy after the publication of the Florence letter. He hoped to inherit his old rival's strength, but instead encountered open opposition. A political squabble in Virginia turned into a Blaine-Sherman contest, rousing tempers in and out of the state. In New York, Platt's organization sought to unite the state with a candidate acceptable to Blaine, rather than accept Sherman, who was first in the field in 1888 with no competitors. Facing this opposition, Sherman never succeeded in overcoming his weakness in New York.[16]

Sherman's other serious problem was his home state. His power was concentrated in the North. Cincinnati and southern Ohio were the province of Joseph B. Foraker, who had risen to national stature when he defied President Cleveland's request to return battle flags to the ex-Confederate states. In the first half of 1887, while Foraker gained fame waving the bloody shirt, newspapers prominently mentioned the governor either as a presidential or as a vice-presidential candidate if Blaine should run again. "Almost by magic," Foraker wrote, the party divided into factions. Sherman, fearing divisions in the Ohio delegation, insisted that the Ohio state convention of 1887 endorse him for the nomination. Only this, he wrote, would put an end to "sneering remarks about the course of Republicans in Ohio, exceedingly offensive to me." [17]

Foraker, who needed Sherman's support to be re-elected governor in 1887 with a majority large enough to make a national impact, reluctantly agreed to wait his turn. The

Ohio state convention which met in July 1887 nominated him for governor on a platform that included an endorsement of Sherman's presidential ambitions for 1888. This tied him firmly to Sherman's candidacy, but he exacted a great price in return: complete control of the state executive and central committees. On that, he insisted, he would have "no fooling or nonsense of any kind with Mr. Sherman, or any of the gentlemen who represented him." [18]

Foraker fastidiously kept to the letter of his pledge to unite the Ohio delegation behind the Senator, but rumors of a "Foraker movement . . . made by his consent and by the advice of the friends of Mr. Blaine" continued to damage Sherman's prestige. Foraker admitted in his memoirs that only his open commitment to Sherman prevented him from becoming an avowed candidate. In the end, Sherman got his unanimous delegation, but it did him little good. At Chicago, Foraker's followers paraded about "flaunting their large Foraker badges side by side with small Sherman badges"; they haunted the hotel corridors "to cheer for Blaine" and organized "small but lively anti-Sherman meetings outside the Ohio headquarters to demonstrate the boldness of Sherman's opponents." [19]

Given Sherman's weakness and the minor initial strength of all the other candidates, Elkins, despite Blaine's hesitation, thought he could convince the other candidates that they should withdraw in Blaine's favor, rather than create a difficult and bitter fight that would make the nomination worthless. Success in this depended on Sherman. But this was no simple task: staying in the presidential race when others would have been hopelessly discouraged was an old Sherman habit.

Elkins's principal weapon for coercing the other candidates was the New York delegation. But what it did would not be for Blaine, but for the New York state party. Blaine's withdrawal precluded organizing the delegation explicitly for him and made concentrating on a single candidate far more important than working for Blaine. Yet the two were related. "In my judgment," wrote Senator Frank Hiscock in late February, "Unless New York concentrates upon a candidate, Senator Sherman is certain to be nominated." Such unity, he acknowledged, was impossible "without the assistance, in a confidential way at least, of Mr. Blaine." Hiscock was simply remembering the experiences of 1880 and 1884 when New York had divided between the organization candidate and Blaine. Each group needed the other. They found it easiest to agree upon the candidacy of Chauncey Depew, attorney for the New York Central Railroad and popular among New York Republicans. The national convention could not possibly nominate him because of his railroad connections, but by putting Depew forward, the New York delegation could keep together to seek a candidate at the convention or to nominate Blaine.[20]

In May 1888, with Elkins's men canvassing the West and South, and with the press barrage for Blaine at its height, the community of interests between the Platt organization and the Blaine men was also at its apex. Platt, with their support, dominated the New York state convention which shouted for Depew, eulogized the recently deceased Conkling, and named his slate of uninstructed delegates-at-large. Platt had reached the end of the long road back from the disasters of 1881 and 1882. As he wrote in his autobiography, he had finally obtained "supreme and undisputed control of the New York State organization for the first time in a number of years." [21]

The New York leader's main interest in the national convention was to show his power. Through most of May, Blaine appeared the best candidate for his purposes. Platt cooperated smoothly with Reid, Depew, Phelps, and Elkins until the end of May. Depew was openly asserting that "I do not expect to get the nomination, but I firmly believe Blaine will." Platt predicted sixty votes for Blaine from New York; Elkins arranged for California to lead off the Blaine boom at the convention, confident that from there "Chauncey and 60 votes from New York [would] decide the matter." Convinced that he controlled over two-thirds of the convention, Elkins began stampeding the other candidates. "If nominated Blaine will not decline," he assured Clarkson on May 6. "Sixty delegates from New York will be for Blaine," he wrote Harrison on the seventh. "Everything now points to Blaine's nomination," he informed a Harrison lieutenant on the eighth.[22]

With New York apparently under control, Elkins went after Sherman's supporters. He had a long talk with Charles Foster, in which he argued Sherman's weakness and the "desire of the party for Blaine's nomination even against the politicians." Elkins audaciously suggested "a meeting of other candidates and in case of failure to agree, and feeling Blaine's nomination would come, why not make it unanimous by having Sherman declare in advance for him." But Sherman was neither pessimistic about his prospects nor did he accept Elkins's protestations that the Blaine forces were "not opposing him anywhere." On the contrary, he saw "an active and vigorous contest" made by "leading friends" of Blaine. Elkins renewed such attempts until the convention, but Sherman refused to withdraw and remained convinced that "Blaine is a candidate, has been from the beginning and will be until defeated." [23]

Most politicians agreed. The activities of Blaine's friends had become so patent that the press rung with charges that Blaine's original declaration had been duplicitous. "If Mr. Blaine is aware of what the elastic Elkins is doing, and lets it go on," went a typical comment, "he is acting no honorable part." Blaine, considering his nomination at the head of a divided party "a stupendous blunder," sent Reid an open letter from Paris in mid-May explaining that "I could not accept the nomination without leaving in the minds of thousands . . . the impression that I had not been free from indirection, and therefore I could not accept it at all." [24]

Blaine's Paris letter, which Reid published on May 30, shattered any hope for an easy success. Tom Platt felt "sick and discouraged." He would have to plan anew. Reid brought forward Russell A. Alger as a possible candidate for the Blaine men. Elkins, at a conference with Hiscock, Depew, Phelps, and Reid on June 1, pressed the Harrison connection. Phelps, who wanted to run for Vice-President on a ticket with a western general, concurred. Platt, however, resisted a candidate with more ties to Elkins than to himself and talked of a Depew-Harrison slate. But no one was at all sincere, and the tenuous alliance between Platt and the Blaine men was clearly breaking down.[25]

Platt, in fear of losing control of his delegation, moved to protect himself no matter whom the convention nominated. He immediately began courting Gresham, a strategic move giving him leverage against both Harrison and Blaine. He even bargained with John Sherman to keep him in the race until the very end, thereby insuring himself against moves to either Foraker or McKinley. And through all these feints he maintained his links with the Blaine men. Elkins went off to consult with Harrison, and Platt promised not to commit himself to a new candidate until Elkins could report on the conference. Despite heavy pressure to abandon Depew for a more available man, Platt continued to support the New Yorker to hold his delegation together.[26]

This left the New York delegation where Elkins wanted it. Although he had argued for Harrison in New York party councils, in all likelihood, Elkins never intended for

New York to switch its support before the national meeting. When he finally conferred with Harrison at Indianapolis just before the convention, he left the Hoosier with the impression that he no longer thought Blaine's nomination a possibility, and that Harrison could expect the Blaine strength after early ballot obligations were discharged. But in reality, Elkins was still seeking to nominate the old leader, and therefore did not want Harrison to be too strong on the first ballot. Elkins had convinced himself that the party was full of "discontent" at Blaine's withdrawal that had to "be allayed in order to induce harmonious action in the convention and in the campaign." By the time the national party met, he had progressed from the idea that only Blaine could unite the party to an active effort to keep the national convention in turmoil until Blaine's nomination became inevitable. "Boys," Elkins told Blaine's two sons, "it *must* come. It's no matter whether Blaine wants the nomination or not; we want him." [27]

III

The Blaine men organized the national convention proceedings down to the last detail. Clarkson brought his own carpenter from Des Moines to reinforce or nail shut doors and to install turnstiles "the same as at base ball parks." He had the tickets printed under his personal supervision at the last moment. The temporary chairman, John M. Thurston of Nebraska, entered the hall flanked by Blaine's two sons and made an adroit speech eulogizing the former candidate. The permanent chairman was Morris M. Estee of California, whose delegation was unique in its open advocacy of Blaine.

Despite such elaborate preparations, it was enormously difficult to control the convention once the first ballot showed no candidate clearly on his way to success. When instead the early leader, Sherman, had barely one-quarter of the delegates, and votes were scattered among fourteen candidates, control became virtually impossible. Observers were not sure what the lines of division actually were or who was behind several of the minor candidates whose names had not even been placed in nomination. Amid such confusion, however, there was plenty of room for skillful manipulation.[28]

The lack of one or more strong candidates to create solid organization and counter-organization explains in part the complexity of the 1888 convention. But the peculiar circumstances of the thwarted Blaine supporters also contributed to this result. Elkins puzzled all along over "what the men who are for Blaine first last and all the time are going to do with their votes" if Blaine's name was not placed in nomination. At the convention the puzzle was even greater. The motives and activities of the Blaine men never—then or later—became completely clear, and the classic combination against the front-runner took unusual and bewildering forms when it was aimed at a front-runner who had refused to run at all. Nevertheless, contemporaries understood the convention as a search to avoid Blaine. Elkins set the program, but the rest of the party found a sufficient response. Elkins generally operated in the open at Chicago. His tactic was to create a sense of Blaine's impending nomination in order to prepare delegates for a dramatic shift. No one was sure what was happening, but, quite deliberately, everyone knew that something was up. The California delegation on its arrival in Chicago announced Elkins's plan. Its spokesman, M. H. DeYoung, informed reporters of his delegates' intentions to vote solidly for Blaine until the rest of the convention wearied of stalemate and followed them. At about the same time, New York finally caucused and announced its support of Depew whom the newspapers expected would at some point withdraw in favor of Blaine.[29]

Before the first ballot, the Blaine men conferred with Platt, Hiscock, and some Foraker supporters. Elkins claimed 500 votes for Blaine among the Sherman, Alger, Harrison, Allison, and Gresham delegates, and in New York. But the conference recognized that Blaine simply could not kill off Sherman without splitting the party. Therefore, they resolved to support another man against the Ohioan, hoping that a deadlock would destroy two candidates at once and prepare the way for Blaine. However, they realized that shrewd counter-moves against them might turn their feint toward another candidate into a nomination. Thus, the Blaine managers and their allies needed a candidate whose nomination was acceptable if they lost control of the convention. They chose Harrison and proceeded to convince his supporters that they were sincerely working to nominate him.[30]

Balloting on the first day, Friday, June 21, was so obviously inconclusive that after three votes the convention recessed without even a division. During this break, the New York delegation determined to make its move: when the convention reconvened that night, Depew withdrew his name. Sherman's managers responded by moving an adjournment which carried overwhelmingly. The vote showed the convention's uncertainty. Sherman, Allison, and Alger supporters apparently voted strongly for the motion. Harrison's Indiana delegation voted against adjournment. But the Blaine men—whoever they were—remained invisible: California was solid for adjournment, but New York largely against it. How fully they would back Harrison was anybody's guess.[31]

The field began to mass that night against Harrison who was assumed to be the coming front-runner. At a conference Friday night, the Sherman, Allison, Alger, and Gresham forces, controlling a majority of the convention, tried to form a coalition. But the threat of Blaine complicated the alignment of forces. Many feared that Harrison was only a blind for the old leader so that killing him off was doing Blaine's work. Blaine's opponents could hold together simply by keeping their votes frozen and forcing adjournments when dangers threatened. But this too might play into Elkins's scheme. The Blaine newspapers argued that a lengthy deadlock would justify even the committed and instructed delegates in going over to the old leader. The classic strategy of trying their candidates in turn by lending each other votes was even more dangerous. If Blaine's strength was as great as Elkins claimed, once delegates were released from local obligations they would be hard to "deliver" to the designated candidate. A dark horse was still more dangerous. Elkins would be under no restraint against someone whose candidacy had not depended on Blaine's withdrawal.[32]

Fortunately, the combination faced only one day's balloting before the Sunday recess. Two trials Saturday morning showed no tendency toward Harrison despite his fifty-eight votes from New York. But a scattering of votes for McKinley gave point to widespread rumors that he was the convention's "Garfield." McKinley very wisely arose to forbid the use of his name, which protected him against being used by either side without Sherman's prior approval. No one knew who his supporters really were. The Associated Press dispatches carried rumors of a plan to encourage dark-horses—McKinley in Ohio, Shelby M. Cullom in Illinois, and ex-Governor Porter in Indiana—so that Blaine could be legitimately contested against them. When the convention recessed at noon, Chauncey Depew gave substance to all these speculations by predicting to reporters that Blaine would be nominated by acclamation when the delegates reconvened at 4 p.m.

Depew's announcement confirmed every suspicion

about Elkins's machinations, causing enormous excitement among delegates and managers. His claim that the friends of "nearly every leading candidate" had already "given their consent" revealed how false most of the bargaining had been. The Harrison men were "angry and unmanageable" over the way they had been "cheated." Allison's managers were suspect. Foraker appeared "a discredited man." Reporters suspected that Alger had been offered the vice-presidency for going to the "plumed knight." But the move was premature. When the convention reconvened, Elkins's arrangements for the prospective "stampede" were still incomplete. A motion to adjourn for the weekend carried by 492 to 320 votes. The Blaine forces were obviously disarrayed. California voted for adjournment, New York against it. A leader of the California delegation explained that "we all voted for an adjournment, supposing we did it at the request of New York." Apparently only the Harrison supporters uniformly opposed the motion.[33]

New York's vote was a subject for wonder. Some observers thought it was to keep the Harrison forces from turning to the anti-Blaine coalition. Others guessed that the New York Blaine men wanted a few more ballots that night to cement the deadlock. But Platt in his autobiography talks of how "we suddenly broke away" from Depew to support Harrison. The New York leader probably decided that Blaine was no longer the best prospect to support. The sudden unveiling of the Blaine movement had evoked "great bitterness" at the convention. Indiana delegates threatened to knife him during the fall campaign. The hall buzzed with talk of "a second convention" were Blaine nominated by these devious means. Such hostility, threatening the existence of the party, gave Tom Platt good reason to dissociate himself from Blaine and to consider Harrison as a serious possibility.[34]

Frank Root noted an important distinction in Blaine's various supporters. The state leaders whom Root called "politicians" had different motives from the "adventurers"—Elkins and his friends. The adventurers without local interests to defend were much less inhibited in their activities for Blaine than were his other supporters. Elkins on Saturday afternoon had claimed a majority of the convention. But many of these delegates were tied by local pledges or instructions, and Elkins could not persuade key people to take the political risk of switching them to Blaine. Men like Platt had to keep commitments back home, maintain unity in their delegations, and prepare their organizations for the upcoming campaign. These considerations always took priority over nominating a particular candidate. Only men like Elkins could afford to be gamblers.[35]

Elkins had counted on pressuring John Sherman into releasing his delegates to open the way for a move to Blaine. Sherman's own managers had broken under the strain of Foraker's threatened defection and the apparently imminent shift to Blaine. Murat Halstead, certain that the Ohio delegation was "already broken," advised Sherman to withdraw in favor of McKinley. Hanna offered the same advice to "save the party from the Blaine lunatics."

Most observers predicted that by Saturday evening the convention would be a straight contest between McKinley and Blaine. This was probably what Elkins wanted. Undoubtedly, the anti-Harrison coalition would have split apart. Sherman's managers had been caught between Foraker's power in the state and Elkins's operations at the convention. Only McKinley had had the presence of mind to keep things under control by leaving the final decision to Sherman.[36]

Hardened by his pride and his bitterness over past failures, Sherman rose to the occasion. He peremptorily wired Hanna: "Let my name stand. I prefer defeat to retreat." His withdrawal, he was convinced, meant the success of Blaine's "deceptive and I think dishonorable" course. Elkins had come very close on Saturday, successfully creating the strain, uncertainty, and misjudgment among the other managers that are the prelude to a "stampede." In fact, only a voice from outside the convention stopped him. The Blaine men's chief error was in underestimating the thoroughness with which Sherman had tied his opponents in Ohio to his will. Foraker, despite his preponderant power in the state, complained of being "under a yoke" in presidential politics, and even Elkins's tactics at the convention failed to remove it.[37]

The adjournment Saturday afternoon, which offered the hard-pressed managers a day and a half for cool consideration and hot bargaining, considerably diminished Blaine's prospects. The deadlock presented the leaders of the large state delegations with a substantial opportunity. In 1880, when the convention had been at a standstill, all the big delegations, to whom the other politicians looked for guidance, were frozen as leaders of the Grant and anti-Grant coalitions. In 1888, however, the collapse of factions had produced a far more open convention. The two largest states were much more flexible, and it did not seem impossible to break the Ohio and Illinois delegations. Platt and Quay, therefore, each tried to put together combinations to break the deadlock and become the president-maker. Platt experimented with Harrison, Alger, and Gresham. Sherman thwarted the Alger experiment which depended upon Foraker carrying Ohio to the Michigan candidate. Quay discovered similar difficulties in the way of supporting McKinley. Both Platt and Quay had been in contact with Gresham for several months and conferred with him in Chicago before the convention. Neither went to Gresham, not because he refused to make promises—as Mrs. Gresham claimed in her biography of her husband—but because they soon found better things to do with their votes. Even Mrs. Gresham was aware that Platt's overtures on Saturday and Sunday were "a feint" which—as intended—"produced consternation in the Harrison and Blaine camps." [38]

Platt and Quay were both demanding explicit pledges of the candidates that they could name a man to the cabinet and control the patronage of their states. But it was hardly essential to accept such proposals. Quay had demanded a written pledge from Harrison, and Platt had asked for the Treasury post. Harrison refused both demands without sacrificing their support. Sherman, on the other hand, found that his explicit pledges to Quay were a one-way street. They embarrassed him, but did not prevent Quay from seeking a new candidate. Such pledges were by and large simply bad politics for a candidate. He could hold out vague hopes to any number of people, but explicit pledges made unreliable friends and many enemies. By 1888 most presidential aspirants knew this: the Harrison administration would convince even Quay and Platt.[39]

When the convention adjourned, the Sherman, Allison, Gresham, and Alger managers again tried to coordinate their efforts to stop Harrison and Blaine. McKinley was still their compromise choice, but when they repeated their pressure on Sherman to withdraw, Platt came to his aid with a promise that he would swing New York to Sherman if Ohio went for McKinley. Sherman, meanwhile, tried to force New York to his support. He offered Depew the vice-presidency and Blaine the State Department if Reid and Depew would carry the New York Blaine supporters to him. This would force Platt to follow if he wished to maintain control over a united delegation. Thus, whoever controlled New York, Sherman remained a live threat to the other candidates, and any strategy based on his withdrawal was impractical. This made a common front among the four candidates that much more difficult.[40]

Two related courses of action suggested a way out of the deadlock. One was to get Blaine himself to disown his managers' schemes. A number of delegates sent cablegrams warning him of "the bad feeling and probable demoralization of the party if his representatives [were] permitted to continue their tactics." Most delegates anticipated a reply from Blaine forbidding the use of his name. The second possibility was to reconsider Harrison as a candidate. For a number of reasons, he emerged during the recess as the most satisfactory compromise choice. New York's vote on adjournment and Platt's course immediately afterward separated to some extent the Harrison and Blaine movements. Platt carefully publicized his independence of the Blaine men over the weekend. The Saturday session also showed that despite the pro-Blaine slant of Harrison's pre-convention campaign and public knowledge of his financial involvements with Elkins, his supporters were angry enough to hold aloof from Blaine. Their vocal threats that they would defeat Blaine in the fall elections in Indiana upset both the Blaine and the anti-Blaine sides.[41]

Both courses were successful. The pressure on Blaine paid off as anticipated. On Saturday, he sent two telegrams forbidding the use of his name and asking that the dispatches be made public, which they were on Monday morning. Meanwhile Elkins received a message from Andrew Carnegie, with Blaine in Scotland, in a pre-arranged cipher, which merely repeated Blaine's constant advice:

"Take Trump [Harrison] and Star [Phelps]." In perhaps the most statesmanlike act of his career, Blaine withdrew to avoid a split party and to achieve his ambition to be Secretary of State again.[42]

The way was now clear. Both the Blaine and the anti-Blaine groups had arrived at Harrison.[43] Elkins, now all for Harrison, conferred with Platt who had become louder and louder for Gresham over the weekend in order to exact terms. Elkins let the New Yorker think that he would become Secretary of the Treasury and accepted his man, Levi P. Morton, as Vice-President. Platt in turn agreed to support Harrison on Monday. After one ballot Monday morning, the California delegation switched to Harrison, who for the first time forged into the lead. Clarkson at this point arranged for Allison's withdrawal before the next ballot and threw his support to Harrison. Quay turned to Harrison when he learned of Clarkson's move, as did the Massachusetts delegation. The eighth ballot put Harrison far over the top with 544 votes, resulting in a nomination which, if it was not greeted with much enthusiasm, met with an almost unanimous feeling of relief.[44]

The result for the party was curious and equivocal. Whose candidate was Harrison? He had, in the end, the support of both wings of the convention. He acknowledged in a letter to Blaine that only "the help of your friends made success possible." Yet Sherman was certain— with good reason—that only his own last ditch resistance to Blaine had produced the nomination. Allison had started the final break. Quay apparently had arranged in advance to be chairman of the national committee. Platt thought he would become Secretary of the Treasury. Elkins's position was the most curious of all. Elijah W. Halford, soon to be Harrison's private secretary, explained that

Every friend of General Harrison should feel kindly towards Mr. Elkins, and indeed towards all the close friends of Blaine, as well as towards the splendid New York delegation, whose candor and unanimity, *misunderstood for a time,* probably, really dictated the nomination of Harrison.

Yet three days before, Halford had written of the New York delegation voting against the adjournment "to throw dust in the eyes of the delegates and the people." The dust obviously had still not settled. Convention organization had, as usual, revolved around opposition to the group with the best avenues of communication before the meeting. But in 1888, that group, the Blaine men, was so amorphous that the dominant organization and counter-organization had produced a bewilderingly open convention. Harrison was everyone's candidate: the party had arrived at the classic available man.[45]

IV

Harrison made good use of the circumstances of his nomination. Being in everyone's debt, he let everyone expect his reward for his election, refusing to tie himself to any one group or to make explicit promises. The party, hungry after four years out of power, was in a particularly good position throughout the campaign. There was an enormous amount of infighting, but most of it aided rather than damaged the chances of the ticket, whatever its long-range effect on the party.

For the first time in memory, organizing the national committee provoked no major friction. Quay wanted the national chairmanship and had arranged at the convention to have it. Platt supported him in return for a place on the executive committee for his lieutenant, J. Sloat Fassett. Elkins, realizing that after his role at the convention he ought not to take any official position in the national committee, had already committed himself and Blaine's supporters to the Pennsylvania leader. He lent his voice to the pressures on Harrison to appoint Quay, and concentrated his campaign efforts on an attempt to make his adopted state of West Virginia Republican. Clarkson, who became temporary chairman after the convention, agreed to take a "working place" wherever Harrison wished, rather than continue as chairman.

Quay, by taking the chairmanship, gained not only prestige, but insurance against divided control of the campaign in his home state. Platt had done the same in New York. Both men extended their rapprochement with the Blaine men from the state to the national levels. The quarrels of stalwarts and half-breeds, which had always been largely incidents of New York and Pennsylvania politics, had at last vanished completely.[46]

When the national committee held its organizational meeting in New York on July 11, Clarkson took command, smoothly completing the arrangements made in Chicago. The executive committee represented most of the party's strength. Clarkson, who became vice-chairman, was close to both Allison and Blaine. Five other members had supported Blaine; two were Gresham men; Dudley, the committee's treasurer, and John C. New were Harrison's friends. Quay, the chairman, and Fassett, secretary of the committee, represented the two state parties in the area where most of the money would be raised and spent. Only Sherman's supporters were missing, but even he could approve of Quay's selection as chairman. Harrison correctly described the organization as "a Republican and not a personal" one.[47]

The committee was an improvement over that of 1884. Then, Blaine had had to swell its membership to disproportionate size to avoid the accusation of making it a personal organization. He had selected an inept national chairman, a gout-stricken chairman of the executive committee, and had left direction with a then little-known member from New Mexico. In 1888, of the twelve men, six were effective operators from 1884, and the officers were all master politicians whom party leaders all over the country would heed and respect. Whatever a national committee could do they were well equipped to carry out.

Grover Cleveland single-handedly defined their task. Before the presidential message of December 6, 1887, Clarkson was convinced that Foraker's successful bloody shirt campaign in Ohio that fall had "made the platform the next year" unless "the blunders of the White House . . . change the present complexion." Soon after the tariff message Clarkson took the lead in pressing for a campaign emphasizing the tariff and playing down the traditional Southern question. Harrison was amenable to a tariff campaign, but Indiana's large Negro vote made him reluctant to abandon the issue of Negro rights. Late in July, Clarkson wrote urging him to cease his advocacy of voting rights. The national committee feared that "the argument of old issues" would drive eastern "tariff Democrats" away from the Republican ticket. Harrison finally acceded. He told Negro audiences that the race problem would be solved if the protection argument broke the solid South. Privately, he knew better: "There would be no tariff question now," he wrote Whitelaw Reid, "if the labor vote of the south had not been suppressed."

Many Republicans were unhappy over this strategy. Reid took Harrison's advice to discuss southern voter frauds in a "temperate" way "separated from any war associations." The candidate self-righteously claimed that he "would not be willing . . . to purchase the Presidency by a compact of silence upon this question." Prominent midwestern Republicans such as Foraker and John C.

Spooner of Wisconsin, who faced audiences still enthusiastic about the war but dubious about raising tariffs, railed against the national committee. But the committee largely had its way and 1888 became the year of the great tariff campaign.[48]

The Republican party, controlling the Senate, had to take legislative action on the tariff question. The Democratic House had passed the Mills bill which reduced the embarrassingly large surplus in the treasury by lowering tariffs. Some Republicans preferred simply to reject the Mills bill and await vindication in the election. Most of them, however, thought that the Senate had to put forward an alternate plan to reduce the surplus. Otherwise they feared that the President might call them back into special session and put the onus for continuing the surplus on the Republicans. Moreover, manufacturers wanted to know what protection the party would offer them. Most important of all, midwestern Republicans needed a moderate measure as a campaign document so that they would not have to run on the extreme protection plank passed at the convention.[49]

An informal caucus on July 25 finally resolved in favor of a Senate bill. Sherman reluctantly approved only after the entire caucus promised to stand by whatever bill the finance committee wrote. This unanimous pledge was a new departure in tariff making. However, it must be remembered that the caucus had not agreed to pass a tariff but only a Senate bill for the Democratic House to reject. Hiscock, who as Senator from the most important doubtful state had a major voice in the decision, gave assurances that no one need entertain the terrible possibility "of the Democratic house accepting our bill." [50]

The strategy was eminently successful. Allison's committee reported out a moderate bill to reduce revenues without sacrificing protection. Republican Senators got thousands of frankable words into the *Congressional Record,* and the Senate adjourned without the bill coming to a vote. The party was now equipped for the campaign. Its protective tariff platform promised protectionists "the entire repeal of the internal revenue taxes, rather than the surrender of any part of our protective system," while the "Senate" or "Allison" or "Aldrich" bill and the attendant debates offered an excellent set of campaign documents for the low-tariff areas.[51]

V

Blaine had bewailed the manufacturers' failure in 1884 to support his agitation for a protective tariff. Pennsylvania especially had disappointed the national committee. Four years later, the Keystone state took the lead in financing the ticket. Both contemporaries and historians have almost universally attributed this change to the greater prominence of the tariff issue, which enabled the Republican managers, in the notorious phrase of James P. Foster, president of the Republican League of the United States, to "put the manufacturers of Pennsylvania under the fire and fry all the fat out of them." This explanation is only partially accurate and taken by itself creates a seriously misleading impression of the financing of the 1888 campaign.[52]

James M. Swank, secretary of the American Iron and Steel Association, had been one of the many voices calling for Quay as chairman of the national committee. But the widely accepted notion that he dictated the choice lacks both proof and logic. After 1884, the Association's opinion on a suitable national chairman would hardly have merited serious consideration. It had supplied a chairman once and failed to raise the expected funds. Quay was not drafted at the insistence of the steelmen. He wanted the post. Swank's endorsement was merely the Association's final surrender. The Pittsburgh steelmen had already moved into Quay's camp; even Thomas M. Bayne, their representative in Congress and Jones's political manager in 1884 was now part of his organization.[53]

Swank's one real power was over the iron and steel schedules in Republican tariff bills. This single-minded interest severely limited his influence in any other question. When Hanna sought his support for McKinley's pre-convention campaign in 1896, Swank acknowledged his complete inability to back a candidate for the nomination in any but the most unusual circumstances, as in 1888 when Sherman was the only avowed candidate. Had Blaine been a candidate then, he admitted, "I would not have known what to do. Probably I would have done nothing." [54]

In 1888, Swank's concern was the metal schedule in the Senate tariff bill. He brought all the pressure he could to set the tariff on steel rails at $15.68 a ton instead of the $14 per ton that the Senate Finance Committee was considering. "We would not for one moment," he assured Allison, "think of using any improper means to secure the favorable consideration by your Committee of the steel-rail duty." But he warned the Senator that the $14 rate would make it "difficult or maybe impossible to secure the $35,000 or $40,000 of additional collections which I hope to make from the steel-rail manufacturers." [55] The committee agreed to the higher rate, the very first point in the schedules which the Democratic minority report attacked. This obviously was an impressive display of power. But it must be noted that in return Swank specifically promised a *second* collection from the steel-makers, who had already sent the national committee $37,000. In short, he had committed all his resources to win the one point on the tariff schedule.[56]

Swank reminded Allison of the work that the Association had already done for the party in printing and distributing 1,387,864 tariff tracts. Historians have assumed that this indicated an "almost bottomless" purse. Actually this was hardly a remarkable contribution. Swank merely printed the tracts and shipped them in bulk. State committees, Republican editors, or *ad hoc* local groups such as the Republican Clubs distributed them to voters. An eight-page tract—about the median size—cost roughly half a cent to print and ship. Swank at one point printed 700,000 documents for $4000. He assured a Minnesota politician that for $200 he could have an eight-page speech translated into Norwegian and Swedish and 25,000 copies printed in each language. Swank, by advertising the number of tracts he was shipping both in the *Bulletin* of the American Iron and Steel Association and in "confidential" leaflets to Republican politicians, got a great deal of credit out of his numbers game and the roughly $10,000 that had cost him some difficulty to raise.[57]

The steelmen intended to raise $100,000 for the committee. Joseph Wharton agreed to supervise the collection and used this leverage to press Allison for a tariff schedule to his liking. But Wharton got only the least part of his request when the Senate bill reduced the duty on nickel ore. This bipartisan measure, which enabled Senator Henry B. Payne, the Ohio Democrat, to sell ore from his Canadian mines to Wharton's American Nickel Works, represented no political sacrifice. On the other hand, Allison rejected the demand for a higher tariff on nickel and nickel alloys.

The steelmen apparently raised somewhere between $75,000 and $80,000—a substantial sum, but hardly a large percentage of the campaign fund. Certainly this was not enough to make its donors the masters of a national party. It would be a strong talking point when next the metals schedule came up—no more than that and no less.[58]

The largest and most famous Pennsylvania fund was the one that Thomas Dolan and John Wanamaker raised. Dolan was the president of the Manufacturers' Club of Philadelphia and prominent in utilities and woolen manufacturing. Wanamaker was the leading retail merchant of Philadelphia. The Philadelphia business community had a history of opposition to Quay and a long memory for the irregularities in the state treasurer's office. By the time the delegations had returned from Chicago, they knew that Quay had charge of the campaign. But they still hoped to gain influence with the candidate. Quay's opponents late in June therefore organized what was virtually a counter-committee under Wanamaker to raise and distribute funds in competition with the national committee.

Understandably, Quay vigorously resisted the original plan. This produced a stalemate with Quay in control, but no prospect of substantial funds from Philadelphia. Only a high office would tempt Wanamaker who had no economic interest in the protective tariff. Quay turned to Dolan who was closer to the state organizaton to help him bring Wanamaker into the campaign. Late in July Quay offered Dolan and Wanamaker the chairmanship of a finance committee that would be directly attached to the national organization. Dolan and Quay held out the prospect of a cabinet position for a Pennsylvanian, probably promising it to Wanamaker who was assumed to be "not a politician" and therefore easily managed.[59]

Wanamaker, however, managed quite well for himself. With Dolan's support, he insisted on direct authority from Harrison. Quay reluctantly conceded, and one of his men asked Harrison to request Wanamaker's participation.

Harrison's response was vague and made no promises. The two businessmen "accustomed to the directness and precision of great business transaction"—as their intermediary, Charles Emory Smith, euphemistically expressed it—demanded a clear guarantee that Harrison had not already given away Pennsylvania's place in the cabinet at the convention. New consulted with Harrison for them and conveyed the candidate's assurances that "everyone's claims will receive due consideration after principal event occurs and not before."

But even this was insufficient. Dolan and Wanamaker demanded the kind of promise that Harrison had refused to Quay. They were willing to compromise only to the point of accepting a letter from a close Harrison associate stating that he had discussed the question of a cabinet post with the candidate who agreed to the men's announced terms. Harrison, unable to evade their demands any longer, had Michener write a letter to Smith which Dolan and Wanamaker found "entirely satisfactory." "The work will now be pushed with energy," Smith promised.

Even Quay was ignorant of these more definite agreements between Harrison and the Philadelphia men. Smith, after the election, reminded Harrison of "the importance of not letting Quay know of the movements that were made outside of his knowledge." Everyone in Pennsylvania wanted credit for victory, and this mutual competition, for all the suspicion and distrust it created, redounded to the benefit of the ticket, if not to the prospects for harmony in the new administration.[60]

The committee as finally organized was an advisory board of businessmen with a smaller executive committee and a treasurer who could both raise and spend the funds independent of the national committee. Quay had reluctantly agreed to these conditions. According to Wanamaker's own statement, the businessmen raised $200,000, although rumor raised the figure a good deal. Contemporaries believed that part of the money was used to buy Republican presidential votes in New York and part was bet on the outcome—apparently to Quay's distress. All such stories are uncertain since the national committee after the election "made a bonfire of all the written matter which had accumulated in their headquarters." But if the story is true, this action was not *quite* so frivolous as it sounds. In October, betting odds in New York strongly favored Cleveland. If deals with local political movements in the city were to succeed, the local leaders had to believe that the Republicans would win. Otherwise they could safely renege on their agreements without fear of retribution. That one could influence elections by juggling the betting odds on the candidates was a regular part of the political folklore of the period. Someone like Wanamaker would be just the man to believe in its efficacy. Perhaps the politically more sophisticated Quay did not.[61]

Pennsylvania was not the only source for funds. Mark Hanna raised a good deal of money—perhaps $100,000—among midwestern businessmen. Farther west, ambitious Republicans in the territories denied statehood under the Cleveland administration, raised tens of thousands of dollars for the national committee.[62]

New York Republicans were active as usual. A small group, including Horace K. Thurber, Cornelius Bliss, J. P. Morgan, Whitelaw Reid, and Levi P. Morton, met privately at Thurber's instigation to pilot the course of the national advisory committee. They too wanted to establish their own claims rather than be lost in the accounts of the national committee. Thurber, a partner in the great wholesale grocery house of Thurber, Whyland & Co. and the president of a steamship company, was bent on making a political reputation. Besides working with the national committee, he also spent his own funds buying various "movements" of Democrats quarreling with Tammany. He was badly burned when local politicians took his money—as well as several other people's—and failed to deliver the votes. Thurber then joined the hue and cry for election law reform that arose in New York after the campaign. He had learned how the party professionals could exploit the businessmen going into politics. Everyone in politics had sensed "the buoyancy in the market almost as soon as the canvass opened" and had made the most of his opportunities. B. F. Jones, very much on the sidelines, noted ruefully that "the National Committee has been very successful in making collections." Suddenly money was everywhere.[63]

Why was the party so wealthy in 1888? While some of the money came from men interested in tariff legislation, men like Wanamaker and Thurber were not at all interested in protection. Surely one reason was the range of people who might expect rewards from a party out of power. In 1892 and 1896 the "out" party would again show this remarkable fund-raising ability while the party in office would be wracked with dissension and jealousy. The decentralization of political effort during campaigns, the uncertainty of who did what, and the complete destruction of records, made participants overestimate their own contributions, since there was no definite way of knowing what anyone else had done. A new candidate had the advantage over an incumbent in his ability to enlist everyone in the party hopeful of any political future from tide waiter to ambassador.

More businessmen than ever thirsted for such glory. The Cleveland administration by increasing the respectability of politics had made businessmen more forward and public in their party commitments. There had always been a large number of politically active businessmen, but because politics had for a long period been held in low popular esteem, businessmen who were also politicians tended to play down one or another of their identities. Arthur E. Bateman, although he was a delegate to the 1888 convention, did not want to be considered a "politician." The Democrat Abram S. Hewitt humorlessly remarked in 1888 that "I do not intend to meddle with politics as long as I occupy the office of mayor." On the other hand, no one thought of Zachariah Chandler, Tom Platt, Simon Cameron or his son Donald as businessmen despite their extensive commercial activities. Each of them earned his living from business rather than politics, little as they usually separated the two spheres. The idea of a ruling oligarchy of professional politicians surrounded by passive businessmen who simply contributed funds, as expounded by Matthew Josephson and Herbert Croly, is simply a myth growing out of the nineteenth-century reformers' habit of confining the term "politician" to pejorative uses. The large numbers of businessmen whom one encounters at every point in Gilded Age politics had in 1888 become more public in their behavior, assuming, as Wanamaker did, that they were giving politics a higher tone and more efficient and honest methods of operation. In 1884, Sherman's managers had been amazed to discover that hundreds of the delegates to the Republican National Convention were engaged in mercantile pursuits. After 1888 it would not have surprised anyone.[64]

Of course, the emphasis on "economic" rather than "sentimental" questions—Clarkson's categories—helped to make businessmen more open in their political activities. It undoubtedly also brought into politics men not previously active. In fact, the naive way in which they rushed in boasting of how much money they were raising and spending proved quite incendiary, feeding the flames of the antitrust sentiment to which the President had appealed in his tariff message. The long, sterile debates in 1884 over Blaine's record had demonstrated the public's confusion over the proprieties of politicians' involvements in business. But men like Hanna and Wanamaker, naively accepting the common moral distinction between venal politicians and world-building businessmen, had assumed that while politicians would be suspect for mixing business and politics, businessmen would not. Deeply in politics, they still did not think of themselves as "politicians" and failed to employ the caution habitually exercised in discussing such things. Hitherto rare and desperate incidents like the dinners at Delmonico's for Dorsey in 1881 and for Blaine in 1884 were becoming commonplace.[65]

James P. Foster's "fat frying" notice was the most famous statement about financing the 1888 campaign. What has been forgotten is that Foster represented an amateur group founded in response to Cleveland's tariff message only a few months before the campaign. It was rather less important than the "Young Republicans" of today. The national committee in 1888 considered it a "Sunday School political organization." When Foster tried to get official status and support for his structure of clubs he was first ignored, then insulted, and finally refused funds. Most of the clubs had "only a nominal existence," as Ostrogorski correctly noted. The national league was scarcely "a living body." Here, then, was a new group in politics, capable neither of delivering votes nor of setting tariff schedules, naively advertising that it hoped to extract money from the corporations in return for tariff favors. Clarkson's policy of attracting new blood with economic issues had in this instance proved embarrassing. Foster had produced a first-rate Democratic campaign document which was even circulated in translation.[66]

The simple fact of good times was another important reason for the increase in fund-raising activities among businessmen. In 1884 depressed conditions had seriously hampered collections. But the tradition that presidential campaigns disturbed business was recognizably false in 1888. Business forecasters predicted in June that a brisk trade would remove the "stigma which usually attaches to 'Presidential Years' among business men" and would induce them to "contribute liberally of their time and money for political purposes." Fund-raisers, noting the industrial prosperity, looked forward to excellent collections.[67]

This greater wealth, however, did not mean tighter organization. These forays of the business community into political financing in no way helped to centralize or bureaucratize the party as Josephson assumed, following Robert Michels's "iron law of oligarchy" and much contemporary reform sentiment. *The Nation*'s fears after the 1888 election that the country had moved "one step nearer to the possibility, which now stares us in the face, of the purchase of the entire Administration from the National Committee of the winning party" were misplaced. Rather, almost every newly active group in 1888 further diffused power, creating new centers of administration of the party's funds and increasing uncertainty as to who was in charge and who would be rewarded. There was more money than in the past but no more clearly defined lines of power. The decentralization of the party had in no way been checked. In fact, there was no reason to do so: it was proving very profitable to the ticket.[68]

VI

The national committee planned to concentrate its efforts and money on a few points. New York, New Jersey, Connecticut, and Indiana were the main doubtful states. The Republican party with its larger base of safe states had somewhat more leeway in its planning than the Democrats. The opposition had to carry New York plus either Indiana or both Connecticut and New Jersey, while the Republicans could win by carrying either New York alone or Indiana plus any other state offering at least four electoral votes.[69]

This last statistic is important in explaining the persistent Republican urge to crack the South. A Republican West Virginia, which seemed possible in 1888, would have offered new freedom to Republican managers from the exactions of New York politicians, and seriously altered the balance of power between the parties. It would also have provided a new kind of power for Elkins who had adopted West Virginia as his home state. A Republican victory there would be, as one enthusiast described it, "the Gettysburg of the Democratic party." [70]

The Republican managers, unlike the Democrats, could choose between a New York and an Indiana strategy. Harrison had agreed in advance to the committee's concentrating on New York, but the question could always be re-opened. Important elements in the party disapproved of Platt's and Quay's exclusive preoccupation with the Eastern states. Platt, in complete control of the New York campaign, was sure he could carry the state. The party was united as it had not been for many years, while the Democrats were badly split between the Cleveland and Hill factions. He wanted the national committee to concentrate almost all its resources on New York. Although this was not done quite to the extent that Platt desired, within the state the committee was completely subservient to the state organization. The two committees, Clarkson noted just before the election, worked in "a perfect union of harmony and activity not known before since the war." [71]

While the national committee concentrated on the Eastern states, some of the normally Republican states of the West, in turmoil over the tariff question as well as trust and railroad problems, clamored for funds. Minnesota was heavily for tariff reform, and party leaders widely feared defections. Most politicians, however, thought that although there would be reduced pluralities and perhaps the loss of some seats in Congress, the state would remain Republican. Thus the national committee had little motive for giving aid. Nebraska, with its rapid population growth and unstable economy, was already on its way to the political upheavals of the nineties, and the Republican state chairman needed money. Iowa, rocked by agitation over railroad regulations and tariff reform, was becoming a much closer state than previously. Although the state was unlikely to go Democratic in 1888, Allison, because of his important role in tariff legislation, was able to wrest $3000 from the committee to aid Republican congressional candidates there.[72]

The politics of the upper South was changing as well. Republicans saw real grounds for hope in Delaware, West Virginia, and Virginia. Delaware actually elected a Republican Senator, but since its three electoral votes were one too few to matter in the national outcome, the national committee summarily refused aid. Nor would it spare funds for West Virginia despite Elkins's well-managed campaign which came within 2000 votes of success. Virginia too was as close. Quay, however, had no faith in the Virginia Republican leadership. In this he was correct, for they made a deal with the Democratic state committee which according to the Democratic chairman produced Cleveland's small margin in the state.[73]

The national committee thus avoided spending its money in the states that were traditionally safe for one or another party but that had become doubtful in 1888. The changes taking place in the political climate of the late eighties were too uncertain for the national managers to evaluate. More and more states were becoming competitive between the parties. But there were always intricate local reasons that made it difficult to tell whether the changes were the result of long-term trends induced by changing populations, economies, and interests or simply fluctuations caused by factional quarrels or popular leaders. If the committee had aided such states there would have been no limit to the dispersion of funds. California, Delaware, Maryland, Michigan, Minnesota, Nevada, New Hampshire, North Carolina, Rhode Island, Virginia, and West Virginia all fell into the category of marginally doubtful states in 1888. And throughout what was considered the Republican heartland—Ohio, Illinois, Wisconsin, Iowa, Kansas, and Nebraska—there were surprising alarms and portents of the coming upheaval which first threatened to destroy the Republican party, and then finally wrecked the Democrats. Thus, Quay understandably made the decision that despite pleas from other states, he would concentrate resources on the traditionally doubtful ones. Of these, Indiana was pledged to financing itself, but important influences were working to change that agreement and bring the campaign back to the ancient track of struggling for New York and Indiana.[74]

The Indiana state organization had never been a party to this agreement and the state chairman continued to demand money from the national committee. He spread stories of his rival state chairman's lavish funds and of the enemy's plans of "importing hundreds of illegal voters . . . and perpetrating the greatest of frauds." The Democrats quickly knew that the Republican National Committee would not operate in Indiana, but hearing rumors of the special funds being collected, believed that Harrison would have large sums to spend. Given the even balance between the parties in the state and the absence of emotional issues to affect voting patterns, the Democratic managers thought that the "floating vote" would be the margin.[75]

Late in September Quay tried to enforce his policy of not aiding Indiana by canceling Blaine's plans to campaign in that state. But Harrison, anxious to make Blaine his ally against the easterners, insisted that he come as planned. Blaine gave several well-received speeches in Indiana and moved completely to Harrison's support against the Quay strategy. Most of his friends followed his lead. Not only were they anxious to strengthen Harrison against their old enemies, but rising doubts about New York and Connecticut and the possibility of victory in West Virginia or Virginia were all adding weight to the Indiana side.[76]

The Blaine men were well equipped to pressure Quay. Harrison's friendship was once again up for grabs and Blaine and his friends reached for it. Reid wrote to Harrison expressing his doubts about the committee's loyalty and offering to "see that a few thousand dollars were forthcoming" for the Indiana campaign. Harrison used the offer to prod the national committee. He had sent two of his lieutenants to confer with Quay, and they had returned with a mere $6000 and the discouraging advice to collect their own funds "in the Western field." But Reid's letter opened new possibilities. "We have not felt," Harrison replied, "that we could *ask* any help in New York, outside of the Nat Com'tee—but you & other friends can of course direct your personal contributions." Harrison professed belief in his managers' loyalty, but admitted having heard disquieting rumors. Reid understood the message perfectly and promised "a sum equal to the remittance you mention from the National Committee, (six thousand,) within a week from this date." He stressed that the money could be freely used "as the circumstances and your judgment may indicate." [77]

Harrison also applied pressure of his own. His friends advised contributors to stipulate that their donations to the national committee go directly to Indiana. Some people went even further. Murat Halstead, collecting for the committee in Cincinnati, began sending money directly to Indiana. "I have done this," he explained to Harrison, "because it looks as if the National Committee was not dealing as liberally with Indiana as would indicate that they appreciated the state of affairs." Decentralization and competition made Harrison master of the situation. Blaine returned from his western trip and immediately met with "all parties in authority" to argue "the necessity of every aid to Indiana." Dudley presented a detailed canvass of the state to show that money for "Indiana recruitment" would bring victory. He wrote the famous "blocks of five" letter which advised the Indiana county chairmen on purchasing "floaters," on the day of Blaine's arrival in New York. Obviously the committee had realized the necessity of supplying Indiana before others did so and earned recognition for the victory. In fact, the desperate scramble to receive credit for the election-day funds led to this one great and nearly fatal mistake of the campaign.[78]

Harrison's habit of encouraging everyone's expectations worked best at a distance. Men who assumed they had created personal rather than merely political obligations too easily turned competition into conflict. New and Dudley, long at odds, competed on the national committee while Louis T. Michener, an associate of Dudley's worked to undermine State Chairman James N. Huston. Michener in the 1920s recalled having taken "full authority" on the state committee ten days before the election when Huston collapsed of exhaustion. But contemporary sources indicate that Huston worked night and day, slept at headquarters, and directed the committee to the end. Yet Michener's faulty memory probably had a basis in his activities: he undoubtedly believed, even at the time, that he was running the Indiana campaign. Mrs. Gresham thought that he was the *de facto* chairman. In short, both men were struggling for power in Indiana.

Huston, as chairman of the state committee, would channel the money for election-day expenses to the county chairmen. But Dudley and Michener wanted credit for supplying the money. Dudley took the remarkable step of writing directly to the county chairmen. He blundered in offering scandalous but obvious advice about political techniques which, as Michener observed, "had long been used by all parties in the state." But the heart of his letter was the statement, repeated twice in slightly different forms, that "there will be no doubt of your receiving the necessary assistance through the National, State and County committees. . . ." [79]

Dudley's action was highly irregular. "You have made a mistake," Quay reportedly told him, "in attempting to deal with anyone in Indiana except Chairman Huston of the Indiana State Central Committee." Huston himself issued a statement that "Colonel Dudley has had nothing to do with the management of the Indiana campaign." He denied that Dudley had been in the state at all or that the state committee had even conferred with him. All this may have been true: Dudley dealt with Michener, not Huston. For a moment, competition had gotten out of hand. Fortunately for the Republicans, Dudley's statements about purchasing "floaters" was so much like equally explicit Indiana Democratic circulars that the opposition could not press the issue with great moral fervor. Politicians hoped that the letter came "too late to be disastrous."

Probably this publicity did little more than inflate prices. A Bloomington newspaper considered it noteworthy that instead of the standard $10 the parties in some cases bid "as high as $15 for a single vote." Since from all accounts the Indiana Republicans had most of the money, this inflation may have aided them slightly.

Still, the effect of such funds is easy to overestimate. Allan Nevins, for example, makes much of the widely discussed Republican vote-buying in Bloomington. But the Democratic newspaper there boasted that "the fight was for the 'floats,' and although the Republicans had loads of 'boodle,' the Democrats got a good share of them." Both parties' newspapers noted that the Democrats had actually gained ground since the previous local and national elections. In dead center politics, men tend to dwell on the minor episodes that seem to make up a definable margin of victory, especially if they can thereby impute the results to the efforts of particular people. After the election Quay and Harrison had a famous exchange about the efficacy of "Providence" versus that of "men . . . compelled to approach the gates of the penitentiary." Since the men were evenly divided between the parties, perhaps Harrison had the better argument. Providence might not care, but in a closely divided electorate chance might very well decide.[80]

VII

In New York, Platt's convention strategy had succeeded in uniting all factions for the campaign. Cooperation between the state and national committees was near perfect. Most important of all, Platt had achieved a temporary and forced harmony with Warner Miller and the upstate Republicans by nominating Miller for governor. It was indeed a hungry party. After six consecutive defeats in the state, the prospect of victory over their scandal-wracked and divided opponents had finally induced several months of harmony and activity.[81]

Republican managers gleefully viewed the New York Democrats "divided into angry and greedy factions," and geared their entire strategy to exploiting these divisions. Tom Platt followed every turn in the labyrinth of Democratic infighting, preparing ingenious traps for his opponents. In New York City, a rising but out-of-office Tammany Hall faced the decaying County Democracy. Both sides fielded full local tickets which meant that in the competition for New York offices, Democratic district captains could trade their followers' presidential votes for Republican organization votes for the mayoralty and local offices. Democratic leaders urged loyal support down the line but acknowledged their inability to control the local politicians engaged in a "war for extermination." [82]

The County Democracy was particularly vulnerable to Platt's penetration. He had cooperated with them two years previously to prevent Henry George's election as mayor. Democratic politicians suspected that he had also helped organize the committee of Independents that had forced the County organization to renominate their unpopular mayor, Abram S. Hewitt, in 1888. During the mayoralty campaign, Hewitt got open Republican support in several instances.[83]

Platt was able to subvert the County organization because of its members' extreme isolation in the Democratic Party. They were battling not only Tammany, but Governor Hill as well. Platt observed with great satisfaction a "committee of Democrats and Independents" opposed to Hill which William M. Ivins and William R. Grace of the County Democracy led. "Have we not the materials here," he asked, "for creating much bad feeling and by so doing weakening both Hill and Cleveland?" Grace and Ivins both claimed to support the Democratic national ticket and promised the administration that the County would "do all that its means [would] permit in pushing an active National Canvas here" if the national committee provided funds. But Cleveland had not only thrown his weight to Tammany against the County organization but had worked to undercut Grace's anti-Hill campaign.[84] With the more respectable County leaders setting the pace in ticket splitting, their underlings, willing to do anything to defeat Tammany, had no reason to withstand Platt. In fact, there were rumors in October that Grace himself had decided that Cleveland's cause was hopeless and Grace was conceding that the County organization would trade Harrison for Hewitt votes. Evidence from four years later suggests that these rumors of Grace's collusion with the Republicans were probably true.[85]

Nor did Platt's machinations with the County Democrats preclude his collusion with Tammany politicians as well. His henchmen in the city government could expect more from Tammany than they would get from the reform Republican whom Platt had run to insure against Hewitt's victory. Platt, because he was using the Democratic split to elect a President rather than a mayor, had a remarkable freedom in his dealing with Democrats desperate to win in New York and scarcely enthusiastic about their presidential candidate. Wherever Harrison support could be purchased, he had an open market.[86]

Of the politically independent groups in the New York electorate, the Prohibitionists were the most important. Their vote had been steadily rising since 1884 when they had denied Blaine far more than the margin of votes that elected Cleveland. The Democratic managers counted on them for victory. William L. Scott of Pennsylvania, one of the leading Democratic managers in 1888, thought that "the most important thing for us to do is to work the prohibition movement in New York for all there is in it." The great Prohibitionist spellbinder, John P. St. John, was well subsidized by the Democratic National Committee in 1888 and hoped to raise New York's prohibition vote to 75,000. His campaign speeches expressed his hatred of the Republican party and emphasized tariff reform about as heavily as prohibition of the liquor traffic.[87]

This part of the Democratic strategy was largely thwarted by Warner Miller, the Republican gubernatorial candidate, who held many prohibition votes in the party by vigorously campaigning for a high license bill against the wishes of Platt and his lieutenants. Miller realized that he was placing "the entire liquor interest" against his chances but was convinced that by stopping the defection of "temperance Republicans" and bringing back some of the Prohibitionists, he could insure the success of the national ticket—and perhaps win a place in the cabinet. Some of his political associates described his strategy in baseball jargon as a "sacrifice hit." The prohibition vote, instead of swelling to seventy or seventy-five thousand as was feared, dropped from its high of almost 42,000 in 1887, to a little over 30,000. The votes that Miller lost by his stand were not necessarily lost to the presidential candidate. Many of the so-called "Blaine Irish" leaders campaigned for Harrison while avoiding the state ticket. Democrats anticipated that Hill would get *"very many* Republican votes among the Hotel and Saloon men" but did not expect that these votes would carry over from Harrison to Cleveland. Most spectacular of all were instances of open "Harrison and Hill" tickets and banners displayed in parts of the state. Miller lost, but the "sacrifice hit" was successful: "There is no mourning in my house," he assured Harrison after the election. "The success in the nation is sufficient." [88]

Hill personally did his best for the national ticket. All

of Cleveland's close New York political associates were convinced of his good faith. But to what extent he had been able to control his followers, and by how much they had augmented his votes by agreements with the Republicans, it is impossible to tell. Such rumors were to plague Hill for the rest of his career and probably had some basis in events, especially in New York City and Brooklyn. A Brooklyn Democrat complained to Cleveland of "Republicans high up in the scale of respectability deliberately voting for men they considered unworthy merely to secure two or more votes for their Presidential candidate in exchange for a single vote for one in whom they had no interest." [89]

Platt's strategy of taking advantage of Democratic divisions in New York, and of spending his money to win over disgruntled and desperate Democratic leaders was a success. The revelations of the New York *Mail and Express*—a Republican newspaper—of the large sums spent for election-day bribery confirmed the suspicions of the Democratic state chairman that the Republican committee was "going along inexpensively" during the campaign "saving its money for election day." This was the strategy for a united and hungry party. The managers counted on individuals all over the state working for the ticket in hope of reward without too much prodding from the center. They could simply wait for opportunities and gather the money to take advantage of them when they came. A confused and faction-ridden opposition was sure to provide them if only they waited. The Republican strategy was by no means certain of success. Clarkson, shortly before the election, could only assure the candidate that everything that organization could accomplish had been done. Beyond that the state remained genuinely doubtful, and would depend not so much on organization as on the "vest-pocket vote"—that is, the people who did not go to the polls with their tickets held high in the air for the boss to see that they were voting correctly.[90]

No one can precisely estimate the efficiency of a national organization. Harrison was elected with a minority of the popular vote. Had he lost, which was easily possible in that close contest, the Republican organization of 1888 would not have become legendary in the folklore of American politics. All one can say is that the leaders made few mistakes, profited from their opponents' embarrassments, and concentrated their resources well. Their success came largely from their opponents' difficulties and the fortunate shape the party had assumed in 1888, which was not the work of any particular leadership group. The national leaders did take good advantage of their circumstances by sensibly limiting the role of the national organization and by giving other groups their head. The party unity and success they achieved in 1888 was largely a historical accident. The weakness and disorder of the national party had been curiously profitable. The wavering electorate had given its last nod in the direction of the political world it would soon be leaving. Being the "out" party proved an advantage in the delicately poised national party balance of the eighties.

In the end, 1888 was an Indian summer for the Gilded Age. Men did what they had done for so long, discounting the changes they saw and hoping that they still had time for one more try at the old game before the season ended. Their hopes were realized: despite the darkening skies that local politicians kept reporting, the political climate was not yet ready to turn. But when Harrison took office it would be winter indeed: he would face not only the swollen expectations of the party that had elected him, but also an unpredictable electorate making demands that the party could no longer ignore.

V

1892: Disappointment

Patterns to which a generation of politicians were accustomed wavered in the 1888 election. The Republicans gained in parts of the upper South while the Democratic party made serious inroads in New England and the Midwest. Even before the fateful fifty-first Congress convened in December 1889, the state elections threw a glaring new light on the uncertainties of the previous year, shattering Republican hopes in the South while increasing the Democratic momentum in the North.[1]

The test came in Virginia. The administration supported the Republican gubernatorial campaign with prominent speakers. Clarkson cracked the patronage whip over dissident factions and promised national committee funds. But the effort, begun so hopefully, was a total failure. Clarkson's threats failed to achieve a united party, and he could not raise money. Finally, at a last-minute White House dinner the administration prevailed upon Arthur E. Bateman, whose railroad interests involved him in Virginia politics, to contribute $17,000. The Republican candidate's crushing defeat was one which he shared with the administration and the national committee.[2]

Results elsewhere were even more startling. Foraker

lost in Ohio; Iowa elected its first Democratic governor; Massachusetts barely went Republican for governor and became extremely doubtful for 1890. In New Jersey, the Democrats substantially raised their narrow margins of previous years; Rhode Island elected a Democratic governor; the Democrats swept all the state offices in New York. Democrats were elated: "I feel sure," wrote Calvin Brice, "that the party is steadily growing." [3]

The Republican debacle was limited only by the number of states that did not hold general elections. Worried leaders realized that the party's troubles extended as well to Wisconsin, Minnesota, Indiana, and Illinois. The election of 1889 had revealed a shift away from the Republicans even before the party had had a chance to carry out any part of its platform. One year later, the party would experience a much worse defeat, losing seventy-eight seats in the House as well as state-wide elections in Illinois, Indiana, Massachusetts, Michigan, Nebraska, Oregon, Pennsylvania, Rhode Island, and Wisconsin. Contemporaries incorrectly saw this as the adventitious result of revulsion over the McKinley tariff, the Reed rules, and the agitation for a "force bill,"—in short the actions of the fifty-first Congress. But the legislation of this first Congress under Republican control since the 1870s did not cause the change. Rather these efforts were a response to the party situation which the elections of 1889 had already made clear.[4]

A growing immigrant population, which was becoming increasingly Democratic due to nativist and temperance pressures in the Republican party, combined with more and more serious agricultural discontent threatened the permanent eclipse of the Republican party. It was not clear that the nation was turning to the Democratic party, but simply that it was turning. The old moorings, the old loyalties, were becoming less and less relevant. Politicians worried over the preferences of the "young men" continually pouring into the electorate, men to whom the Civil War was history rather than memory. They worried over the "Irish vote" and the "labor vote"—groups whose political posture left the politicians of the era endlessly uncertain.[5]

Politicians were deeply aware of the cultural sensitivities that modern students have found to be so important for the political preferences of the electorate. But these revolved largely around state and local issues. Party leaders in the administration and in Congress sensed—dimly and confusedly to be sure—that what the electorate wanted from Washington was positive government in the economic sphere: stimulation of business, aid to the farmer, action against trusts, public improvements. Speaker of the House Thomas B. Reed reflected this assumption in his belief that the nation desired forceful government and would accept his methods of controlling the obstreperous House—which, after a brief excitement, it did. Harrison also held this attitude toward government. In a letter offering a Supreme Court appointment to George Shiras, Jr., he wrote:

> I have desired to add to the bench, not partizans on the one hand or, on the other, those who held constitutional views of that narrow kind that would put the general government under such limitations as to make it impossible to exercise the general powers conferred by the Constitution.

Republicans simply did not believe in the doctrines of Herbert Spencer. They believed in such policies as protective tariffs, appropriations for rivers and harbors, subsidies to shipping and railroads, federal supervision of elections, federal aid to education, and a variety of other positive governmental programs. Republican leaders saw a cranky, sullen, and unstable electorate whose interest in the old issues had declined steadily from the early eighties through 1892. People wanted something done. The Republican party under Harrison set out to offer something positive to all the groups it hoped to attract.[6]

In doing this, their sense was undoubtedly correct, but the performance bordered on the grotesque. Like the businessmen new to politics in 1888 who said too much and spent too obviously, they set out to satisfy demands with an embarrassing naiveté. They planned large-scale "political profit-sharing," a competition to see which groups could cash in the expectations held out to them in 1888. However, the pressure groups that succeeded were the ones already in the party, not the groups like labor and agriculture that were becoming disaffected or required wooing. The veterans got "the old flag and an appropriation," the protected industries obtained the McKinley tariff, and the "boys" who canvassed in 1888 secured almost all the fourth-class postmasterships within a year. The reformers got Teddy Roosevelt as civil service commissioner and the West got the admission of six new states and the Sherman Silver Purchase Act. The widely diffused antitrust sentiment received a sop in the Sherman Antitrust Act.

The taste was bitter, even to the initiated. Senator Orville H. Platt said that the antitrust law was not "honest" but simply a name "that we might go to the country with." Sherman saw "so much selfishness and greed" during his labors over the tariff bill that he hoped he would "not live long enough to have any connection" with another. Corporal James Tanner's dubious conduct in the pension bureau rapidly became too much for Harrison's Secretary of the Interior, and Tanner was forced out with much intraparty bitterness. The Independent press was disgusted with Clarkson and Wanamaker, while

Clarkson felt he had been made the scapegoat for the administration and waxed increasingly sarcastic over Roosevelt's strictures. The President, never popular among the party leaders, sank even further in their esteem. It was a poor rehearsal for McKinleyism at a time when the party could not afford disaffection. The delicately balanced set of interests that had composed the successful coalition of 1888 could not meet the demand for performance. The party's center of gravity remained in the states and Congress, not the presidency. It was structured to compromise interests and balance favors, not to innovate. In this, it conflicted both with the thrust of Republican ideology and with the demands of the nineties. That the Democrats were even less equipped to meet these challenges was small consolation as the Republicans prepared for the mid-term congressional elections.[7]

II

The administration was poorly equipped to stem the Democratic tide in 1890. Harrison's cabinet selections had been politically weak. His assets as a candidate proved to be liabilities once in office. He had created more expectations than he could satisfy at once and as a president elected by a minority of the popular vote, he was not in a strong enough position to make the impatient wait for their rewards. His election had come from the temporary union of so many different and uncertain elements that it was not a question of pleasing a number of factions as it had been for Garfield, but rather of putting together a brand new coalition. All about him Harrison saw competing centers of power whose diameters could no longer be measured by the traditional yardstick of their role in the nomination and election just past. Blaine had to go into the cabinet, but his enemies would have to know that he had no influence over their prospects. It would not do to choose between Platt and Miller in New York, or Sherman and Foraker in Ohio, or Quay and his current or potential enemies in Pennsylvania. But was it possible for a President not to choose?

Harrison thought that it was. His cabinet officers were "not to be State bosses," he informed Elkins. Their "influence in local matters would be less rather than more" for entering the cabinet. He would prevent them from using their relation to the administration "to weaken or destroy the proper influence of any other Republican leader." Harrison apparently dreamed of keeping frozen for four years the moment of party history that had given him his nomination and electoral victory: jostling factions would continue to compete evenly for favor with an administration that served as a balance wheel forever preventing any side from gaining a clear-cut advantage.[8]

Harrison undoubtedly had no choice but to adopt this strategy. Appointing powerful state leaders to the cabinet would have driven their state rivals into the opposition. His administration, elected by a minority of the popular vote in an electorate increasingly unpredictable in its loyalty, could scarcely afford factional opponents within the party. But extended over an entire administration, this strategy of expectation had to turn into a strategy of frustration. Politicians would not forever accept the excuse that one's debts were multiple and contradictory as a reason for not paying them.

In the crucial New York State cabinet appointment, Harrison found that both Miller and Platt wanted a post. Elkins lobbied for Platt to whom he had promised the Treasury, but Miller and the Union League Club of New York organized a counter-lobby against the appointment. When the two factions could not unite on a candidate, Harrison felt that "everyone ought to set me at full liberty to make my own choice," and sought other recommendations. Reid submitted a list of possible compromise candidates, and Elihu Root reluctantly offered a few names. Harrison appointed Benjamin F. Tracy, who appeared on both lists, as Secretary of the Navy. This was hardly the backing that would give the administration any power in New York.[9]

Similarly in Pennsylvania, Wanamaker's appointment as Postmaster General upset Quay, whose support of Wanamaker's aspirations to a cabinet position apparently did not extend to so threatening a position. The President, admitting "the lack of experience and knowledge in practical politics" of his cabinet, persuaded a very reluctant Clarkson to become first assistant postmaster general with the understanding that he could resign as soon as he distributed the patronage. Harrison had not only made a politically weak appointment, but had strained his relations with the chairman and vice-chairman of the national committee.[10]

This was the story of the entire cabinet. Blaine was the one strong figure, but he was already piqued at Harrison's delay in naming him. Only days after the election Blaine prepared to fight for the leadership of the party if he felt that Harrison did not consider him "worth consulting in the organization of an Administration." Even after Blaine's appointment to the State Department was assured, Elkins, anxious for a cabinet place for himself, protested that to have only one cabinet member from the "Blaine element" would "reach the verge of injustice." Blaine's friends considered the cabinet except for Blaine "a pretty scrubby lot."[11]

Harrison's politically obscure cabinet had driven no one of importance into immediate opposition, but it had strained the loyalty of many important Republicans and made it difficult for the administration to bring any power to bear over the party. The state leaders, Elkins observed, were "more discouraged than is usual following a new administration." Considering the prospects for 1890, he judged that of the cabinet, only Blaine and William Windom had "any aptitude for office or politics." The others "were unable to help the President and do anything toward helping in the Congressional campaign." The national committee was another weak reed. Quay, following the model of Zach Chandler under Hayes, had tried to keep the committee as a possible source of power over the President. Immediately after the 1888 election, he had delegated Clarkson to "raise an organization fund" and to "begin . . . the work of detail [sic] organization for 1890 & 1892." But the 1889 election in Virginia amply demonstrated the failure of Quay's policy, and when Harrison turned to the committee for organization in 1890, he found it a shambles. Of its officers, Dudley was a thoroughly discredited man; Harrison had alienated Fassett by refusing to appoint him collector of the port of New York; Quay, deeply embarrassed by scandals and intraparty opposition, was also near the breaking point with Harrison and Wanamaker over patronage quarrels. Only the reluctant Clarkson, recently resigned from the "minor cabinet," remained of any service.[12]

Clarkson had tried to solicit funds for the 1890 campaign and to rejuvenate the League of Republican Clubs. Both efforts failed. He and Harrison finally achieved a makeshift organization. They pressed into service two obscure New Yorkers, James J. Belden and Lemuel E. Quigg, as part of an abortive policy of building up Platt's enemies. With Thomas Henry Carter and Clarkson, they made up what one of them later called an "unhappy quartet" to manage the congressional campaign. Clarkson had enlisted a weak team: Belden, a Syracuse banker and Congressman, sixty-five years old and something of a back number even in his home district; Quigg, Reid's Washington correspondent, age twenty-seven; Carter, a Montana Congressman and friend of Harrison's son Russell, an unknown man.

The committee could not raise money. Harrison and his cabinet, Clarkson claimed eighteen months later, reneged on promises to raise $300,000 from businessmen. Clarkson in desperation collected some money from the shipping lobby and raised an additional $40,000 on his own credit. The ensuing electoral disaster swept away his remaining loyalty to Harrison. The administration's ship subsidy bill was not up to his promises, and Harrison, John W. Foster, and Wanamaker, he claimed, did not keep their pledges to redeem his notes. Clarkson continued to serve the President, but only for want of any other political possibilities. Reflecting on his experiences with the administration, he complained in 1892 that Harrison gave his political allies "neither gratitude nor confidence. He was a purely intellectual being. He had no bowels." [13]

Newspapers and journals called the election "the great political revolution of 1890." *The Nation* noted that the Democrats had carried a majority in every section of the country. Elkins expressed a typical contemporary judgment in blaming the defeat on the Reed rules, the Force bill, the McKinley tariff, and "the course of the President since he came into office." The old Blaine reflex re-asserted itself with increasing force. Elkins, like many others, began looking to the mythical Plumed Knight who would lead "the Blaine column, constituting three fourths of the party" and bring back "the old leaders, who had been set aside."

Blaine was the one name behind which Harrison's opponents could rally. The President's popularity reached its lowest ebb in the winter of 1890–91 after the electoral setback of the fall and the lame duck Congress's failure to pass the Lodge federal elections bill. Rumors of friction between Blaine and Harrison, which had some basis in fact, cast Blaine in his traditional role of alternative candidate. He personally did little. A dying man, shattered by serious illness and the deaths of two of his children in early 1890, he was scarcely able to carry out his duties as Secretary of State. Few of his political friends ever saw him. Nevertheless, he was the only realistic prospect for the growing opposition to Harrison.[14]

Harrison's opposition grew in large part from fear of Republican defeat in 1892. The 1891 elections, although not so disastrous as those of 1890, were still disturbing. Clearly, many of the old Republican states were in danger. The party had lost ground in New York where it expected gains, while the Democrats elected governors in Iowa, Rhode Island, and Massachusetts, and came close to victories in Michigan and Nebraska. The West seemed more and more unstable. A delegation from the Northwest argued successfully in November 1891 that the national convention should be held in Minneapolis because "the doubtful States are now to be found in the West and Northwest, owing to the flocking in of the foreign population and the growth of the Alliance movement." Republican politicians responded with a call for Blaine, whose stand for reciprocity provisions in the McKinley tariff might take the sting out of western opposition to protection without alienating the East. Low tariff advocate Joseph Medill, who had never been a Blaine enthusiast, honestly believed that only he could win.[15]

Another part of the opposition was using Blaine's name to attack the President. Quay, never previously a Blaine man, became one of his most persistent supporters. As early as August 1891 he tried unsuccessfully to have the Pennsylvania state convention endorse Blaine for President. Platt led the opposition in New York, but others usually in conflict with him in the state were also hostile to the President. Belden started a Blaine club in Syracuse late in 1891. Warner Miller was openly hostile to the President. Clarkson, despite his position on the national committee, was wholly for Blaine early in 1892. A. L. Conger, the national committeeman from Ohio, claimed that all but the Indiana member of the committee opposed the administration. Dudley was organizing for Blaine and against Harrison in his home state. Senators Henry M. Teller and Edward O. Wolcott worked for the Maine man in Colorado.[16]

This movement for Blaine made despite the potential candidate's own lack of either inclination or organization suggests how hard it was to put together a national coalition. Blaine was a known quality. He represented a cluster of associations, perspectives, and old alliances which might be resuscitated. His health made him an unlikely candidate, but this mattered less to men facing the enormous problem of putting together a national coalition than their view that he was a possible focus for cooperation. In the Gilded Age one did not so much need an organization to nominate a candidate as one needed a candidate in order to create national organization. The unyielding decentralization of politics in the nineteenth century remained the basis of political behavior.

As in 1888, the problem was in Blaine's intentions, now wrapped even more deeply in mystery because of his delicate position in the President's cabinet and his steadily deteriorating health. Even his oldest political friends could only speculate on his plans, but the closest ones generally anticipated that his health or his inclinations would eliminate him as a candidate. The New York *Tribune* in March 1891 began to talk of renominating Harrison. Depew was convinced that the nomination was Blaine's for the taking but doubted that he would accept.

The candidate himself simply vacillated under this shower of attention.[17]

The administration, however, was not waiting for Blaine to make up his mind. Harrison in 1891 took vigorous steps to insure that the party would not repudiate him. In February he appointed Charles Foster of Ohio as Secretary of the Treasury. Foster cooperated with Sherman on Ohio appointments, and the two men made it seem, one of their enemies complained, "a crime in our state . . . for a man to be a friend of Blaine's." Aware that he could not trust his national committee, Harrison carried out a thorough re-organization in July. Quay resigned along with Treasurer Dudley. Both men had long since parted ways with the administration, and they promptly came out publicly for Blaine. Harrison made Clarkson chairman and promised vigorous support for his activities. The administration bid as well for Platt's loyalty by finally naming Fassett, another national committee officer, as collector of the port of New York.[18]

Elkins played a crucial role in Harrison's re-organization plans. Through the first two years of Harrison's administration he continued to walk the tightrope between Harrison and Blaine which he had mounted before the 1888 convention. He was still close to Blaine, whose son Emmons worked for his West Virginia Central Railroad Company. Russell Harrison remained in his debt. But the senior Harrison usually turned a deaf ear to his patronage suggestions and passed him over for the cabinet. Elkins remained on civil terms with the President, but continually complained about his appointments. After the 1890 elections it seemed as if he too might go back to his first loyalty. Foster's appointment to the cabinet over his objection seemed about to push him over the brink. He voiced his disappointment to Russell. Such ingratitude had convinced him, he claimed, that "the best thing for a businessman is to let politics go." But Elkins remained the

President's crucial link with Blaine and his followers. Harrison brought Elkins into his plans for re-organizing his administration in mid-1891, and apparently promised him a cabinet position when one became available. Elkins began to work for the administration, planting favorable articles and conducting some of the negotiations with Platt that led to Fassett's appointment.[19]

Elkins's most important role, however, was that of emissary to Blaine. Harrison wanted assurances that Blaine would not enter a contest with him for the nomination in 1892, and Elkins, the administration decided, was the man to make the approach. "I think it is time," Charles Foster bluntly wrote to Elkins, "some of Blaine's real friends should see him. There is danger of friction between him and the President." Elkins saw Blaine and got what seemed like assurances, although Blaine was apparently too proud to commit himself in quite the way that Harrison would have liked. When the expected cabinet opening occurred at the end of August, Elkins applied all the pressure he could to Harrison to make the appointment. But until Blaine committed himself, Harrison waited. Finally, Elkins's efforts were successful. Blaine agreed to withdraw and after various inexplicable hesitations addressed an open letter to Clarkson on February 6, 1892. His motives were as cloaked in ambiguity as they had been four years before and some people still thought him a candidate. But unlike 1888, most of his old political friends had already gone over to the President and now Elkins as a member of the cabinet was truly in the enemy camp. Unpopular as he was, Harrison had shored up his position considerably by the re-organization of 1891.[20]

III

Blaine's withdrawal brought forth a number of other candidates. Platt and Quay again approached Gresham, who, doubting the chances of success, refused. Cullom began cautiously to advertise himself; Alger with trepidation became Michigan's favorite son; ex-Speaker Reed began a movement; even Clarkson's name was put forward. If Harrison did not make a concerted movement for renomination and Blaine was out, the party clearly was again up for grabs.[21]

As always, Ohio had its aspirants. First in the field was McKinley, whose victory in 1891 for governor made him a prospective anti-administration candidate. By January 1892, his friends in Ohio openly discussed the possibility. Although McKinley assured an administration emissary that he favored Harrison's renomination, Hanna, his political manager, privately admitted that the governor "has had the feeling that lightning might strike him" and conceded that he had done "a little work in that direction." Sherman, too, became a candidate and once again called on Hanna to work for him. Hanna could not refuse, which placed him in the potentially embarrassing situation of working for two candidates from his home state. However, Hanna's road was none too rough, since Sherman did not have any real chance for the nomination. As the convention approached, Sherman, with few illusions as to his chances, made Hanna a free agent to operate as he wished at the convention. Hanna, as we shall see, made a real effort to nominate McKinley, although legend has it that he was relieved when he failed.[22]

This points up the ambivalence with which Republican leaders approached the nomination. Although as the convention approached people began speaking more optimistically—as they always do—few believed that a Republican could be elected. For the first time in a generation the contest was uneven. This did not lead to a dearth of candidates, only to a certain hesitancy among them. The winter Blaine boom served to test whether or not anyone dared press his ambitions. After Blaine's withdrawal, widespread doubt that Harrison would seek another term gave uncertain encouragement to secondary candidates, such as Sherman, Alger, McKinley, and Cullom. It was an unstable situation with everyone waiting for someone else to make the first move. Blaine, with his national following, might be able to defeat a President in open conflict. He had done it in 1884. But any one of the others could only be a sacrificial lamb to open the way for a third man. Yet if no one made a move, things would drift, as Hanna said, "until we could do nothing else but take Harrison." In such circumstances, the administration, as the only source of national power actual or potential, gained strength.[23]

From Blaine's withdrawal through the spring conventions in the states, opposition to the administration beat a muffled drum. Reports of hostile sentiment abounded, but the President's enemies could do no more than work for uninstructed or favorite son delegations. As the conventions drew near, Blaine still seemed the only man around whom the opposition could rally. Many people suspected that the President's enemies were actively fomenting discord between the two men. The administration girded itself for a battle at the convention and the opposition, led by Quay and Platt, began its own counterorganization.[24]

Harrison was embarrassed for men to round up delegates. His Indiana friends lacked the necessary national connections. Michener worked among southern delegates in the spring. But he cracked the patronage whip with a heavy hand and aroused a great deal of criticism. Thomas V. Cooper, now a firm administration man, worked unsuccessfully early in the year to build a coalition against Quay in Pennsylvania. Then in May he was sent across country to sound out delegates from Ohio to California. The administration put its office holders to work. Harrison officially disapproved of federal officials attending conventions, but as an Indiana state committeeman explained, "We can not afford at this stage of the game to be too virtuous in our actions." In short, the President's forces were active throughout the spring, but lacked a leader in the contest with such nationally known opponents as Platt, Quay, and Dudley.[25]

Elkins emerged as the administration's main political advisor, but he was clearly not the man to build harmony in the party. He had promised to make Platt Secretary of the Treasury and after failing to deliver on his promise had gone over to Harrison in order to enter the cabinet. Platt, Carter told the President, "regarded Elkins as the receiver of stolen goods." Not in a position to lead himself, he still wanted to keep control over the administration's political future. His instrument for this was his protégé Carter. Only Clarkson, chairman of the national committee and in many ways the most available bridge between the factions, stood in the way.[26]

Clarkson was in an ugly mood: wracked with pain from arthritis, in serious financial straits, and fearful of being pushed into political obscurity—as in fact he was. But he was too valuable an ally and too dangerous an enemy summarily to force out of his post. By May the administration badly needed Clarkson to avoid a serious convention fight and a possible dark horse. Probably no one but Blaine could hope to defeat the President, but an openly hostile convention would destroy any chance of Harrison's re-election. Platt and his friends threatened "to make martyrs of themselves" as had Grant's convention supporters in 1880. Yet both Platt and Quay appeared ready to compromise with the administration. Cooper was optimistic that Pennsylvania's two Senators, in view of the defeat they had suffered at the hands of antimachine Republicans in 1890, would come over to the administration if Harrison made some gesture toward "conciliation." Similarly Fassett thought that he could bridge the gap between Harrison and Platt in a White House conference. Harrison, however, was simply not the man to make gestures that implied that he was in any bargaining for his renomination. In a letter meant for Platt's eyes, he icily declared that he could say nothing "to any who have been disappointed in their expectations of appointment for themselves or their friends." [27]

Curiously, it was not appointments which were at issue—there was little left to distribute—but rather the President's very attitude. Platt hungered for respectability and deeply resented the President's view of him as simply an office-seeking low politician. His friends explained that his only demand was for "deference and respect." He wanted the President to "assign him that position as a gentleman and Republican leader that he occupie[d]." Obviously, if such men were even to tolerate Harrison's nomination, he would need a leader who had their confidence, a man whose word they would accept.

Elkins thought that he and Carter could do the job. Late in May they both went to New York to smooth the way for Harrison's renomination. Elkins quickly discovered the truth of Carter's judgment that "to send Elkins to New York was like shaking a red flag in the face of a bull." Carter, unwilling to assume command unless he was sure that Clarkson was unavailable, visited the chairman and found him "wary, full of complaints against Harrison and yet careful to show that the breach might be bridged." Carter advised Harrison to make terms with Clarkson and put him in charge of his convention organization. To do this and to isolate Platt, Elkins optimistically arranged a conference with Clarkson and Quay in Washington.[28]

Clarkson's attitude, however, dashed Elkins's hopes and

left the administration "badly frightened and greatly irritated." Lemuel Quigg, Reid's reporter and liaison man with the administration, saw Clarkson immediately after his interview with Elkins and jotted down his response:

> "Why," said Clarkson indignantly, "he talked to me as he might have talked to an Alabama nigger who was wanting to jump on the safe side. He blustered about having 580 delegates solidly pledged. He said the President would be nominated on the first ballot and that there was no danger of a stampede to Blaine."

Quigg asked him what he replied:

> "Oh, I simply laughed at him. I told him he was crazy; that he was talking moonshine; that Blaine could lift his finger and leave Harrison without delegates enough to serve as pall-bearers."

The administration must have been desperate, for after weathering Clarkson's anger, Elkins still asked him to call on the President. Clarkson sarcastically replied that there was no point in his going "if everything was going along so beautifully."

Clarkson was convinced that Harrison would not be nominated because "a large and stubborn opposition . . . in the delegation of every doubtful state" made his reelection impossible. "To be successful in the present condition of the country," Clarkson told Quigg, "Harrison must be renominated by acclamation; because we are not only renominating him but 150,000 other officeholders." Moreover, he did not see how Elkins and a few Hoosiers could defeat "men like Platt, Quay, Fessenden, Alger, Filley and Teller," who not only opposed the administration but personally hated Elkins as well: "He got what in their judgment belonged to them. His going to New York fanned the fires." Elkins had finally picked his side.[29]

IV

Blaine had assured his friends that he would not be a candidate, but some of them no longer trusted his judgment while he was "subject to persistent pressures of all sorts and from all directions." The opposition, unable to unite on any other candidate, worked on him incessantly until on June 4, when the convention was assembling in Minneapolis, he resigned as Secretary of State, making his break with the President complete.[30]

An interview that Quigg had with Tom Platt at the end of May throws some light on the Secretary's state of mind before his resignation.

> Platt seems to be confident that Blaine will take the nomination. He said that when he saw Blaine yesterday they went over every point of the situation, the chances as to the nomination; the chances as to money; as to the final election,—and Blaine all the while manifesting the keenest interest. Right in the midst of the talk, Platt says, Blaine looked up and said, "But if I am elected, I shall have to stay here in Washington during the summer months of the long term of each Congress, and that will kill me." Platt insisted that it wouldn't . . . that he (Blaine) was already pretty well committed and could not withdraw now without making many of his friends feel that he had not treated them fairly. "You ought not to have listened to us," Platt said, "so long as this unless you were willing to go in. We have now the right to assume that you will take the nomination; isn't that so?"
>
> "Do you think so?" Blaine asked. "I haven't said much."
>
> "But what you have said encouraged us to think we could depend upon you. Now, for God's sake, do not write any more letters. Let the thing take its course."

Blaine made no answer to this appeal but Platt says he "looked at me with what I felt sure to be a significant and promising glance." [31]

Harrison's opponents, who were not even friends of Blaine, apparently had played on his ambitions, his hostility to the President, and his fear of seeming a perennial Hamlet, to make him the passive focal point for a cynical coalition.

The opposition, then, had strong leadership but an improbable candidate who might at any moment decline to run, do something rash, or literally die on their hands. Blaine's resignation was probably more than they had expected. Platt told Blaine to "let the thing take its course." Clarkson expected, or hoped, that Blaine would do nothing and would "accept the result if it came to him." Blaine may have decided on his own to end the embarrassment of being a candidate while in the cabinet or perhaps, as contemporary rumor had it, the President had demanded that he either withdraw from the race or from the administration. Whatever his motives, the resignation could only be disastrous to his chances. It made him overtly the anti-administration candidate, rather than a figure who could unite the party.[32]

Against this opposition of malcontents, the administration had a clear record on which to run, a definite candidate but no established political leadership, and a widely diffused and uncertain political strength heavily weighted toward office holders in the South and the Republican states. Harrison's position was somewhat similar to Arthur's in 1884 except that the opposition of 1892, lacking a viable candidate, was much weaker. Harrison's convention organization was much like Arthur's: federal office holders and associates from his home state with very little central direction. It is hard even to name his manager.

Michener had a large role at Minneapolis, but probably not as large as he claimed. He had wanted to be Harrison's manager, but was not instructed to begin any work until after Clarkson's final refusal. At the same time Carter was ostensibly put in charge of the campaign. Many of Harrison's friends expected Elkins to lead the administration forces at the convention. Russell even made plans to go to Minneapolis until the White House said no.

During the convention, telegrams went back and forth between Washington and Minneapolis as the President, his private secretary Elijah W. Halford, and Russell sent orders to the various managers. Michener complained of fighting a battle with "a general fifteen hundred miles away." A. M. Jones of Illinois and Chris Magee, both state opponents of prominent anti-administration leaders, played major roles on the convention floor. Several Indiana friends holding federal appointments apparently took orders directly from the White House, and no one emerged from the convention with the reputation of a president-maker.

The administration deliberately avoided publicizing its leaders. Morris M. Estee of California, an old associate of Elkins, urged the White House to have its newspapers claim that "we had no management at all but that the people pushed it along." He feared that singling out any leader would convince the President's opponents that the promises had already been made. Probably he was also working to cover up the part that Elkins had played in organizing Harrison's forces. Certainly the Secretary of War's close political friends such as Estee, Carter, Richard C. Kerens of Missouri, and Powell Clayton of Arkansas were much in evidence at Minneapolis, although Elkins's personal role—whatever it was—remained well hidden. The newspapers gave much credit to Depew—which men on the inside found "amusing." The most usual estimate was simply to attribute the nomination to federal office holders, a point on which the President became very sensitive.[33]

The Minneapolis convention was a dull one. The President's forces held together largely because there was nothing to draw them away. Clarkson had carried a majority of the national committee into opposition, but Harrison's strategy was simply to minimize all contests and to compromise at every possible point. His managers assumed that the Blaine men needed a supercharged emotional atmosphere in order to block the President. As long as the proceedings were quiet and orderly, they could only lose strength with each passing day. The opposition essentially had no strategy except to speak as bitterly as possible of the President and to delay the proceedings and fight for every inch of ground. They could only hope that the administration forces would crumble. But this was unlikely, for if there was no enthusiasm for the President, the opposition was unable to muster any either. "Without Blaine," *The New York Times* reported, "the Blaine men have not seemed to care much who was nominated." By the time the convention opened, many suspected that the opposition would turn to McKinley. But Harrison's managers knew from their polls that they had a majority against any candidate.[34]

The opposition could do little but delay proceedings: "It is evident," wrote Michener, "that they are determined to delay us in every possible way in the committee on credentials." This kept the convention from organizing, holding up all other business, but it was unlikely to have any serious effect unless some sensation "stampeded" the Harrison delegates to another candidate. Rumors spread of defections among leading administration supporters, but they were easy to disprove at the convention. Some of the President's managers optimistically advised abandoning all contests to end the delaying tactics, but most of the leaders feared that this would frighten some of the delegates and give plausibility to rumors of defections.

Instead, Harrison's managers turned to a technique that had been used by the stalwarts in 1880 and President Arthur's supporters in 1884: they called a caucus in another hall to demonstrate their strength publicly and make it difficult for anyone to defect. This method had held the "306" together in 1880. It had not worked in 1884: Arthur's first ballot total was substantially lower than attendance at the caucus. In 1892, the move, which Michener attributed to A. M. Jones, was completely successful. Slightly more than half the delegates attended the meeting held on Thursday afternoon. The first test vote of the convention that evening proved the success of the meeting. The Harrison men polled 463 votes—exactly the number of delegates that the newspapers reported attending the "Market Hall meeting." [35]

While it would be naive to attribute as much as contemporaries did to this piece of showmanship, it did come at just the right moment and may have held firm some of Harrison's wavering delegates in the face of an attempt to nominate McKinley. He had been the most likely dark horse throughout, but only on Thursday did the opposition seriously consider uniting on him, a development that provoked Hanna to predict that he could be "nominated easily."

In making this assertion, Hanna assumed a great deal. He needed strong support from a number of large states— beginning with Ohio. Hanna had previously persuaded Foraker to switch his support from Blaine to McKinley if the latter's chance came. In addition, Hanna hoped for substantial support from Iowa, Massachusetts, New York, and Pennsylvania. He wanted Sherman and Allison to influence Governor Gear, chairman of the Iowa delegation, to "give McKinley some votes on the first ballot." But Gear did not believe that the attempt would succeed or that Allison would wish him to go against the President. Hanna also expected to get most of the Massachusetts delegation but instead won only 11 of 30 votes. New York and Pennsylvania proved similarly disappointing, as the President received 27 votes in the one and 19 in the other.[36]

The Pennsylvania vote was particularly damaging. It demonstrated the ability of Magee, who had been secretary of the Market Hall meeting and a prominent Harrison leader, to carry a respectable block of Pennsylvania Republicans against Quay's wishes. One of the more prominent Harrison managers telegraphed the White House that "To Chris Magee belongs credit for checking the stampede to McKinley." The Ohioan had simply not done well enough in the large states to serve as a magnet for the small state delegations and the southerners. In the end, he and Blaine split the opposition vote and Harrison won easily with 535 $\frac{1}{6}$ votes.

Although this was a substantial majority of the convention, it was a far from impressive victory for an incumbent President, and made the nomination a dubious one. The President's renomination, reported Hanna, "seemed to fall like a wet blanket upon those in attendance." Many expressed doubts over the wisdom of running any candidate for a second term. John Hay, writing what was meant to be an encouraging letter to vice-presidential candidate Reid, saw prospects for victory only through Democratic divisions and in spite of having Harrison on the ticket. No one knew where to look for either the leadership or the political support to re-elect an administration—an attempt that had not succeeded in two decades.[37]

V

The Republican party in 1892 had scant hopes for success. Clarkson, before the convention, had argued that it would be difficult to elect any Republican. Right after Harrison's renomination Hanna expressed fears that even Ohio might go Democratic. A close friend of the President with a reputation for optimism, R. R. Shiel, was "very doubtful" of victory in Indiana and thought Illinois equally dubious. He commented on the sharp change from elections past:

> Four years ago we only had three or four doubtful states and we could draw from all the other states and concentrate in those doubtful states. This year we have only got four or five but what are doubtful and have but four or five that we can expect to draw from to aid us in the doubtful states.[38]

The gloomy prophecy was true: almost the entire nation had become politically doubtful since 1888. Most damaging of all, New York seemed hopelessly lost, and the party, accustomed to making its fight there, was unnerved. Unable to carry the Empire State, it drove further and further afield. The national committee was forced to spread its resources thinly, while the prospect of defeat in New York weakened the party in the rest of the country. In the Midwest, where voters had a long tradition of breaking with the party on state issues but voting Republican nationally, Democratic politicians reported that for the first time the Germans and Scandinavians in Wisconsin and Illinois, seeing that "New York [was] safe, that Cleveland [would] be elected . . . [were] willing to cut loose from the Republican party altogether." Initial doubts of success, especially in New York, began an accumulation of disadvantages that ended in a Democratic landslide.[39]

These poor prospects made organizing a national committee unusually difficult. Harrison began by fixing on Cornelius N. Bliss as treasurer. Bliss had been highly successful in raising money for the New York state committee in 1888 and had vigorously supported the President's renomination. With Platt still hostile, the White House sought the counsel of Bliss and Reid as to what kind of an organization would heal the wounds in the crucial state. But when the committee met on June 27, even the primary step of selecting a chairman proved impossible. Clarkson, who seemed the best man to bring together the various elements of the party, wanted the job. But Harrison no longer trusted him and would do no more than assign him a place on the executive committee. The other suggested candidates were either nonentities or men like Chris Magee who would alienate major state leaders.[40]

Elkins stepped into the breach with a proposal to conduct the campaign himself through a figurehead chairman, William J. Campbell of Chicago. Campbell had long been active in Illinois politics, but was known nationally only as an attorney for packing-king Phillip Armour, a connection which would not help the ticket in the Midwest. Elkins planned that Campbell as chairman would run a western office in Chicago while Carter as secretary would be Elkins's foil in running the New York headquarters in collaboration with Reid, Hiscock, and their followers. This was a counsel of desperation: Campbell would not take the chairmanship; Carter was reluctant to be secretary; and Reid had already discovered that Platt controlled all the New York committees and that any attempt to organize against him would be fatal to the ticket.[41]

The organizational meeting was an embarrassing failure. The President met no open conflict, but he could not organize the campaign. The committee put through El-kins's plan simply to buy time. Within a week, Campbell named an executive committee, arranged a meeting, and announced his intention to resign, calling on the commit-tee he had named to select a new chairman. In effect, the administration had taken the responsibility for naming the chairman away from the national committee. As Campbell was making his announcement, Harrison, in a White House conference with Carter, Elkins, Jeremiah Rusk, Halford, and Michener, desperately—and unsuc-cessfully—sought a new chairman.

When the new executive committee met on July 16 to accept Campbell's resignation, only Carter and Clarkson remained as possibilities. The committee chose Carter who unhappily accepted. Everyone knew that he had not wanted the position. Finding a new secretary was em-barrassing as well and for several additional days that posi-tion remained unfilled until Louis E. McComas, a former Congressman from Maryland, agreed to serve. Members of the executive committee publicly conceded that "the campaign had had a most unfortunate start." [42]

The committee as finally organized was not one to in-spire confidence. The chairman was an unknown man and could not control his committee. Of the other members, only four—DeYoung of California, Fessenden of Con-necticut, Garret A. Hobart of New Jersey, and Clarkson—had experience on previous committees, and of them all but Hobart had opposed the President at the conven-tion. The committee was scarcely in operation before late August, and when Michener visited headquarters early in September he found activities at a standstill. Most of the skilled managers had not yet started work; Clarkson either from illness or indifference worked only four or five hours a day; several of the committeemen present were simply incompetent. "Nine-tenths of the work," he reported, "falls upon the shoulders of Carter and McComas." This unfortunate situation continued throughout the campaign, with Carter usually lacking skilled assistance and politicians in the states constantly complaining of a dearth of literature and other forms of aid. The organization reflected the doubtful prospects and unhappiness with which it began. Clarkson told a New York Democrat late in September that "both these National Committees are organized for business and both of them are afraid they will be successful." But on that score the Republicans did not act as if they had much to fear.[43]

The one bright area was the campaign's financing. Bliss directed fund raising in relative independence of the committee. Seeing that prospective contributors lacked confidence in the party's organization, he urged Harrison to appoint an advisory committee as in 1888.[44] This would also insure money to run the New York campaign whatever Platt's attitude. After weeks of negotiation and a personal appeal from the President, Thomas Dolan once more agreed to head the new committee. He and Bliss made a successful team. Clarkson years later claimed that the committee had raised $6,000,000. This was a wildly exaggerated figure, but it does show that he recalled a well-supplied committee. The more usual estimate was somewhere between $1.5 million and $2 million. Clarkson blamed the need for large collections on "mercenary newspapers and greedy speakers," and for this there is contemporary evidence. Newspapers demanding financial aid for their support of the ticket formed "a very large part of the Committee's business," Clarkson noted in August. Labor and foreign language newspapers especially were a heavy drain on funds. In addition, committee members were amazed at office holders who demanded salaries and expense accounts for their part in the campaign.[45]

By 1892, the national committee no longer relied on

assessments to raise any large part of its funds. Years of attack on the system had made it an increasingly less reliable way to raise money. Teddy Roosevelt's energetic direction of the Civil Service Commission in 1892 dealt the final blow. Members of the national committee were furious over his investigations. They accused him of being "intent upon his own magnificence and personal identity" and described him as a "chattering monkey." But Clarkson, who had tangled with him all through the Harrison administration, recognized that Roosevelt was on the right track. Clarkson carefully analyzed the new circumstances to which the party had to respond in its fund raising. He denied that the committee had violated the civil service laws. Assessments were an "old barbarism." The party could not "honorably accept, much less assess and coerce subscriptions from clerks or officers whose salaries are all needed to support their families." Clarkson understood that the run of patronage jobs, the little postmasters, letter carriers and tide waiters, were for the party's "poor," a kind of welfare program—much like the Civil War pensions. It was not simply that the reformers were right on humanitarian grounds, but that such collections were poor politics and unprofitable. "I would rather go into any city in America to-day," he wrote to the White House, "and try to raise $10,000 from liberal [Republicans] among businessmen than $1,000 among office-holders." Collections ought to be from men of means whether in office or out, "particularly the outs."

Clarkson, however, did not have in mind the tactics of 1888 or the unfortunate 1890 campaign, which he caustically described as "playing the mendicant upon manufacturers and corporations." Rather, he hoped to put the party's finances on the basis of "free but systematic donations from its generous men,—who will always give when they are shown the party's needs." In 1892, Clarkson was only voicing a hope; in four more years a radical change in the situation of the parties nationally, and of business's relationship to them, would change Clarkson's hopes from a national committee chairman's dream to a reality in a way beyond his wildest imagining, with leading business-men of both parties aiding in the work.[46]

VI

The traditional lead-off of the Republican campaign was the early state elections in Maine. Manley, the chair-man of the state committee, feared that Blaine's hostility to the President and his inability or unwillingness to cam-paign would reduce Republican majorities. He also dis-covered that Democratic manager William C. Whitney had galvanized the Maine Democrats into their most seri-ous effort since 1880. A week before the election Manley complained that the opposition had more money and more speakers in the field than he could muster. Assess-ments were disappointing and the national committee had to supply most of the funds. In the end Manley got enough money and Blaine wrote a satisfactory public letter en-dorsing the ticket and pleading ill health.

Still, Manley expected the result to be disappointing: "Our votes will not fall off, the Democratic vote will, for various causes, increase." He was well aware of what stu-dents of voting behavior have since corroborated, that campaigns change few votes: they bring out those who will vote the ticket. He had no way to prevent the Democrats from getting out their vote. Manley's prediction of a vic-tory by 12,000 votes was accurate. The Republican total had risen 3000 since the low point of 1890, but the Demo-cratic total had gone up 10,000. As Maine went, so went Vermont: Republican pluralities in September were the lowest in a presidential year for the previous quarter-century.[47]

The South looked discouraging as well. Neither Harrison nor Carter had any faith in the party's chances even in collaboration with the Populists. The early state elections in August, September, and October bore out their convictions. Nevertheless Republican managers schemed to win Southern states and convinced Harrison to back their strategy as a tactic to divert Democratic funds from the West. The national committee through Chris Magee spent time, effort, and considerable sums on arranging fusions with southern Populists and on buying off factional Republican tickets. Elkins made a major effort in his adopted state of West Virginia, which, although still Democratic, had become a close state in the eighties. As late as October 26, the White House was still urging the national committee to find more money for these efforts.

This signal exertion was not based on rosy optimism. The disastrous Georgia election early in October had soured the President on the Southern strategy. But the party was desperate. The committee's estimates two weeks before the election told a frightening story. They showed 210 safe Republican votes of the 223 needed to elect a candidate. This was an enormously inflated figure, 64 votes too high in the final outcome. Even so, the remaining 13 votes meant carrying either New York or Indiana or a combination of Southern and border states. The situation in both of the traditionally deciding states was such as to make clutching at straws in Delaware and North Carolina understandable—however futile it might be. Moreover, since several of the fourteen states labeled "now safe" were really still doubtful, even imagined victories in the South or in Indiana might not be enough. For all the irons it had in the fire, the committee had to turn back to the difficult task of carrying the Empire State.[48]

The President's opposition had centered in New York even before the nomination. When Harrison won at

Minneapolis, his New York supporters hoped to see Platt toppled from his uneasy position as party leader. Platt had retained control of the state committee for the previous four years, but he had faced open opposition in the party since the close of the 1888 campaign. Worse yet, the Republicans had never won a state election under his direction. One editor caustically described Platt as "very strong at the caucuses and very weak at the polls." This was a dangerous situation for the leaders of a party that had by no means accepted the role of a minority and still expected to win elections. Many hoped that Platt's defeat at Minneapolis would be his downfall. Politicians warned Harrison of Blaine's fate in 1884 when he left the New York party in the hands of his enemies and suggested a figurehead such as Depew for the new leader. Platt, of course, knew that such suggestions were a blind for a campaign directed by Elkins.[49]

Reid seriously investigated the possibility of such an anti-Platt organization. Quigg canvassed the state committee, digging into its members' financial and political interests, to see if they could be reached. His report is one of the most illuminating political documents of the era. Of the thirty-four-member committee, he found that twenty were bound to Platt "by personal and financial ties, which, in my judgment, would be likely in any event to keep them a compact and devoted band, ready to do his will in his way." Most of these men held state political offices or aspired to elective office. Several were editors dependent upon Platt for the solvency of their newspapers. Others had various financial stakes in Platt's continuing control. The opposition members were tied to the White House: some held federal offices or were sponsored by administration officials; others were connected with Elkins's financial interests or linked to Depew through dealings with the New York Central.

To test the accuracy of his work, Quigg went to Platt with a list of the committeemen and asked him who on it were his friends. Platt checked off the twenty names that Quigg had already determined and boasted: "It's my committee . . . I propose to control it, too, whether I shout for Harrison or not." Quigg's conclusion was unequivocal: "Platt's control is complete and I don't suppose it could be shaken without such a fight as would make success in November uncertain and probably impossible." Platt was in a dangerous humor, Quigg reported, and had to be appeased. He advised Reid to confer with Platt at once and "treat him as if you thought he was the greatest and purest man on earth." [50]

Platt continued to sulk for almost two months. It became more and more apparent that Platt had no ulterior political aim, but was simply in an irrational rage at the administration. He felt personally slighted in a way that one would not expect from a hardened politician. Reid, after several interviews with him, explained that

> . . . he is excessively sore over the whole chapter of his relations to this Administration. . . . On the whole, probably the thing that has stung him the deepest is a little thing:—he has never been asked to call; his opinions have never been asked, and his few letters to the President have never been replied to excepting through a secretary! [51]

Platt's frustration stemmed in part from his sense of the split between state and congressional politics on the one hand and president-making and the conduct of the executive branch on the other—a difference running throughout the period. He complained to Reid that despite his "great and acknowledged services" in the 1888 campaign, he had never received the deference or cooperation from the President and his cabinet that he felt due him. His power in the crucial state of New York had, to his bafflement, failed to create an influence with the administration that would have given him respectability in the party. His power was not threatened, but his legitimacy was in question, and Platt, who had perhaps never recovered from his traumatic descent of 1881, was in a genuine status panic.[52]

Harrison too had his back up and resisted the direct interview that Platt desired. But he realized the need for some conciliatory gesture when he received a letter sent through Hiscock which was essentially an ultimatum. Platt's complaints were of the ephemeral kind that Reid had reported: the President did not consider him a gentleman. The letter contained an explicit renunciation of any desire to bargain for future favors. Yet the sanctions that the letter threatened were as concrete as the complaints were vague: that Platt would "withdraw practically from active politics," a course which his "large following" would understand as "absolutely hostile to you—and as such have its effect." He even threatened to thwart Bliss's attempts to raise funds by persuading wealthy Republicans that the cause was hopeless.[53]

This letter, odd as it was, eased the situation. Platt was demanding an apology to which Harrison did not feel he was entitled, but he was asking for nothing else. Platt was a satiated political power who admitted that the President had satisfied all his patronage requests after denying him the treasury department. Actually Harrison did not even have to apologize for anything he had done; he only had to deny his contempt for Platt—a small and harmless lie. He did this directly in a letter to Platt assuring him that he had never acted out of "personal disrespect."

Harrison discussed directly the discontinuity between presidential politics and congressional and state power:

I have never sought (and it is rather uncommon in politics, I think) to require personal loyalty of those who received appointments from me. Up to the very meeting of the Minneapolis Convention I was making nominations upon the recommendation of Senators and Members of Congress whose opposition to me was not only pronounced, but bitter, and those who opposed me at Chicago in 1888 have, as you know, had generous recognition.

In short, state party leaders did not need to name the presidential candidate—or even like him—to profit from his elevation. "Post convention loyalty to the ticket and to the party," Harrison wrote, "should be rather the test when honors are to be distributed." [54]

Platt's direct reply to this letter was vague, looking toward an eventual conference "with a few friends" that the President had suggested, but his more important response was to begin visiting national committee headquarters and organizing the New York campaign. Thereafter, he was fully committed to carrying the ticket: raising money, urging his followers throughout the state into action, and, in an unusual move for him, making a short public speech early in October which produced a letter of thanks from the President.

By all reports, the New York party after late August was united. In addition to Platt's activity and Bliss's successful fund raising, Reid contributed mightily in money and publicity. Both parties, overcoming initial difficulties, were well organized in New York by September to face an electorate that experienced politicians considered the quietest and most indifferent in memory. Under such conditions, prospects for overcoming the Democratic margins of the three previous years, while not quite non-existent, were obviously slim.[55]

Prospects of reversing the Democratic trend in the West

were no better. From Ohio to the Pacific, the party faced enormous difficulties. Many states in the midwestern heartland of the party—Ohio, Illinois, Wisconsin, Michigan, Minnesota, Iowa, Kansas, and Nebraska—were politically doubtful.

In Ohio, the party had been rocked by one of its most open factional battles since the Civil War era—the senatorial contest in 1891 between Sherman and Foraker. Somehow, Harrison had managed to antagonize both factions. Hanna, after the Minneapolis convention, threatened to sit out the campaign, while many of Foraker's supporters blamed the administration for their hero's defeat the previous year. Knowledgeable observers in both parties reported that in Cincinnati, Republican boss George B. Cox would trade presidential votes for his county ticket to compensate for losses he would sustain from Sherman men knifing his local candidates. Understandably, the state campaign was lackluster and many of the usual sources refused to contribute funds.[56]

While Republican politicians fought each other, the Democrats were embarked on a brilliant "still hunt" campaign. This strategy called for minimal publicity, small meetings, and much canvassing to reach wavering Republicans without arousing partisan feelings or inviting vigorous counter-moves by the opposition. It was a strategy worthwhile only when the opposition was not putting forth its full effort and when voters ordinarily fixed in their predilections were reachable because of hard times or specific local irritations. Democratic politicians were aware of the now uncertain state of political loyalties that had been unchanged for a generation: "There never was such a time," the Democratic state chairman wrote, "to go for Republican farmers who have always been and are now blind to argument. I instruct our fellows to rub their noses in the depleted condition of their pocket books." In this quiet way, he hoped to "steal" the state away from the Republicans. The Democrats came within an ace of success, actually producing a victory for one Democratic elector.[57]

In Illinois and Wisconsin, ethnic tensions over Republican-supported school language laws as well as agrarian discontent, which found partial expression in a desire for tariff revision, made both states dangerous ground. In Wisconsin the Democrats, emphasizing the tariff in the country and the Bennett school law among the German population, succeeded in carrying the state through the same "still hunt" technique. In Illinois, the brilliant John Peter Altgeld, who combined reform and the political ambitions of the burgeoning Chicago ethnic communities, led a well-run organization to victory. In both cases, the state parties were solidifying the majorities achieved two years previously. They generally attributed their success to agrarian discontent and the increasing immigrant populations in the midwestern cities.[58]

Farther west, where agrarian discontent expressed itself in the Populist movement and the demand for remonetization of silver, the Republicans had even greater problems. With both major parties generally pro-silver in these states, the protest vote in the West was against the traditional majority party, the Republicans. This presented the possibility of fusion on silver with the Democrats. Although the Democratic candidate had called free silver a "reckless and dangerous experiment," in a nationally publicized pronouncement in February 1891, Democrats and Populists, with the encouragement of the Democratic National Committee, effected fusion arrangements in Oregon, Nevada, Colorado, Idaho, Wyoming, Minnesota, North Dakota, South Dakota, Nebraska, and Kansas.[59]

Fusion is always difficult. Some Democrats refused to surrender their own organization or vote another ticket, and Populists of Republican antecedents could be driven back into their former party by a fusion with the Democrats. This opened opportunities to counteract the fusionists, but the Republican National Committee could not stretch its funds far enough to offer substantial help to local committees. The West, they hoped, might go Republican even without aid. Moreover, Republican-Populist fusions in the South seemed a more promising investment.[60]

The national committee adhered to its policy of refusing aid to the West except in the case of Nebraska. There, the Democrats and Populists were cooperating informally. Even the conservative Nebraska Democrats who publicly supported Cleveland privately advised party members to vote for the Populist candidate to keep the state from going Republican. Republican managers struggled along on their own money until late in the campaign when an administration agent visited the state and realized the danger of a Populist victory. As a result, the national committee provided funds for Nebraska in the final days of the campaign. With a Democratic ticket still in the field, the Republicans barely won.[61]

A Hoosier in the White House damaged rather than benefited the Indiana party. The situation was much like the New York Democrats under Cleveland, in which there were almost two different parties, one focused on the state capital and the other on Washington. The chairman of the state committee, John K. Gowdy, continually complained of the national administration's meddling in state affairs. The national committeeman, J. N. Huston, was even more hostile to the administration. He had nearly retired from politics in disgust until the Indiana delegation at Minneapolis elected him committeeman in rebellion against Michener's attempt to name someone close to the administration. As the party organized in the summer of 1892, the state chairman, the national committeeman, and the President's troubleshooter and troublemaker Michener were all intensely hostile to each other.[62]

The campaign began haltingly. From Washington, Michener and Halford sent forth advice and men to be put to work, but in Indianapolis chairman Gowdy had little money and could not adequately staff his headquarters. Assessments—as everywhere—had shrunk, and the state finance committee, headed by banker and national committeeman Huston, scarcely functioned. In October, the White House began taking a more direct hand in the Indiana campaign. The administration pressured and cajoled Huston into action. Halford wrote a flattering letter; emissaries visited him; Carter commissioned him to make the county-by-county poll that the state committee had been unable to do. But this campaign directed from a distance did not run smoothly. By mid-October everyone was discouraged, and letters begging for aid poured out of Indianapolis. Carter did not want to send funds at this point, preferring to have the state organization tap local sources first and then turn to the national committee only for its election-day expenses.[63]

This traditional political logic, however, no longer applied. The state committee was so poor that it needed funds in mid-October to complete the organization required to make use later of election-day money. "There is no use," warned an Indiana leader on October 18, "of sending us aid if they do not send it within the next week." The national committee was in a difficult position since it did not yet have clear information from Indiana. All state committees report desperate straits when they write to national headquarters for money. Carter was too late in recognizing the gravity of the situation, and then his fund-raising efforts were unsuccessful. On November 1, Carter and Dolan were still trying to raise money for

Indiana without the "specific data concerning the counties, precincts and wards" to convince contributors that the chance of carrying Indiana was worth any investment.

Carter never believed that the state could be won and worked only in response to White House pressure. The state committee's emissary offered only "generalities" while the Democratic state committee's poll showed a Democratic majority of 18,000. This was for public consumption, but the Republican managers had no figures to dispute their claims. Carter had no reason to trust the state's management. Michener had sent him an incredible telegram demanding funds and telling him that if they were not forthcoming the curses of the Republicans of Indiana "will follow you to your dying day." Such histrionics, of course, suggested that the men in charge had thoroughly lost control of the situation.

When Halford went west just before election day, the national committee had finally sent funds, but it was obviously too late. The state leaders still lacked the reliable polls which would pinpoint areas in which to use the money. They did not even have a tally of Marion County (Indianapolis) whose sizable Negro population had a reputation for purchasability. The Democrats, meanwhile, had an accurate "inside" poll showing a 6000-vote majority —close to their actual margin of 6482 votes.[64]

VII

When the results came in on election day, Republican leaders were not really surprised at the Democratic victory, but its magnitude startled them. The opposition had carried eight of California's nine electoral votes as well as the electoral votes of Illinois and Wisconsin for the first time since the Civil War; they had almost swept Ohio and had carried all the traditionally doubtful states, winning New York by over 45,000 votes. It was the first decisive victory since 1872 and following in the wake of the elections two years previously was an ominous portent for the Republican party. The Democrats had gained among precisely the groups that were growing most rapidly: city dwellers, immigrants, Catholics, labor. Republican leaders did not assume that a Democratic majority was emerging in the nation. Politicians never do that. A worse Democratic defeat four years later would spawn the myth of the "First Battle" instead of being seen as the beginning of a long era of minority status for the party. But such fears seemed in the back of their minds as they commented on the return.

A dominant theme was that of the "unexpected." The Populist victory in Kansas was "a great surprise to the managers and leading members of our party. The unexpected has occurred here and elsewhere." A Nebraska Republican blamed "our unexpected defeat" nationally on organized labor and the Catholic Church. In Maryland, neither party's managers understood the result: "Both agreed that they got something they didn't expect, and it is a question which class was surprised the more— the local Republican or the local Democratic politicians." Republican politicians sensed that the electorate, especially the new groups gaining a measure of political power, were extremely unstable, and at this point the Democrats had profited from their discontent. The Homestead strike of that summer, coming in a highly protected industry, had weakened the force of Republican tariff arguments in 1892. Yet Republicans were aware that shifting economic conditions could change labor's mind. One year's liability could become the next year's asset. Working-class groups struggling to organize themselves were an element of the population up for grabs between the parties, and astute Republicans, if they did not welcome the rise of organized labor on economic grounds, did not fear it politically. Men like Elkins, Kerens, Hanna, and John B. Milholland maintained excellent relations with Terence Powderly, Samuel Gompers, and other leaders of unions and workingmen's political organizations, and understood thoroughly that they represented pressure groups that would deal with either party.[65]

But in 1892, Republicans, who had often done well in the cities, saw the city and immigrant votes as a major threat. In explaining the loss of Indianapolis, a Republican leader pointed out that the increase in the Democratic majority in Marion County was "not more than that national increase from immigration." Manley, as shrewd a politician as the party had, was humiliated that "the slums of Chicago, Brooklyn and New York should settle the destinies of this country for four years" and cited sample returns to illustrate his point. Shelby Cullom flatly asserted "We lost Illinois by the tremendous democratic vote of Chicago." Elliott Shepard, editor of the New York *Mail and Express,* said the same thing by blaming the Catholic vote, although had he been writing from Chicago or Milwaukee, he probably would have added the Lutherans. In any case, discontent seemed rife in the land, and all the discontented people at the moment were voting Democratic.[66]

Republican leaders tempered their pessimism when they looked at their opposition: a coalition of various, excitable, and unhappy groups. Senator Orville H. Platt analyzed the Democrat's plight with considerable insight:

> The Republican party has been defeated in this election because the Democrats have induced all the people in the country who think that they want something which they have not got, to vote the Democratic ticket in the expectation that that party if in power will give them what they want. Socialists, anarchists, communists, hood-

lums, as well as farmers, laborers, and people of small means, and the discontented everywhere, expect now that all their ideas whether reasonable or wild, are to be carried out in practical legislation by the Democratic party. . . . Much of the discontent prevailing in the country has foundation in the conduct of the capitalistic classes, and the people whom I have described will not be content with any reasonable correction of existing abuses. They want to cut deep. I think we have got to let the Democratic party struggle with this problem a while now. It is little that the Government can do in dealing with capitalistic abuses. . . .

Faced with these massive and insistent demands, the Democratic party was ill suited to compromising them in any politically viable way:

The Democratic party has as much wealth and as much aggressive capitalistic influence in it as the Republican party. . . . Either the Aristocracy in the Democratic party or the proletariat is to direct affairs in the next four years, or there is to be a fair compromise between them out of which good may come. I can't tell which it will be at present. I think the proletariat is on the top, and that conservative men have got to unite without reference to party. . . .

Such prophecies of impending political revolution were far from unusual in the 1890s, although Platt's realism and calm were particularly impressive. Of course, Republicans like Platt could preserve their equanimity while viewing events from the sidelines. The burdens now facing the Democracy were more onerous and direct.[67]

The conservative Democrats who controlled the party had much to fear. "[O]ur majority in the House is too large," a blunt New York Democrat wrote to the President-elect—meaning that it was composed of too many western and southern silverites. Harrison noted bitterly how "Mr. Cleveland's National Committee made combinations wherever they could in the silver states—abandoning their own organization and voting with the wildest inflationists." Cleveland's supporters were an amazingly varied lot. They included John Peter Altgeld of Illinois, described to Cleveland in September 1892 as "a very clearheaded, conservative man of the business type . . . the very antithesis of a 'rainbow chaser.' " Eugene V. Debs in Terre Haute, Indiana served as chairman of a "Committee of One Hundred" of the "Grover Cleveland Democrats" which held meetings to agitate for his nomination in the spring of 1892. William Jennings Bryan worked for the ticket in several states. Henry George campaigned actively for Cleveland. Even the Populist candidate James Baird Weaver looked with favor on the Democrat's success.[68]

Cleveland, because of the reform cast of his first administration, his tariff message, and his being out of office, functioned as the candidate of expectations much as Harrison had in 1888, unlikely as either man was for the mold in which the times had cast them. The political atmosphere was rich with expectation and pungent with disappointment at the failure of those hopes to find any real fulfillment in the politics of the early nineties. This instability frightened politicians who had been accustomed to count their votes in advance for a score of years. But whether it would continue, or whether there would be a smashup which "conservative men . . . without reference to party" would have to pick up, waited on the actions of the new administration and the moods of an electorate in transition.

VI

〰

1896: Opportunity

"The best thing for the Republican party to do is to wait," Orville Platt had written after the defeat of 1892. It did not have to wait for long. In May 1893, shortly after the Cleveland administration had taken office, a stock market panic ushered in the major depression that had been threatening since 1890.[1]

The fragile coalition behind President Cleveland rapidly fell apart, leaving the Democrats with a divided party, a set of unsuccessful economic policies, and the brunt of the nation's anger as terrible industrial depression succeeded the panic. Political moorings, strained since the late eighties, gave way completely in the most massive shift in voting behavior since the founding of the Republican party. In the first two years of Cleveland's second administration, every occurrence—the repeal of the Sherman Silver Purchasing Act, the Pullman strike, the Wilson-Gorman tariff, the bond issues, the actions of the Supreme Court—brought a further decline of the Democratic party.[2]

Change in political sentiment was amazingly rapid. The voting behavior of a heretofore safe Tammany district in New York City, the 14th Congressional District, gives a striking example. In 1892, the district went Democratic by a comfortable 8825 votes. When the Congressman resigned at the end of 1893, Tom Platt put up Lemuel Quigg in a special election in January 1894. His canvassers found that "great numbers of Democratic workingmen are going to vote for Mr. Quigg." Platt instructed his men to play down partisan issues and stress the Wilson bill, then being debated in the House, "as a matter of bread & butter & not a matter of politics." Quigg's election, his canvassers were supposed to point out, would "not affect the Democratic majority in the House of Representatives but simply serve as a warning to the Democrats that they must go slow in the passage of laws that interfere with industry." Thus, Platt did not expect a shift in party loyalties but a protest by voters considering themselves Democrats and looking to Tammany Hall for political favors. Platt's strategy succeeded, and in the light vote one would expect in a special election, Quigg squeaked through with a plurality of 949 votes.[3]

Between January and November 1894 the economy slid into the trough of the depression (June 1894); the Wilson bill turned into the Wilson-Gorman tariff and became law without the President's signature; the scigniorage bill was vetoed; major strikes took place in the soft coal fields and on the railroads; Coxey's Army made its march; a host of pioneer muckraking and radical works were published; an ugly spirit of jingoism suddenly burst forth; the great Pullman strike occurred, and Cleveland took his fateful stand on it. It is impossible to determine how each or any of these events affected the 14th Congressional District of New York, but when elections took place less than ten months later, Quigg found himself the Congressman of a safe Republican district with a majority of 5977. "I doubt," he wrote, "if there is any other district in the United States showing the same percentage of change."

Quigg was wrong. In fact, had he looked at his political neighbor, the 15th Congressional District, he would have found a swing between 1892 and 1894 of 16,503 votes against 14,802 in his own district. The shift between January and November 1894 in that district—also the scene of a special election—was greater as well by 2319 votes.[4]

Quigg's fate was more typical than unusual. His explanation for it was quite direct. The results were due to "the terrible effects upon the working people of the Democratic party's industrial policy here at Washington." One need not accept his faith in the tariff as an explanation of economic depression to realize that the electorate's rejection of Democratic policy was national in scope. In fact, he was probably close to correct in attributing the workmen's actions to their views on the tariff. In any case, the example of Quigg's district could be extended to many other parts of the country. When one notes that there were no Democratic Congressmen in all the states between Ohio and California, it becomes apparent that the fountains of the deep had indeed opened in American politics, and—contrary to earlier expectations—the Democratic party had been engulfed. Republican presidential hopefuls would be charting a new land of political possibility.[5]

Indeed, if there was ever a time when promoting a Republican presidential candidate seemed worth one's full efforts, it was after the Democratic disaster of November 1894. In putting through the repeal of silver purchasing and the Wilson-Gorman tariff, the Democrats had presented their whole economic policy, and still the depression continued. In addition, they had profoundly alienated labor in the Pullman strike. The way was clear for a candidate offering an alternative economic policy, which is to say a candidate with a reputation as a protectionist, a moderate "friend" of silver, and popular with the so-called labor vote—in short, a successor to the deceased Blaine.

McKinley was inevitably the man. Reid, who quickly realized this, urged Elkins that "the natural tendency of the old Blaine guard" ought to be toward nominating the Ohioan, which would "in itself bring the protective tariff issue to the front." "We are far more united on this," he reminded his old cohort, "than on silver or anything else." [6] McKinley had been campaigning for a long time. In 1892 he had shown his strength at the Minneapolis convention. He stressed national issues in 1893 when he was re-elected governor of Ohio. As the depression brought prices down, his identification of high tariffs with prosperity proved more credible than it had in 1890 when he had lost his seat in Congress in the wake of a price rise blamed on his tariff bill. In addition, he attacked the Cleveland administration for not "doing justice" to silver currency, although he tried not to emphasize this issue. Throughout the pre-convention period, and indeed well into the election campaign itself, McKinley hoped to keep the tariff question to the front and ignore the currency issue. As one of his visitors reported in the spring of 1895, "With the tariff the only issue I suppose he feels he would be the only logical candidate." In a wish disguised as a prediction McKinley in 1895 guessed that the 1896 convention would "re-enact the currency platform of 1892, and then stop." He nervously declined to have a book refuting "Coin" Harvey dedicated to him. "It is better," he explained, "not to do anything which may require explanation." [7]

So long as no extraneous issue arose, he was the man of the hour. The only way to fight McKinley was to raise an issue that might throw the election in jeopardy which meant acting almost treasonably toward the party. In the end, only Tom Platt openly battled McKinley and in doing so, as Reid put it, he "committed what in politics is the unpardonable sin of burning his bridges behind him.

. . . [H]e has placed himself in an irregular position utterly unjustifiable, even by the rules of the kind of politics he plays." Of course, Platt's action also had its logic, but not in the game of making presidents. Platt was not looking to win a nation but only New York State, and in his own way he proved as successful as Hanna and McKinley. But the crucial point that must be noted, if one is to penetrate the mystique of the "National Boss" Mark Hanna, is that Hanna had the one popular, available, and in every way logical candidate for the Republican nomination in 1896.[8]

Historians in recent years have studied the campaign of 1896 as thoroughly as any presidential election in American history. We certainly know more about it than about any other episode in Gilded Age politics. There is no need for another narrative of events. However, Hanna's achievement has still to be placed within the context of late nineteenth-century president-making.[9]

II

Mark Hanna retired from business immediately after the congressional election of 1894. Undoubtedly it had convinced him that the chance of making McKinley President was now worth his full-time efforts. Before that time, he had covered all the traditional roles of the Republican businessman in politics. In the late sixties and seventies, he was a local politician engaged in the affairs of his city. He attended the primaries and worked as a poll watcher on election day. Like almost everyone in the nineteenth century, his interest in politics went much deeper than a simple defense of his economic interests: he enjoyed the game and was ambitious for honors and power. In short, he was typical of his age and especially of the Midwest, where almost all businessmen were active in party politics. Hanna took part in reform and businessmen's movements until he gained a foothold in the regular organization and in those part-political, part-civic organizations such as the school board that one would expect from a rising business-man with political interests. In short, he followed a well-worn path.[10]

Elkins, the great president-maker of the eighties, in moving from local to national political importance, had easily and naturally followed his earliest political patron, Richard C. McCormick, in the path of the territorial businessman-politician. So Hanna had a model for his own course in the activities of his close political associate, Charles Foster. Foster, as a Congressman for several terms in the seventies, had gained a reputation as a "business-man in politics" who introduced "business methods" into campaigning. In fact, he was considered a pioneer in po-litical techniques that have come to be especially identified with Hanna. Allen O. Myer, a Democratic politician from Cleveland with an unsavory reputation himself, wrote a description of Foster's methods which sounds like nothing so much as a muckraking attack on Hanna:

> The first appearance of the use of money to effect results by influencing people corruptly, was with the advent of Charles Foster, of Fostoria, O., as a candidate for Congress in '70, '72, '74, '76 and '78. He lived in the town in which he was born. He was a man of affairs. He was engaged in mercantile pursuits and profited by the opportunities pre-sented by the war. He accumulated a fortune and branched out into investments in manufactures and rail-road improvements. . . . In looking about for other worlds to conquer his restless genius led him into the field of politics. He was nominated for Congress. The district was Democratic. He introduced business methods into his campaigns. He did not trust to noise and excitement. He perfected the party organization; a thorough poll was made. This enabled him to form an accurate estimate of

the number of votes he needed. Knowing this, the places were found, the prices were ascertained, and the money was placed in proper hands the night before the election, and such voters as could be reached by money were "fixed."

Myers described Foster as "the pioneer and apostle of Boodle in Ohio" and predicted that he would leave "nothing but a ruined reputation and an apt pupil in the person of Calvin S. Brice." This was written in 1895. A year later he undoubtedly would have had in mind a different pupil of the system that had "brought disgrace upon the name of Ohio." [11]

Even in matters of public policy, Foster and Hanna displayed striking similarities. Both shared the same matter-of-fact sense of business-politics. Neither could imagine that there could be anything offensive about business methods in politics or envision serious conflict between business interests and those of the Republican party. In his role in effecting the compromise of 1877, Foster was truly in his metier, working upon what C. Vann Woodward described as "the intertwining of economics and politics." He favored subsidies to the Texas Pacific in order to Republicanize the state of Texas. On the other hand, he reluctantly voted for the compromise electoral commission bill which Hayes opposed because "the great business interests of the country will hail it as a measure of peace, safety, and relief. It will unlock capital, it will permit business energy to exercise its functions freely and unrestrained." [12]

Since he held elective offices, Foster outwardly had a very different career than Hanna, just as McCormick's differed from Elkins's. But in terms of adopting the various roles within the party organization, the parallels in both cases show them consciously or unconsciously following an already marked road. Foster was probably the man who pushed Hanna beyond the politics of his home city. In 1880 Hanna joined Foster on the state committee as a member of the important finance subcommittee. He also became active that year in raising funds for the national committee. Here again Foster's influence was likely, since Foster took an active role after the convention in managing Garfield's interests. After cooperating with each other through the eighties in Ohio politics and in Sherman's 1888 bid for the presidential nomination, Foster went into Harrison's cabinet as Secretary of the Treasury. Here too he attempted to carry Hanna with him by inducing the President, in September 1891, to ask Hanna to be treasurer of the national committee. But with McKinley's election as Governor of Ohio imminent, Hanna had finally moved beyond Foster and was seeking an even larger prize in national politics.[13]

Hanna was no more Foster's disciple than Elkins was McCormick's. The important point is that they trod paths already blazed and, up to a point at least, did what close friends and associates had already done. There was a variety of traditional roles for businessmen in the Republican party, going back to its origins, and sometimes even similar career lines. When late in 1894 Hanna resolved to devote all his time to nominating McKinley, he was simply adopting the role of businessman–president-maker in the new conditions that the Democratic debacle had created. His was no new role and, what is more, he was—even then—not alone in assuming it. He had by far the most likely candidate. But there were other possibilities, and some of them had their Hannas as well.

III

The traditional account of the campaign of 1896, coming from Croly's biography of Hanna, paints a conflict between this new type of businessman-in-politics, and the eastern "bosses," the old-fashioned state politicians. According to the story told by several of McKinley's friends, Hanna went East early in 1895 to confer with all the major eastern politicians, including Nelson W. Aldrich, Platt, Quay, and Manley. Their meeting at the Fifth Avenue Hotel was kept so secret that "the newspaper did not get an inkling" of it—a circumstance surprising to anyone familiar with nineteenth-century newspapers, and which surprised some of the people who told the story. The conferees agreed to carve up the country, distributing patronage and cabinet positions, and to make McKinley President. McKinley, when Hanna reported back to him, was morally outraged (or, in the more reasonable and sophisticated version of Paul Glad, "thought the bosses' price too high") and refused the offer, deciding to run a campaign of "the people against the bosses." [14]

Except for anecdotes told many years later, there is not a shred of evidence for any of this. Rather it is based on the picture of presidential politics of the era after McKinley's inauguration. Republican administrations kept the national conventions after 1900 under tighter control and could usually fix the convention's choice in advance. Important state leaders arranged such details as the vice-presidential candidate among themselves before the meeting.[15] Yet even then, Hanna for a time in 1904 and Roosevelt in 1912 contested the nomination. In the late nineteenth century not even incumbent Presidents had been able to do what Hanna supposedly attempted. His tactic would not have been an old-fashioned method that was abandoned for a new departure, as it has usually been considered, but a revolutionary change that McKinley correctly considered premature. In all likelihood it was none of these things at all. Probably the incident simply never occurred in the form that legend gave it.

Hanna and McKinley's other managers communicated with politicians all over the country, discussing presidential prospects and seeking delegates. But with other candidates already in the field, the election two years off, and the politics of the Eastern states in the enormous flux we have noted, no one could have expected any firm commitments. Quay and Platt were both struggling for their political lives. It is impossible to imagine what kind of agreement they could enter upon for delegates who would not be elected for another year. The whole past history of Republican president-making showed that to commit oneself to a struggling leader was simply to supply a pawn he could trade off for state power when the time came. This would be especially true of McKinley in 1895 since his popularity was greatest with the insurgents battling Quay and Platt. Hanna, if the tales are true, was adopting the unfortunate strategy of Arthur's managers in 1884, and without even holding the cards of current patronage which they had possessed. This story leads to the unlikely conclusion that Hanna was politically naive.[16]

The picture changes and makes more sense, however, if we see Hanna as a typical rather than a unique figure in Republican national politics. The unusual feature of the 1896 campaign was how early everyone leaped into the presidential field when they realized during the passage of the Wilson-Gorman tariff that the opposition had virtually collapsed. Clarkson, for example, noted in October 1894 "the current belief that the whole country is coming to us on a tidal wave" and set out on a thirteen-state tour in Allison's interest. Historians have misleadingly contrasted men like Clarkson with Hanna as the politician versus the businessman. Clarkson was a state politician and businessman much like Hanna except that up to that point he had been politically more successful and economically less so. By 1894 he was not simply an Iowa politician, although he represented that state on the national committee, but a New York businessman on the board of directors of a telephone company and involved in an unsuccessful enterprise to put a bridge across the Hudson River. Like Hanna, he dabbled in president-making. Only his business failures in the depression of the nineties drove him back into hungry office-seeking under Roosevelt instead of the more elegant game of nominating presidents. In the end he matched none of Hanna's successes either in politics or in business, but they were men seeking the same prizes by the same methods and should be distinguished largely by their respective successes and failures.[17]

Speaker Reed was in the field just as early, and his manager again was of the Hanna type. Joseph H. Manley, who has appeared many times in these pages, had had a long career in Maine politics as postmaster of Augusta under Garfield and Harrison, chairman of the state committee, member of the Maine legislature and national committeeman. But he too was now more than a state politician. He owned a newspaper and was president of a gas company in Augusta, had an interest in the Boston & Maine Railroad, and was in the coal and railroad business with Elkins. Thus, although much more widely known as a politician than as a businessman, he was by the nineties another of the businessman-politician president-makers who formed a characteristic type in the party.[18]

Elkins, another beneficiary of the political changes of the nineties, had become a Senator in 1895 and found it hard to be both an old master president-maker and a freshman Senator. He hoped to gather such old associates as Kerens, Reid, and Carter to "take a hand in the contest" as he had done for "nearly twenty years." But he had lost his fluid position of the eighties. His post in Harrison's cabinet had limited him to backstage maneuvers in 1892; being a Senator restricted him still further. He could have openly supported the ex-President, and in 1895 Elkins seemed to be working for a Harrison-Elkins ticket. But with Harrison's withdrawal, he found it difficult to support anyone but Allison, who by this time had emerged as leader of the Senate Republicans.[19]

Elkins had acquired one great weakness for presidential politics: a political base in West Virginia. Republicans there, led by Governor Albert B. White, were for McKinley, and Elkins, so Reid explained to the Ohio candidate, would "therefore have to follow the lead of his delegates." Wary of McKinley's popularity in his home state, Elkins tried to maintain friendly relations with him. Several of Elkins's old associates had simply gone with the action in president-making by moving close to McKinley. Through them, each side sounded out the other: Elkins interested in the vice-presidential nomination, and McKinley looking for the West Virginia delegation. McKinley used Elkins's pretense of friendship to write him in April 1896 asking his support for an instructed delegation. "I know that a simple hint from you," he unctuously intoned, "would make it easy for the people to do what is in their hearts to do." Elkins tried to duck the request, arguing that the state had not instructed since 1880, but could not prevent McKinley from pressing his case with friendly West Virginia Republicans.[20]

Elkins was no longer the "political adventurer" that Frank D. Root had distinguished from the state "politician" supporters of Blaine in 1888. Like Quay in 1884, he now had to fear a popular candidate who could work through actual or potential dissidents to force him into line. Caught between the conflicting demands of state and national power, he soon had to abandon his efforts. "I am not taking any particular interest in the contest," he wrote to Reid in March. "West Virginia or part of it, at least, is for McKinley. . . ." By the end of April he had surrendered, allowing his state to instruct for McKinley without a fight and publicly conceding that McKinley's nomination was inevitable.[21]

IV

The Ohio men had turned the Blaine strategy of 1884 on Elkins in 1896, a pattern which their campaign followed in most of the states where there was a contest. Like Blaine in 1884, McKinley looked like a winner even to politicians tied to another candidate for state political reasons. This doomed the attempts to form a "combine" against him by putting forward favorite sons. Reid pointed out that they were safe from this traditional strategy for halting a front-runner because once delegations left their local candidates they would "not be going for anybody to beat McKinley, since he [was] their second, if not, in fact their first choice." The campaign of "the people against the bosses" was not a novel or daring technique, but a well-known way for a popular candidate to bring the state leaders around by allying with their local enemies. While Hanna talked about "the people against the bosses," Quay, for example, complained to McKinley of "the alliance Hanna seem[ed] to have made with the municipal thieves of the two great cities of our state." [22]

Quay was in the midst of a desperate battle with the aptly named "Hog combine," a curious combination of urban machine politicians, state leaders, and reformers which Clarkson described as "so powerful that they would crush any other man." At the 1895 state convention Quay had to run himself for chairman of the state committee when he discovered that no one else could defeat the opposition candidate. Even then his usual free spending and delegate persuasion failed to control the convention. Finally he pandered to reform by coming forward as what one of his publicists called the "Republican Tilden." It was a full-blown exercise in the progressive rhetoric of the nineties, decrying "the growing use of money in politics" and "corporate control" and promising "proper control of corporate power," "civil service," and the "overthrow of the lobbyist and jobber!" [23]

Quay was easily as perfect a hypocrite as McKinley. In fact, one has to wonder if Quay's success with this technique in 1895 was not the inspiration for the Ohioans' strategy. According to the legend, they got the idea after a visit to a group of eastern politicians that included Quay. In any case, their technique was new neither in the practice of attacking the most powerful man by working through the lesser bosses, nor in the "good government" rhetoric that accompanied it. Political methods were an effective issue in the mid-nineties, and the people most vulnerable to attack because of it were also the most eager to turn it on their opponents.

McKinley and his organization kept in frequent contact with Quay while they maintained pressure on him by cautiously collaborating with his enemies. Of these, the most important were his Pittsburgh opponents. McKinley received a $6000 contribution for his pre-convention fund from a group of Pittsburgh politicians and businessmen which included Philander C. Knox and Chris Magee. Hanna appreciated the money, but what impressed him was Magee's personal contribution of $1000 which, he wrote McKinley, was politically "very significant." [24]

Since they had support in Pittsburgh as well as great strength in Philadelphia, some of McKinley's close advisors urged open warfare on Quay. But the major was already doing too well through the local opposition to make that necessary. In both of the large cities, Quay's enemies were electing McKinley delegates. Chris Magee was particularly successful. Like Harrison in 1892, McKinley did not need to capture the Pennsylvania delegation, but only to split it. This Magee and others could do on their own, leaving them with a tractable Quay whom Hanna was anxious to have for his national organization.[25]

Quay duplicated the previous year's strategy by throwing his own name into the breach. But while he was a reasonable state committee chairman, no one took him seriously as presidential material. To forestall open conflict late in May, he took a ceremonial trip to Canton as a public expression of capitulation. No one knows what the two men agreed, but one can infer that Quay promised not to make any last-ditch national effort against the Ohioan's candidacy in return for McKinley's agreement not to contest Pennsylvania. Quay's consultation with Platt immediately afterward suggests that he was trying to avoid an open battle at the convention, and his success in holding 58 of Pennsylvania's 64 votes is hard to explain except through such an arrangement with McKinley.[26]

In summary, both McKinley and Quay came out clear winners in the mythical battle between the people and the bosses. The struggle for a presidential nomination was not in any real sense a struggle against state political leadership. Sensible men found ways to make each level of power work for the other provided they did not want the impossible: power in both places at once.

V

New York was in many ways analogous to Pennsylvania. Platt was another surprised beneficiary of the revolution in voter preferences of the early nineties. When in 1893, New York suddenly went Republican for the first time since Conkling's retirement, Platt could only attribute the result to "Divine Providence." This victory, which aroused dormant hopes, led to a full-scale political war between Platt and his enemies, organized into committees of thirty and committees of seventy and led by such long-time opponents as Whitelaw Reid, George Bliss, and Warner Miller. This battle culminated in the "Platt-Strong War" of 1895 in which—much as in Pennsylvania—a motley coalition of dissident politicians, reformers, and businessmen, inspired by reform mayor William L. Strong of New York City, attempted to depose Platt. They lost the first round in the state convention, where Platt retained control by a series of timely concessions to up-state support.[27]

The McKinley campaign provided these dissidents with a new forum. As Platt dangled presidential hopes before Governor Morton to control his New York appointments, the opposition inevitably gravitated to other presidential candidates. Reid would not openly oppose the governor, but he followed a strategy of hinting at the insincerity with which Platt was using Morton's name, and of quietly working for McKinley. In preparation for the state convention of 1896, anti-Platt leaders organized McKinley clubs throughout the state and hostility became intense enough to bring a brief moment of cheer to the demoralized opposition.[28]

With his enemies supporting the major, Platt became the leader of the anti-McKinley forces. In fact, what Hanna insisted upon calling the "combine" scarcely existed outside of Platt's efforts. Leading politicians representing all the candidates except McKinley met several times during the winter to plot strategy against the front-runner. But their agreements, for all that Hanna tried to make of them, came to little more than a canvassing of the states to see who had what strength and whether they could line up enough votes to stop McKinley from a first-ballot victory. They encouraged favorite son candidates in several states to withhold votes from the Ohioan. But on any questions of importance they trusted each other too little to make the mutual concessions that might have made the combination effective.[29]

Only Platt fought McKinley to the last ditch. Quay, as we have seen, played his own game and made his separate peace. Elkins, supposedly part of the "combine," actually could not expect to cooperate with Platt who still denounced him for "the bunco game of 1888." Allison's campaign was halfhearted at best. Clarkson worked hard, but got little support. He watched the supposed combination dissolve almost as it was being created. Many Reed and Allison delegates in the South were bitterly hostile— "something which should not occur." Some of his southern managers were forming coalitions with the McKinley instead of the Reed forces. By February Clarkson had to turn down legitimate requests for operating funds "as I have got to the bottom of my own purse and have called on all the personal friends that I feel I can justly call." He coordinated plans with Quay and Platt to use their corporate connections to raise funds and carry the nomination campaign. In the end, he was amazed at their total failure:

> It seems to me [he wrote to Grenville Dodge] that we have used our influence, or rather the influence that men like Allison and yourself ought to have with great corporations, to very little results in this contest. We have had no money help and no transportation help. Platt is furnishing the money that will bring our Allison delegates from New Mexico, Arizona, and Nevada and Utah to the Convention, when all the country between is filled with railroads that ought to be friendly to Allison.[30]

Most indicative was Illinois, "the heart of it all" according to Clarkson, where McKinley's adversaries distrusted each other too much to mount an effective drive.

While Platt pressed for action in Illinois, Clarkson worried that Reed had the inside track with their allies in the state. Except for raising one contribution of $10,000 for the Illinois campaign, Clarkson did nothing to counteract the efforts of the McKinley managers until well into March, and then he had no money left. "We started too late," he confessed in a post-mortem. "We have balked and feared and hesitated. . . ." [31]

James M. Swank, the highly knowledgeable lobbyist of the American Iron and Steel Association, carefully dissected Hanna's rhetoric:

> You speak [he wrote to Hanna] of a "combine against McKinley." I do not believe it exists except in the sense that McKinley, having the lead, is naturally antagonized by the field. Nor do I believe that any combination such as you suggest can be made in advance of the meeting of the Convention in St. Louis, and it may not then be attempted, and if attempted it may fail. I would not encourage the idea that there exists a "combine" today. How can there be when Reed, Allison, Morton, Cullom, and Quay each hopes to be nominated?

In denying the possibility of a combination before the convention Swank accurately described the president-making experience of his generation. There was simply no substitute for having a candidate. [32]

What Hanna called the "combine," John Hay more accurately described as "Platt men" driven to panic. Even in the West and South Platt seemed to have financed and directed most anti-McKinley operations, hoping to impress New York Republicans with his national power and to frighten them away from McKinley. To Platt the whole campaign was a stop on the road to the solidification of his power in New York, whose end he finally reached at the state nominating convention of August 1896 that presented the "Easy Boss" with his choice of becoming Senator or governor.[33]

Platt's own course was independent of his allies. Governor Morton had limited Platt's options by exacting a pledge from all the leading New York Republicans that they would vote for him throughout the balloting. This insured that he would be more than an easily abandoned favorite son candidate. Platt looked for a way to put forward his candidate that would cut into McKinley's strength in New York and increase his own prospects for state control and national office. He found it in the currency issue. Previously he had argued that the tariff would be "the leading issue in the next campaign" and that any attempt to "crowd the free silver issue to the front should be frowned down." Now he found that by stressing the gold standard he could take the sting out of the opposition by commanding support from the New York business community which until then had largely opposed him.[34]

Platt called for an early state convention to elect delegates-at-large pledged to Morton and to pass a strong sound currency resolution. The convention followed his bidding, but the McKinley men destroyed the effects of this endorsement of Morton and the gold standard by forcing two anti-Platt roll calls and registering about one-sixth of the convention in opposition. This clearly showed Platt's weakness: he could neither trade New York's votes without splitting the delegation nor could he hold up Morton as a serious candidate with solid backing in his own state. Amid rumors that Morton would withdraw his name, McKinley's nomination began to seem so certain that Reid wrote the prospective candidate warning against over-confidence.[35]

McKinley's New York backers multiplied their efforts to elect pledged delegates at the remaining district conventions. By the end of April, even some of Platt's closest political allies publicly conceded McKinley's nomination. With opposition papers calling for Morton's withdrawal, Platt fired his final salvo: an open attack on McKinley's currency record. This could not seriously affect the national outcome. As Reid pointed out to McKinley, "the more the Platt-Morton people work this racket, the easier it made it for the Western and Mountain States to instruct for you, as they wanted to do, in spite of their free-coinage craze." But it served Platt's purpose in New York, which was to force his opponents' business supporters into his corner. He played on the hysteria building up in the New York business community over the free silver agitation, warning businessmen that "they had better do something between now and the convention on other subjects than the silly twaddle of newspapers about 'bosses' and 'boss rule.' "

The strategy was a brilliant success. Long-time opponents conceded that on the currency question Platt had proven "better than his party." Supporters of reform, who were almost uniformly far more anxious about the now threatened gold standard than they were about municipal reform, could no longer attack Platt—at least not until McKinley was safely elected. The opposition was thoroughly silenced and when Hanna came to organize the campaign in New York State he found Platt firmly in control. The now easy boss boasted to Governor Morton that his "eminently satisfactory" interview with Hanna in mid-summer had "created consternation in the ranks of the 'antis.' " Hanna, Platt explained, had no choice "when it was evident . . . that the Republican Party had continued confidence in its present management, and desires them to remain in control." [36]

VI

Ohio presented a particularly interesting case of the relationship between state and national power, and a critical test of Hanna's role as president-maker. Here, if anywhere, he might have shown that he had done something which other state leaders had been unable to do in using his power within the state as a springboard to making a presidential nomination. But an examination of events in 1896 belies that expectation and presents instead a pattern very similar to that of the large Eastern states.

Throughout the eighties, Ohio candidates were hampered by their dual interest in state and national power. Sherman's incomplete control of his own state delegation undermined each of his three bids. There were two distinct centers of power in Ohio: one associated with Foraker which centered in Cincinnati, and the other in the northern part of the state represented by several important figures including Sherman, McKinley, Hanna, and Foster. Anyone from Ohio seeking the nomination could be destroyed if the opposite faction openly opposed him. To forestall this opposition, he had to sacrifice a measure of power in the state in return for convention support.

This, however, was still insufficient since there were simply too few major positions to satisfy the unusually heavy concentration of political talent in the Ohio party. John Sherman monopolized one Senate seat, the other was steadily Democratic, and the governor's chair was occasionally so. The voter revolution of the nineties eased this situation by making Ohio solidly Republican both in national and state elections. But until about 1895, intense factionalism, embarrassing to a presidential candidate in the Republican party, was not simply normal but even inevitable. Hanna and McKinley first tried to meet this problem by simply dominating the party. After McKinley's election to the state house in 1891, they gradually moved to solidify control of the party by putting their own men in all the major offices. They aided Sherman in his contest with Foraker for the Senate in 1892, pushing him into apparent political obscurity. But with a firm power base in southern Ohio and a strong ally in George B. Cox, the local boss of Cincinnati, neither his political potential nor his ambitions had evaporated.[37]

The deterioration of the Democratic party and McKinley's presidential ambitions, both completely obvious in 1894, gave Foraker his chance. McKinley could not afford an open fight in Ohio. But Foraker, with the prospect before him of a Republican Senate seat without a fight with the aged but still entrenched John Sherman, had nothing to inhibit him from literally grabbing everything in sight. Foraker swept the entire state convention of 1895. He nominated Asa Bushnell for governor over Hanna's choice, replaced the chairman of the state committee, and had the convention endorse him for the Senate and McKinley for President. Foraker in his memoirs gloated over the account in Sherman's biography: "The Hanna men were not allowed to surrender—they were captured, and even their side arms taken from them." The McKinley men assiduously spread the story that they had been "taken by surprise." But this is hard to believe. Political circles throughout the country understood that Foraker had gained a triumph.[38]

He was now in an impregnable position. By having the convention endorse McKinley, Foraker put his opponents on their good behavior. He would honor his pledge if they would honor theirs to elect his candidate for governor and not to stand in his way for the Senate. McKinley, to retain his hold on the electorate and keep pressure on Foraker, had to spend most of 1895 vigorously campaigning for the Ohio state ticket. The logical result of this unusual—if forced—harmony and increasing Democratic demoralization was an unprecedented majority for Bushnell and a sure Senate seat for Foraker. McKinley had helped his enemies top his own vote in 1893 and had even boosted his arch-rival into the position of a potential presidential candidate.[39]

Hanna, as he swept on to success in nominating McKinley, had lost all power in Ohio. The new state administration took office at the beginning of 1896 and replaced all of McKinley's supporters. Foraker showed his power at every turn. He made no serious concessions to the prospective presidential candidate in organizing the state committee; McKinley's managers worried about the Ohio delegation well into April. In the end, their candidate's strength elsewhere which promised his nomination kept Foraker in line.[40]

George F. Myers, the famous Negro barber and politician, corresponded in McKinley's interest with a number of small-time politicians whose responses provided a sensitive barometer of political conditions. One of them, Jere Brown, wanted money from "Uncle Mark" for rounding up southern delegates, but also had to follow Foraker's dictation to retain his "present 'posish' " in the Ohio department of insurance. He looked forward to a better job on the federal payroll under McKinley but was determined "to hold on . . . at least until [he saw] the outcome at St. Louis." He would not take chances because "the Foraker people are playing funny. They are anticipating McKinley's defeat." On the other hand, Foraker himself was not strong enough to hold such delegates adamantly against McKinley. Rumor had it that Foraker had told several Negro office holders that "he knew how the colored contingent was and that he (Foraker) understood that if it came to funny business we would be in it."

These black politicians stood delicately poised. "Of

course," Brown wrote Myers, "we let him know that we were as sincere as he was." "We will get in the Band Wagon," he added, "and it makes no difference whose name is on it." However, they hoped to find their dilemma resolved by McKinley's easy success, which would prevent Foraker from drawing a hard line between friend and foe. Brown's closing admonition to Myers was a breezy and cynical reference to Hanna: "Keep Uncle warm and let him believe we are turning the South upside down." [41]

Ohio had proven to be a situation very much like New York and Pennsylvania: potential national power required sacrificing actual state power. A popular candidate had a strong negative power. He could make life difficult for the state leader. But he could not afford to exercise any positive power in the state or the state leader could make life not just difficult but impossible for him. His friends could not control both the state and the national conventions, so that Foraker's success in 1895 was, as it turned out, a godsend rather than a catastrophe. Furthermore, if not for the changes taking place in the electorate which opened a national office to Foraker, the two factions would have lacked this mutuality of interests and Foraker's determined opposition might very well have destroyed McKinley's candidacy. Instead he became another of the bosses who won more than he lost in McKinley's nomination.

Unlike Elkins before him, Hanna had not begun as a president-maker without a state base, but he had had to be forcibly reduced to that position before his activities could succeed. State power was something he would have to win after McKinley's election. When he made his move for power as Senator, he was kept on tenterhooks by Governor Bushnell until the very moment the Senate convened. Only the hard-won agreement of Foraker, wary of open conflict with the new administration, finally induced the governor to appoint the persistent Hanna.[42]

VII

How, then, did Hanna's pre-convention activities for McKinley fit into the history of Republican president-making? To what extent did he represent a new phenomenon in American political life? We have seen that rather than representing a new group or class in national politics, he fell into the traditional role of the Republican businessman–president-maker. Nor were his techniques or rhetoric new. In "booming" McKinley and gathering delegates in the South he did not depart from the past. And it is difficult to accept the picture of a national organization for McKinley that in any way transcended state politics. A few men without state power traveled and worked for the major—men like his cousins "Will" Osborne and Abner McKinley, his friend and manager Hanna, Ohioans like Joseph Smith and Charles Grosvenor, and Charles G. Dawes in Chicago—a small group of president-makers and lieutenants such as Elkins had gathered around him in the past. But mostly he worked through state politicians. Indeed there was no one else to use in American politics. They were the professionals.

Because of the massive changes in voting patterns, however, the Republican party in many localities was an incredibly swollen body of old and new adherents that offered a particularly tempting set of prizes for local politicians and a highly fluid setting in which to compete for them. Hanna and McKinley could take advantage of this because of McKinley's popularity with the rank and file and because of the considerable hostility that active party members displayed at the solidification of local party organization going on in many areas throughout the period. McKinley built on his popularity in a number of the smaller Republican states and his contacts in the South to become a natural rallying cry against the local leaders who were strengthening their control. His popular candidacy offered a test of whether or not they with their augmented power would still be responsive to the "will of the people." In many instances they were, so that in some states— for example, Wisconsin and Missouri—all of the factions competing for control allied themselves with McKinley. In other states, groups opposing the emerging bosses— the anti-Platt men in New York, Quay's opponents in Pennsylvania, the opposition to William Lorimer in Illinois—took up McKinley's name.[43]

Sometimes these party leaders almost against their wills opposed McKinley because state considerations compelled them to support another candidate. In Platt's case, it was Governor Morton. For Lorimer, it was Illinois Senator Shelby Cullom for a while, and then Speaker Reed, to whom Lorimer, a freshman Congressman, had heavy political debts.[44] This was in the tradition of normal state politics, but suddenly it seemed ominous. The rising interest in "bossism" and the threat of ever-tighter organization in many parts of American life had enormously heightened interest in political organization. In the wake of Speaker Reed's new rules to run the House, and the formalization of a caucus structure in the Senate, American thinkers were creating a major body of literature on party government. This fascination with organization helped make Hanna's achievement into a legend.[45]

Politicians themselves tended systematically to over-emphasize the degree to which they controlled events. Charles G. Dawes's role in Illinois offers a particularly illuminating example. Following his diary and letters, historians have seen Dawes as a "veritable Napoleon of politics" who after moving to Chicago in 1894 created an organization that captured the state for McKinley two years later. Were this true, it would indeed suggest a new stage in American political organization, but a closer look at local political materials, such as Joel A. Tarr has made in his dissertation on William Lorimer, shows a very different picture.[46]

The McKinley campaign came on the heels of what the Chicago *Tribune* described as "the most desperate patronage fight recorded in the history of local politics" between Lorimer's Cook County organization and Mayor George B. Strong's Chicago city machine. Although many of his supporters favored McKinley, Lorimer was committed to Senator Cullom, or if he withdrew, to Reed. In these circumstances, a motley horde of Republicans from all over the state supported McKinley both because he was popular—as Blaine had been in the eighties—and in order to take a stand, unsuccessful as it turned out, against the emerging dominance of Lorimer and his downstate ally John R. Tanner.

Dawes emerged as Hanna's liaison man between Canton and Chicago and as a coordinator of the opposition. Despite the breezy optimism of his diary and his letters to McKinley, he was not as successful in the second role as he was in the first. His launching of the McKinley "boom" at an annual Republican gathering in January 1896, accounted as one of his triumphs both by himself and later historians, was apparently a failure. An indignation meeting which he called to protest Lorimer's plans for an early convention was also unsuccessful. Dawes kept busy corresponding with politicians all over the state and unquestionably served McKinley well. But his few agents outside of Chicago and the little money he sent them represented but one small part of McKinley's largely undisciplined strength in the state.[47]

Although local conventions one after another instructed for McKinley, the state convention late in April showed how little Dawes or anyone else had coordinated these efforts. His own diary verifies the estimate of one of Hanna's correspondents that the McKinley forces would "lack leadership on the floor of the convention" while the opposition enjoyed "thorough organization." McKinley clearly had a majority of the delegates and the Tanner forces were eager to negotiate their surrender on the question of presidential preference. Nevertheless, Dawes's account is a continuing story of arguments, factionalism, and general disorganization. He had gaily informed McKinley in mid-March that "The machine has 'unconditionally surrendered.'" But this was nonsense. John McNulta, a veteran Illinois politician who may well have been the most important single leader McKinley had in the state, bargained with Tanner and Lorimer all through April. The McKinley men tried several times to put together an organization to contest the convention with Lorimer and Tanner. But in the end they could not agree and had to surrender everything else in order to get instructions for McKinley. Dawes, who had no other interest at the time, took credit in his diary for the result, but here too McNulta was probably the chief negotiator.[48]

When the convention met, Lorimer displayed complete control. With McNulta and Dawes restraining his opponents, he named the temporary and permanent chairmen—which the McKinley supporters concerned about state power had hoped to contest. Then the convention ratified the entire Tanner-Lorimer slate. But when it came time to discuss presidential preferences, Lorimer, aware of the overwhelming McKinley sentiment, called for an adjournment to bargain further. Dawes "decided to make an issue" of the motion and was easily defeated.

The next day, under the leadership of a Danville politician, W. J. Calhoun, the meeting instructed for McKinley by a surprisingly large margin. Lorimer himself attributed McKinley's success to floor leader Calhoun as did all the Chicago newspapers. While there is no point in belittling Dawes's work, any more than Hanna's, one must not make too much of the mysteries of "organization." McKinley, as Tarr points out, was the popular favorite in Illinois, and there were many politicians with good reasons to back him. But they were not people who took easily to orders from above. That, in fact, was a principal reason why they supported McKinley—however deluded they were to do so.

The result for Illinois politics was to solidify Lorimer's power, as all the local ambitions that went into the McKinley campaign were sacrificed to achieve instructions for the delegates-at-large at the state convention. This was small cost to Lorimer. He was re-elected to Congress, all the backstage leaders of the County machine and his downstate ally Tanner were at last in public office, and Lorimer had gained an ascendancy in Illinois politics beyond his dreams. The dramatic rise in power of men like Lorimer was a new phenomenon in the nineties. There, and not in the McKinley managers—at least before the convention—was the revolutionary change in American political life.[49]

Hanna usually worked through whoever wanted to aid his candidate in any state, which meant a number of more or less independent forces operating on McKinley's behalf. What he seems to have supplied were money and coordination where needed—the characteristic role of the president-maker. At the other traditional role of negotiating with the major politicians, he had no more success than his predecessors. But, as we have noted many times, major pre-convention agreements, unless extremely loose, were nearly impossible. One never became fully committed to a candidate unless he had advantage to gain in state politics or, as in the case of the president-maker, had no state base.[50]

Activities in the South were more direct. Here outsiders

could really do something. Men had to be paid to represent McKinley at district and county conventions. They
required money for what Jere Brown called "legitimate"
expenses "such as taking the boys in and drinking them."
Hanna's work in the South may have been his greatest
single contribution to McKinley's nomination. He had
long years of experience and important allies for this since
a strenuous pursuit of southern delegates had always been
a large part of John Sherman's bids for the presidency.
Like Sherman in the past, he attacked hard and early,
spending money, supporting newspapers, and creating the
victory psychology that was so crucial in deciding the
course of the delegates.[51]

The activities of R. A. Moseley, Jr., chairman of the
Alabama Republican state committee, illustrate the effect
of Hanna's efforts. Moseley, like so many southern Republicans, had corresponded with William E. Chandler for
many years. The Reed managers quickly purchased his
support. However, his main concern was to remain as
state chairman, a point which, one of his enemies wrote,
"he regards as paramount to the Presidential question."
He continually peppered Chandler with pleas for information as to Reed's chances versus those of McKinley,
and watched for every fluctuation of the national temper.
When a district seemed to prefer Morton, he tended to
forget Reed. Even if they wanted McKinley, that too was
all right provided they were willing to support Moseley
for state chairman.

But the McKinley managers had done their work well
and the state was swinging to the Ohioan. Moseley sent
Chandler a packet of letters showing what Hanna's agents
had done in some of the Alabama districts. Chandler's
reply was the tribute of an old pro: "If Mr. Hanna has
covered every district in the United States in the same
manner that he did those in Alabama McKinley will be

nominated; indeed that is the outlook now." Of course, Hanna had not covered every district in the United States that way. In the North it was impossible to do so, and in some places in the South Hanna readily confessed that the situation was "beyond [his] powers to understand or control." Nevertheless, this was a worthy tribute, indicating the importance of Hanna's work in the South. "He had the South practically solid before some of us awakened," Platt later recalled.[52]

Hanna's Ohio Negro allies aided these efforts in the South. Myers, their leader, looked after the Negro delegates at the St. Louis convention. Along with such associates as Jere Brown, he corresponded far and wide, distributing some of Hanna's money and creating the skeleton of a convention organization. The irrepressible Brown boasted to Hanna of their success in the South. "We will be prepared," he wrote, "to capture the enemy by carrying the war into Africa." Brown, for all his cynicism, knew that he had to be on his toes with Uncle Mark because he realized "they do not need a single Negro [vote] sure." Hanna had the right candidate and had made it count in the South.[53]

Hanna also became famous for his use of money. Chandler launched a public attack on Hanna's campaign methods that was based on documents secured from enemies of McKinley, such as A. L. Conger of Akron, and from men like Swank who were more or less neutral but were beholden to some of the Senators opposing McKinley. On this issue it is particularly hard to gather data. There is no question that Hanna both spent his own money and raised money from others. The question is whether this was a new technique, an old one on a larger scale than in the past, or no different from what men like Elkins had done. No firm answer is possible, but Hanna probably had to spend more than Elkins simply because in so many instances Elkins worked through business associates such as Kerens, Manley, Chaffee, and McCormick, who were rich in their own right, and who, one would guess, took care of distributing the necessary funds in their localities. Such decentralized spending, even were it as large as or larger than anything Hanna did, would not have excited the comment that Hanna's methods did.

Hanna had little success in his pre-convention fund raising. On February 1, Dawes wrote that "Hanna is being greatly disappointed in his canvass for funds. The great trouble with our campaign is lack of funds for legitimate purposes." In Pennsylvania, he got far less than he had hoped when the men connected with the American Iron and Steel Association were unable to contribute. Money from men like Knox and Magee in Pittsburgh was more in the traditional line of state politicians able to take care of their own and more besides. Croly records that, in the end, Hanna financed the campaign mostly from his own pocket when his attempts at raising such a fund from others failed.[54]

That he made such an attempt is perhaps more indicative than that he finally footed the bill himself. It suggests that one of the principal differences from past campaigns was not that Hanna was more the businessman-in-politics than others had been, but that he was in some ways less so. He was far *less* able than Elkins had been to make use of his business connections for political purposes. He did not control a "Senatorial Railroad"; the mixing of these two parts of his life, business and politics, was not quite as easy and fluid as it was for Elkins or in fact for many members of the United States Senate. When Hanna traveled in McKinley's behalf, the Pennsylvania Railroad did not put a car at his service as it did for Clarkson's western tour in 1896 in Allison's interest. Hanna was no amateur, but he was to some extent an outsider. He could not use his business connections to affect the politics of a distant state through a local politician who was also a business associate. What Elkins had done with connections, Hanna had to do mostly with money. This may have introduced a minor increment in centralization of control, but before McKinley's nomination seemed assured—which really did give Hanna power—signs of it were hard to find. The opposition campaign, largely financed from New York, was perhaps equally centralized. Money in the sums available for a pre-convention campaign simply did not represent very much power. Only having a winner did.[55]

A third reason for believing in Hanna's almost magical prowess was the control which the McKinley forces exercised over the national convention. This they did, not because Hanna showed unique organizational skills at St. Louis, but because McKinley had the nomination sewed up by the time the convention met. Until shortly before, Hanna and other McKinley men worried about the national committeemen, a majority of whom were not early McKinley supporters. But this threat evaporated as McKinley's candidacy swept all before it. Even so, McKinley did not get the nomination by acclamation. Rather, such large Republican states as New York, Pennsylvania, Iowa, and Massachusetts voted overwhelmingly against the certain victor. In addition the Eastern states got their gold platform, which Hanna and McKinley quickly conceded to assure the nomination but which made neither happy. It was not until well into the campaign that they finally surrendered the hope of soft-pedaling the currency question and concentrating on McKinley's specialty, the tariff.[56]

Most important of all for Hanna's reputation as a national boss were the events that took place after the convention. What happened during the campaign really *was* new in American political practice, and gave some substance (although less than has often been assumed) to the idea of a "national boss"—an idea that commentators read back into the pre-convention period, making something new and almost revolutionary of Hanna's activities then as well.

The other change which later events wrought on the image of the McKinley campaign was, in broadest terms, the emergence of the progressive impulse in national political life. This made incredible the notion that grass roots popularity could have had a significant role in McKinley's victory. It made the rhetoric of the McKinley pre-convention campaign seem not only terribly cynical—which it was—but also suggested that it could not possibly have had any effect. Senator Wolcott's estimate in late April 1896 would later seem to make no sense: "The McKinley strength is really a craze. At the bottom it is based upon a desire of the common people to beat the bosses and has gathered such strength that it has become a furor." Men who advocated giving the will of the people full sway could hardly accept such popular delusion.[57]

Thus, in assessing Hanna as of June 1896, he must be seen as the culmination of the politics of his generation: one of the master politicians operating at a peculiarly fortunate time, and having the only popular candidate in a period when for the first time in the party's history the convention winner was a sure victor in the election. What was to happen after the Democratic convention would reveal the revolution in American political life that was occurring during the nineties and would catapult Hanna into a political pantheon that none of his predecessors and equals—Elkins among the Republicans or Whitney among the Democrats—had attained.

VII

1896: Majority

The Republicans planned a thoroughly conventional campaign. They expected to attack the Cleveland administration by blaming the depression on its tariff policies. The whole party had been geared to this strategy for over two years. Once Manley replaced silver advocate Carter as chairman of the national executive committee in January 1894, the national leadership had studiously avoided the currency question. In late 1894 the congressional committee stopped all discussion of bimetallism in the plate matter it sent to newspapers. After the 1896 convention, the committee busily gathered and even created frankable material on the tariff, having old articles by Blaine and speeches from the convention read into the *Congressional Record*.[1]

McKinley and Hanna shared these expectations. McKinley, on August 1, predicted that the tariff would "notwithstanding the present prominence of the silver question, become the main issue." He resisted pressure to play down the tariff issue to insure cooperation from the gold Democrats. "It must not be forgotten," he wrote, "that I am the nominee of the Republican party and that protection is one of the basic principles of that organization."

McKinley not only thought the tariff a winning issue, he believed it was the universal economic panacea. "My own views have not changed—I believe that the proper settlement of the tariff question will relegate the financial question to the rear." Even as late as September 1, his cousin William Osborne, now secretary of the national committee, still assured the candidate: "We are going to keep the tariff question to the front no matter what these Democrats say." [2]

But under the impact of Bryan's campaign, in which he emphasized silver almost to the exclusion of everything else and absolutely refused to discuss the tariff, McKinley reluctantly shifted his emphasis. Even so he tied together free silver and free trade, and brought in the tariff at any and every opportunity. He was convinced that it was the winning issue among the industrial workers, and Bryan's strategy suggests that he too realized what a sore spot the Democratic tariff record would be. Samuel McSeveney's study of voting behavior in the nineties offers some evidence that in acting this way these politicians correctly understood their electorate. [3]

Osborne argued that a tariff campaign could be "made from the very carts," that it would reach "the masses of the people" who needed persuasion, not the businessmen who already were "all right." Orville Platt argued prior to the Democratic convention that "the gold standard feature of the campaign is too prominent even for eastern localities, and we have got to make more of the protection and prosperity idea." He too believed that a tariff emphasis would win working-class votes while the money question might lead the workers to forget "their determination to return to republicanism as a means of re-establishing business." But at the same time he felt the temptation of picking off Democratic votes by defending the gold standard. "I should not know just how to make a speech if called upon," he confessed, "but I suppose the situation will clear up after the conventions are all out of the way." [4]

The success of the silver Democrats did clear up the situation by polarizing the currency issue between the two extremes of immediate free coinage at a sixteen to one ratio, and overt support for the gold standard. All the people who believed in some form of bimetallism had to choose sides—often to their discomfort. Republican bimetallists complained that their party was defending the Cleveland administration. Democrats and many Republicans feared that Bryan's extreme position would set back responsible bimetallism. David Bennett Hill and William E. Chandler exchanged understanding letters, recognizing the curiously similar position in which each found himself. [5]

McKinley had been a bimetallist through most of his career and was reluctant to offend that segment of the party. But the Republican bimetallists would remain loyal either because of their protectionism or out of fear that Bryan would discredit their position by identifying it with immediate free coinage and the rest of the radical Democratic platform. George F. Hoar lamented that bimetallism had been tied up with "all manner of socialism, and all manner of repudiation and public dishonor." The advocates of bimetallism, he argued, "should look for its success through wise and temperate counsels," meaning, of course, the Republican party. The nation's leading bimetallist theoretician, Francis Amasa Walker, feared that Bryan's election "would be the greatest blow bimetallism has ever received," and ended unhappily writing publicity for the "cowardly and contemptible" gold monometallists. Once they saw that the outright silver states in the West were gone, McKinley and his advisors had no reason to placate the more conservative Eastern bimetallists who in any case would not cost the ticket a single Eastern state.[6]

In the end, Bryan—not Hanna or McKinley—had determined the Republicans' currency campaign and its attendant covert alliance with the gold Democrats. He provided the impetus for frightened easterners to unite across the traditional party lines. "Our Wall Street friends," Reid noted sarcastically, believed that "the silver craze [was] marching over the West conquering and to conquer." Under this pressure, politicians could capitalize on the widely expressed sentiment for rising above parties to overcome the silver menace. Reid ordered his editors to call for uniting "all to whom the honor of the country is dear in one supreme effort to protect it," and to continue such articles "provided the capacity for manufacturing them out of mere wind holds out." Eastern businessmen, as well as writers, ministers, and politicians of both parties would have united against Bryan with or without Hanna. It was Bryan who had shown political genius of a somewhat madcap sort in creating a new—if hopeless—coalition. As in most cases, Hanna responded rather than innovated. But he rose magnificently to his opportunity.[7]

II

McKinley and his managers also cast the formal organization of the campaign machinery in the traditional mold. Hanna had not stated publicly that he would become chairman of the national committee, but his decision to do so neither surprised nor upset the party. On a first-name basis with a number of men whose names counted in the eastern business world, such as James J. Hill and John D. Rockefeller, Hanna, as his latest biographer says, if not "widely known in New York at first . . . was favorably known." Some Republicans thought of Hanna, Osborne, and the other McKinley leaders as new men in the national committee who would be "on trial as to their ability to win a victory at the polls as well as in a nominating convention." But the expert Clarkson, impressed with Hanna's "sense," predicted he would run a traditional campaign by making peace with the state leaders he had beaten at St. Louis.[8]

Clarkson proved a good prophet. Hanna made himself chairman and Osborne secretary, but the executive committee contained only one man who was new to national committee work—Dawes, whom Hanna wanted as paymaster in Chicago. Although he had bypassed the national committeeman from Illinois, he was not cutting the state organization. The Tanner-Lorimer forces considered Dawes a neutral who had restrained their opponents at the state convention; they supported him for the executive committee out of anxiety over the pressures building up in Illinois for the appointment of one of their real enemies from the defeated but not yet destroyed city machine. In the crucial position of treasurer, Hanna retained the able Cornelius N. Bliss from 1892. Quay went on the committee to the great relief of both Hanna and McKinley who feared he would not accept a place. So did Manley, who had supported Reed until the last moment before the convention. By these selections, Hanna demonstrated that he did not nurse pre-convention grudges and had no plans for radical changes in the way that Republicans were accustomed to running presidential campaigns. He had made it a party, not a McKinley, organization.

The way Hanna parceled out responsibilities—always a more important indication than the formal committee structure—emphasized this still further. Quay took charge of the eastern headquarters with control of the southern campaign. Hobart, the vice-presidential candidate, was active at New York headquarters as in previous years. New England was in Manley's experienced hands. Apparently

Hanna himself planned to concentrate his own efforts in the Midwest. He even thought of making his home town of Cleveland the western headquarters but finally settled on the inevitable Chicago, the most convenient center from which to reach the crucial Midwestern states.

Hanna planned to take his time about coming east for consultations and talked of an August vacation. But twin pressures of an increasing silver agitation in the West and South and a responding silver scare in the East forced a change in plans. Reid urged Hanna to come East early. Otherwise he would find the important politicians and financiers away from the city and the campaign moving along "lines of its own." Increasing reports of working-men's interest in silver convinced Hanna of the need to "get out our arguments as soon as we can." This meant organization and money.[9]

Organization came more quickly than funds. By July 15, the executive committee had gathered in Cleveland. Under the direction of Dawes and Henry C. Payne, the Chicago headquarters was busy putting together a staff, organizing a bookkeeping system, and commencing operations. Here McKinley men were heavily in evidence: Ohioans Charles Dick and William Hahn were Dawes's principal aides. The literary bureau which grew prodigiously during the campaign was in the hands of Perry S. Heath, an Elkins protege from the Dakotas, who like so many of Elkins's old associates, had worked for McKinley in the pre-convention campaign.

The national committee had never before been under such heavy pressure at so early a date. The need to "get started in Educational work," as Hanna expressed it, delayed the full organization of the new campaign at the same time as it made such organization increasingly imperative. What was usually a leisurely process, taking most of the summer, was now a great rush to meet the demand for literature, speakers, and assistance, which by July 30 Dawes had already found "enormous." At this point in the campaign, Hanna was only just renting his New York headquarters! [10]

This novel situation resulted, of course, from the enormous interest in silver coming in the wake of the Chicago convention. But this obvious fact has masked the most important immediate political effect of the excitement, which was to stir the Republican state committees to earlier and more extensive activities than they had ever before attempted. They were the immediate source of the heavy pressure on Dawes. Clarkson, who had excellent sources of information about midwestern politics, noted late in July that in the main battleground, "the Mississippi Valley this side of the Missouri River," the state committees were "getting down to such organization in advance of the National Committee that our success is daily being made certain. The instinct of self-preservation in those States is leading the local organizations to go on with the work without waiting on the National Committee." [11]

"Self-preservation" was exactly the word. A fund-raiser for the Iowa state committee reported "whole counties swept from under us by the Silver craze, places where all the County Chairmen and subcommitteemen have left us." He received a report from a usually Republican county that listed one township "as not having a single Republican in it. The County Chairman states that it would be necessary to go into the township and convert somebody before we could get a Committeeman there." [12] Party leaders responded with an immediate and determined effort. "It was necessary to open headquarters and commence our campaign a month earlier than usual," explained Iowa state chairman, H. G. McMillan. "Neither the congressional nor the national committee were prepared to meet the emergencies of the case. . . . As a consequence we were compelled to prepare a large amount of literature at our own expense." He estimated that his committee was doing "three or four times as much work as ever before in a campaign in Iowa." The committee's secretary boasted that they had made "the most magnificent organization that has ever been known in this state." [13]

Naturally this increased activity strained the available funds. In addition, the currency issue dried up local sources of money in the West. Iowa Republicans usually raised "considerable money for campaign purposes among the agricultural counties of the state," but in 1896 contributors told the committee to "let the eastern people that made the platform furnish the money to pay the expenses of the campaign." Dawes got a similar response from Chicago businessmen: "The prevailing impression," he complained, "that money will be easily raised leads each individual to evade or lessen his just subscription." [14]

The continuing depressed economy and the acceleration of state political activity made any available funds that much more important so that the national committee's ability to raise money—which manifested itself late in August—became a substantial lever of power. Midwestern state politicians were clearly more dependent on the national committee than they had been in the past. By August 1, Dawes had already distributed money to Iowa, Nebraska, Kansas, and Minnesota through the respective national committeemen. McMillan of Iowa complained to Clarkson that money coming through national Committeeman Albert Baird Cummins was "hedged about with limitations and conditions" and was being used to advance Cummins's ambitions for a United States Senate seat. Clarkson recognized how things had changed:

The National Committeeman has never been given authority under any Committee for twenty years, to my knowledge, to expend money in his State on his own judgement. Whatever is given has always been given through him, but always with the positive understanding and agreement that it should be turned over to the Chairman of the State Committee for disbursement.[15]

Politicians like McMillan were the most desperate men in the party, facing the loss of all their power if they failed to put down the silver menace in their states. Their commitment to the national ticket went far deeper than was usual in previous presidential elections. Obviously Mc-Millan feared that Cummins would control the state's federal patronage if McKinley were elected, yet he dug into his own pocket and worked especially long and hard to produce a McKinley victory, lest the party leadership in the state be submerged under the silver tide. The situation in the states rather than planning and organization on the national level gave Hanna far fewer problems of factionalism and more control over some of the state organizations than previous national chairmen had enjoyed. What was needed was money, and Hanna, as the campaign progressed, almost monopolized the political supply for the West.

Campaigning began unusually early in the East as well, when leaders began to fear the silver sentiment both in the rural districts and among the workingmen. In Maine, with its early election, the canvass began in July, long before the national committee offered any aid. Leading Maine Republicans set out weeks before the campaign officially opened "to talk in those localities where Greenbackism was strong in 1879." By early September a Maine Democratic committeeman reported that "Republicans are making unprecedented efforts in Maine, expending any amount of money—three times as much as they ever made before." [16]

The Maine election result, a spectacular Republican triumph, was a product both of national committee support and unusual exertions by the Maine Republicans. As in most states, Hanna could assume a remarkable degree of cooperation. The state committees simply outdid themselves. In the East, under the impact of the almost paranoid response to what John Hay described as a "revolt of Caliban," a movement threatening destruction "to everybody with a clean shirt," Republicans in every walk of life offered their services and support. Senator Justin Morrill of Vermont was amazed that he had raised $15,000 in his state, almost all of it from private citizens, whereas in 1892 the state committee had had only $4000.[17]

Of course, the voter revolution which had begun a few years earlier was far more important than anything else. The great change of the period was the breakdown of the Democratic party. Henry Cabot Lodge correctly estimated the implications of the great September victories in New England: "It shows," he wrote, "a Democratic split of astonishing proportions." Thus the same force that made the midwestern Republicans begin early, work hard, and cooperate with the national committee, drove the enormously swollen Republican parties of the East to great efforts as well. But in their case, they had a considerable independence due to their heightened ability to finance themselves through local contributions from frightened Republicans as well as gold Democrats. For unlike the more confused situation in the West, in the East the clear, massive shift in voter preference was all toward the Republican party.[18]

In New York, all these phenomena were amplified. The silver scare reached fearful proportions, with the financial and business community believing that both the farmer

and the workingman—even in New York State—were in-
fected with free-silver notions. Perhaps their greater sen-
sitivity stemmed in part from knowledge of the peculiarly
trying financial condition of the Treasury and the crucial
role of the New York banking community in staving off
another bond sale for gold, which they and the administration feared might throw the election to Bryan.

In July, a group of New York bankers formed a con-
sortium to guard the treasury's gold supply by committing
themselves to acquiring European gold to offset any out-
flow resulting from a speculative raid on the treasury.
Charles W. Curtis, under-secretary of the Treasury and a
dedicated advocate of the gold standard, wrote to his
mother of the "curious spectacle of the U.S. finances
being controlled by a committee, of which J. P. Morgan
is Chairman, and the majority of whom are Hebrews,
while the Secretary of the Treasury sits, practically powerless in his office." Were all the facts known, everything the
silver men said would appear to be true. New York financiers indeed felt cause for terror.[19]

New York Republican politicians were rather less worried than the business community. Upstate free-silver
sentiment, they were sure, would evaporate in a vigorous
canvass. Reid saw two forces working in the party's favor:
"the tremendous drift toward McKinley among working
men, and the strong drift away from the Democratic party
among financial men." The politicians were more concerned about uniting the warring Platt and anti-Platt factions for the campaign. As the summer progressed, it became clear that the national victory of Platt's opponents
had not changed the balance of power within the state.
Platt, who had controlled the state's delegation to the convention, would dominate the state convention and the
campaign as well. While the opposition continued to be
active, Hanna held off taking sides. His appointment of

Bliss as the New York member of the executive committee was a mark of his neutrality. But, by indicating that he would not support those who sided with McKinley before the convention, he sounded the death knell of the opposition. On August 1, he conferred with the New York boss in the interview that Platt found so "eminently satisfactory." Hanna in acknowledging the control that Platt had won, completed the demoralization of the opposition, so that by the end of the year, Platt was the master. He boasted that he would be made Senator simply by having one of his lieutenants "touch the button." [20]

No one knows exactly what passed between Hanna and Platt, but the broad outline of their agreement is clear enough from subsequent events. Hanna, Platt reported to Governor Morton, agreed to "recognize the regular organization." This apparently did not mean any explicit pledges of patronage. Hanna probably agreed to do what he could to quiet the anti-Platt men and he left the New York campaign in Platt's hands. At least one of McKinley's managers, Charles Dick, perhaps having taken the progressive rhetoric of the pre-convention contest seriously, noted uneasily that Hanna seemed to betray the men who had worked for McKinley's nomination in New York and Pennsylvania. There were some hard lessons to be learned: the first was that the McKinley administration would be the golden age of the great state bosses.[21]

A second major factor smoothing Hanna's way with Platt was that, unlike previous years in which New York had been a major field of activities for the national committee, in 1896 the state required no division of labor or of finances. When Hanna agreed to Platt's management of the New York campaign, he was also agreeing (if that is the word) to Platt himself financing the campaign. The New Yorker, whose defense of the gold standard had so gratified the business community, was ready to stand the cost of the campaign from his own sources of supply. As in the pre-convention campaign, he held all the cards in New York, while Hanna was playing and winning an entirely different game in the nation. However many rounds one counts between them in 1896, it was all shadow-boxing.

The national headquarters in New York and the state committee were in minor conflict all through the campaign. This reflected both state political quarrels and a general hostility between some of the men who had been active in the past on the national committee and "Cousin Will" Osborne who had charge of the New York headquarters. Although it is near impossible to measure the effectiveness of particular people in a political organization, impressions by contemporaries tend to support Thomas Felt's statement that Osborne's "special qualifications" for the position he held in the campaign "were limited almost entirely to his unquestioned loyalty." While men like Platt, Clarkson, Hobart, Manley, and Quay acquired an instant respect for Hanna, it did not extend to the rest of McKinley's organization. "There is only one man in the National Committee," wrote Clarkson. "That man is Hanna, of course." But for all the "many funny stories about headquarters" which Platt's men circulated, and the complaints at Platt's course registered by the national committee, the division of labor was nearly perfect enough to enable the two organizations to pursue their separate business with tolerable efficiency: "Uncle Platt," wrote Clarkson in mid-October,

I guess is going along all right in New York, indifferent to the censorship of Hanna and his men and independent of them and able to carry the State for Legislature, Governor, and President on his own lines, equipping himself and his Committee from his own resources.[22]

Platt's independence, like everything else in 1896, goes back to the voter revolution of the nineties. He did not have a close state dependent on national committee funds, special collections, and importing famous speakers. His control over the party and the certainty of Republican success in New York enabled him to solidify his financial base for the campaign long before Hanna could even begin his collections. The often endemic competition for funds between the state and the national committee was apparently muted simply because there was more than enough to go around. Much of the money that previously would have gone into the Democratic war chest or into factional fights eventually made its way into Republican pockets. Platt, who had as good a reputation for honesty and for soundness on the currency question as Bliss or Hanna, had no trouble getting his share. Everything went his way. The Democrats could not mount a campaign against him. Even the Cleveland appointees in the New York post offices and revenue offices worked to defeat Bryan during the campaign.[23]

Thus, in both the East and West, Hanna could assume tremendous cooperation and independent local exertion for the ticket. The type of problems that had troubled party managers for a generation—placating Roscoe Conkling in 1880, getting the administration and the New York and Pennsylvania organizations to work in 1884, smoothing Platt's ruffled spirits in 1892—evaporated in 1896 in the heat generated by the silver agitation and the mysteries of changing voter loyalties. This was true to an even greater extent than it had been in the 1888 campaign when the party had had a new man, a clean state of expectations, and an economic issue with which to raise funds. Now they had all this, but the economic issue aroused infinitely more emotion, the new man was a far more popular candidate, and the expectations were unique in party history. Potential political rewards were far greater than could be hoped for in the closely balanced politics of the eighties. At the same time absolute catastrophe threatened should popular sentiment, dependent on economic and emotional factors largely out of the managers' control, swing in some unsympathetic direction.

One of the traditional roles of the national chairman had simply vanished. He no longer had to compromise delicate interests in state after state. He could simply give all to some and demand all from others. No one could afford to "sulk," to "sit on his hands" in this campaign. The men who were left out of the campaign organization did not try to sabotage the machinery as Arthur's followers appeared to do in 1884. Rather they clamored for a role and were disappointed if they did not get one.[24] There was no creaky state machinery to work carefully into shape. Rather all the engines were oiled in advance of the national committee's aid in 1896. In the East they were even fueled, but not in the main battleground of the West. This would be Hanna's principal task, to raise the funds to feed and supply his army of already willing workers.

III

The need to begin work so early delayed Hanna's fund raising. It was not until the end of July that he came to see the eastern businessmen who, as he wrote, "must be prepared with the ammunition." Pressed by the necessity for "active operations and at once," he wired friends in the East such as Reid to locate the leading financiers. These men were already prepared to help the Republican party in 1896. Before the convention Reid had consulted J. P. Morgan, for example, on the currency plank. Morgan had pledged aid in getting the business community to endorse the platform and in working to boost stock market prices when McKinley was nominated. Once this pressure for a gold plank succeeded among the Republicans and then failed in the Democratic party, Hanna could assume the support he needed to execute his grandiose plans for a massive propaganda campaign.[25]

Nonetheless, collections in August were disappointing. Demands for literature continued to increase so that, contrary to plan, the New York headquarters began printing its own documents in addition to what was being done in Chicago—which intensified the pressure on Hanna. On August 22 he wrote of being "rather discouraged by the difficulty I find in raising the necessary funds for the campaign." At about the same time he warned Dawes that campaign plans would have to be cut back for lack of money. All through August, Dawes lamented that the "outlook for funds to run the campaign [was] very poor." Yet immediately afterwards, money began to pour in, and nowhere was there another complaint about any financial shortage.[26]

Accounts of the campaign have followed Croly in pointing to the important role of James J. Hill who, during the week of August 15, took the discouraged Hanna about on Wall Street, introducing him to prominent financiers and vouching for his competence and honesty. Since Hanna was on a first-name basis with the officers of Standard Oil, including Rockefeller himself, had excellent contacts with Morgan, and had a distinguished finance committee and treasurer, it seems hard to believe that business held back because they did not trust or know him. Reid, in June, had been immensely pleased that Hanna was taking the chairmanship. "Nothing could now inspire more confidence than that assurance," he wrote to John Hay. The problem does not seem to have been one of confidence. Yet Hill's role apparently was crucial. Thomas Beer has Hanna saying of the New York financial community: "It had taken Jim Hill and Bliss working like hell to make these sheep see what they must do. . . ." [27]

Hill's importance probably came from his political position. He had been prominent in the Democratic party for years, and now he became a leader of the gold Democrats committed to assisting the Republican party against Bryan. Hanna at first got more cooperation from them than from his own party. While New York Republicans were still squabbling among themselves, men like Hill, John A. McCall of the New York Life Insurance Company, and Abram S. Hewitt—leading conservative Democrats—had come out in support of the Republican ticket immediately upon Bryan's nomination and had begun helping the Republican National Committee as soon as it was organized. This is not to say that they, rather than Republican businessmen, were the ones who raised Hanna's war chest. Rather their cooperation had an unexpected effect on the entire relation of national corporations to the parties, and one which can be fairly termed revolutionary in the financing of national campaigns.[28]

Totally independent of anything that Hanna did, the emerging large corporations began in the nineties to organize for political purposes in response to a rising tide of antitrust and antimonopoly laws, moves to increase corporate taxes, and other measures of public control. Standard Oil, for example, one of the first of the large combinations to come under popular fire, was permanently in the thick of political maneuvering after 1890. Its officers took an increasingly large role in politics on all levels, especially after the elder Rockefeller dissociated himself from the active management of the company in the midnineties and John D. Archbold—who fully lived up to his last name—took over the reins of management. Previously the Standard had been far more defensive in its attitude toward politics. When its interests were attacked, it responded with every weapon in its arsenal—which included money, lobbyists, and legal attack on offensive statutes, public officials in its pay, and the political activities of its employees. Otherwise, it did not enter politics as a corporation.

Hanna knew Rockefeller well and had long experience in political dealing with the Standard. But before 1896, he had always run up against the corporation's reluctance to act politically as a unit. In 1885, Hanna had approached Rockefeller in search of aid in the Ohio legislative race which would determine whether or not John Sherman returned to the Senate. Rockefeller made a personal attempt to get the corporation to contribute, but his executive committee turned him down. Henry M. Flagler explained that he considered such a contribution "an act of injustice to our Democratic associates" in the company's management since the corporation's interests were "quite as safe in the hands of the Democratic candidate." Thereafter Hanna confined his activities to soliciting individual executives of the company. They could contribute money or use their influence, but the corporation as a whole only responded to direct attacks and of course could not afford to take sides in national politics. The treasurer of the Standard in the eighties, for instance, helped elect his father, Henry B. Payne, a veteran Democratic politician, to the Senate, while Rockefeller himself was supporting the Republican candidate.[29]

By the mid-nineties, large business firms, even groups of firms as in the case of the large life insurance companies, were equipped both in organization and experience to deal in national politics far more effectively than ever before. However, they were inhibited by the considerations which Flagler had cited to Rockefeller: that large corporate directories contained both Democrats and Republicans and the obviously related fact that heretofore neither party posed a threat to corporate interests. Individual executives quite commonly made contributions to both sides, expressing the desire to gain influence with anyone elected, but appropriations from corporate treasuries were unusual.[30]

The conditions of 1896 precipitously changed this, enabling the corporations to turn their assets and their organizations directly into partisan political channels. William E. Chandler, no mean authority on the subject, explained during the 1900 campaign, when money in elections was being widely discussed, exactly what constituted the difference between 1896 and previous years:

> Four years ago for the first time corporations began to make political contributions directly from their corporate treasuries. Prior to that time no such thing would have been tolerated. In every corporation there were minority directors who would have arrested any such contribution by going to law, if necessary. Unfortunately or fortunately, four years ago the democratic minorities in railroad and bank corporations nearly all bolted Bryan and supported McKinley. Therefore, these democrats made no objection to contributions to the Republican party taken from the treasuries of the companies. It was a very dangerous practice to inaugurate.[31]

It was their largesse, rather than their votes, that made the gold Democrats so crucial in 1896, justifying such apparent hyperboles as that of Andrew Carnegie, that the "grand" Democratic Party had "saved the country." The activities of men like Hill and McCall opened the golden door of the corporation treasuries, making, perforce, Republicans of all the leaders of business. This constituted a great deal more than simply adding the contributions of Democratic businessmen to those of Republicans. Rather it greatly multiplied the totals, which, in addition to individual contributions, came out of corporate treasuries and were considered by both Republicans and Democrats on the boards of directors as legitimate business expenses.

Standard Oil contributed a quarter of a million dollars. McCall, long a personal contributor of substantial sums to the Democratic party, now paid $50,000 of company money to the Republican National Committee without even consulting his board of directors. "I consented to a payment to defeat Free Silver, not to defeat the Democratic Party . . . ," he explained, "and I thank God that I did." Richard McCurdy of the Mutual, who less than a month before the election had cautiously refused a donation to the Honest Money League, saw his company contribute $15,000 to the national committee and gave his permission for agents to take an active part in the campaign. Large corporations provided veritable armies of political workers and direct campaign services whose monetary value would have run into the millions. The long tradition of business coercion of their employees' political choices—for which evidence abounds throughout the Gilded Age—suddenly served only one side. All in all, the change in the political sympathies of the directors of leading corporations worked a revolution, permitting, for the first time, a mobilization of business support for a single party in a national election.[32]

Even when the gold Democrats, out of the political needs of the Midwestern and the border states, set up their own organization and ran their own candidates, cooperation with the Republican National Committee was about as perfect as could be expected, strikingly so, in fact, for fusion politics. McKinley's victory was greeted with effusions of mutual praise among Republicans and gold Democrats. Without regard to party, big business had followed the majority of the electorate into the Republican camp, a product not of the work of Mark Hanna, but of the voter revolution of the 1890s, the rise of political organization among large business interests, and the great silver scare— all part of the enormous and little understood upheaval in American life in the 1890s that makes it the watershed out of which modern America flows.[33]

The idea of getting campaign funds from business on a regular and rational basis was not an innovation of Hanna's. The *idea* of assessing business had been in the air since the late eighties. Only the *opportunity* that the capture of the Democratic party by the silverites presented was new. Clarkson in 1892 had looked forward to a day when the party's money would be raised by "free but systematic donations from its generous men" instead of either the "old barbarism" of assessment as in "the heyday of the machine" or "playing the mendicant upon manufacturers and corporations" as in 1888. This became a possibility only when the political loyalties of most of the leaders of American business ceased to be divided between the two parties. It was a national chairman's dream come true and Hanna was its fortunate legatee. He was also the appropriate symbol of a vast transformation in American life which made the Republican party the majority party nationally and united American business and the Republican party in a curious marriage that, if it has not been without its spats and separations, has shown a sufficient endurance in the twentieth century to prove itself a true mating.[34]

In sum, Hanna represented the culmination of a long tradition of Republican businessmen–president-makers. He did not revolutionize the party, but he did see it through a political revolution, one which by giving the national party new voter support and a more stable financial base strengthened the national committee and the presidency, opening up remarkable potentialities for the new century to develop. Croly thought Hanna's career "without prece-

dent and . . . not likely to have any imitators." This estimate is true in so far as it points to the very special circumstances that made Hanna's achievement possible. He
took a system that was long in maturing, used it in traditional ways, and yet made it work under brand-new conditions. He was both a portent of the new century and the
final test of the success of the old politics. Croly is correct
to see him as the culmination of nineteenth-century American life; for of all the institutions of nineteenth-century
America, it is the political party structure that has shown
the greatest resiliency on every level, the most impressive
capacity to absorb new social and economic experience
without major structural alteration.[35]

VIII

Conclusion: The Old Party and the New Century

"There won't be any revolution. You're just a lot of damn fools," Mark Hanna told a group of frightened business-men before the 1896 campaign.[1] Indeed, there was no revolution. The old party, following its accustomed ways, marched on into a new century and a different era. The crisis of the nineties came to an abrupt end, and the American middle class moved confidently to confront the fresh problems of the twentieth century with much the same political devices that the politicians of the Gilded Age had employed. Yet 1896 was also a sharp break from the past: it marked a new set of political alignments, a changed institutional balance between the President and Congress, and an altered relationship between the business community and the Republican party. Most important of all, the Republican party, older and perhaps more grand than ever, was now the normal choice of a majority of the electorate. The era of close national elections was over. The political forms were unchanged, but the substance of national politics was very different.

A heightened organization of political life on the local

and state levels had begun to take shape in the nineties. Hanna's achievement suggested that perhaps the national party would have some greater role as well. But all these developments proved quite short-lived. The national committee continued to have only the power that a national administration gave to it, and its strength under Hanna would not be duplicated in the future. The degree of party organization achieved on other levels proved equally aberrant in the course of American politics in the twentieth century. The increased power of state leaders coming out of the voter revolution of the nineties vanished amidst a vast range of progressive efforts to diffuse power. The direct primary, a logical response to the rise of men like Platt and Lorimer, to some extent institutionalized the desire for weak parties. Similarly, the high level of party cohesion in Congress from about 1895 to 1905 once again proved to be unlike past or future experience in that body.[2]

In general, the increased bureaucratization and centralization of American life was almost completely thwarted in party politics. Only in the nineties, apparently, as the American public underwent what Richard Hofstadter has aptly termed a "psychic crisis," did a greater level of organization take form in political life. Then, with the defeat of Bryan and the return of confidence in the political system, the anti-party reflex reasserted itself. Not only the direct primary, but non-partisan local government, the direct election of senators, women's suffrage, and corrupt practices acts all expressed the hope of breaking the political organizations that had become too powerful in the previous era. The progressives' fear of the "boss" and the "machine" had a real basis in the ominous politics of the nineties. Whatever the progressives wanted—and their wants were bewilderingly various—

powerful political parties were not their preferred means to those goals.

Despite the lack of serious alteration in party structure, the political system had in fact survived a crisis in the nineties. The rise of the Populists and the new demands coming out of the depression were its most obvious indicators. But the dimensions of that crisis are best revealed in the enormous change in voting habits, which demonstrated that a new political universe had emerged within the old forms. W. Dean Burnham has shown that the realignment of 1896 wrought revolutionary changes in the way that people exercised the franchise. The old system's greatest success had been in mobilizing masses of voters from every part of American life. Beginning in the progressive era, the percentage of eligible voters actually going to the polls declined precipitously and the regularity with which they turned to a party for their political orientation shrank as well. The straight-ticket voting and the constant political mobilization for contests on every level ceased to be normal American voting behavior. The modern pattern of voter turnout rising with socio-economic position began to emerge in this era. So too did the large numbers of poorly politicized citizens who voted only in the more dramatic elections and stayed home when merely local candidates were running. The American political system began a lengthy "crisis of participation" from which it has yet to emerge.[3]

American parties in the twentieth century ceased to activate masses of voters as they had in the previous era. Burnham's statistics suggest that many of the poor—urban and rural—failed to maintain a meaningful party identity and simply dropped out of the political system altogether. American politics after 1896 demobilized those who had most cause for discontent with American life. This was

not any one man's doing, nor was it the result of either
conspiracy or violence. Rather, it was an adventitious outcome of the politics of the nineties that endured because
it proved functional in American society.

The alignment of 1896 was the most sharply sectional
since the Civil War era and the least competitive since the
decay of the first party system in the early nineteenth century. The decline in party competition and voting totals
was greatest in the South, but the same effects were striking
in the North as well. The basis of the "1896 system," as
E. E. Schattschneider has observed, was a "big Republican
monopoly in the North" and a "little Democratic monopoly in the South." The Republican party virtually disappeared in that section, while the Democrats won an
average of only about two states outside the South and the
border states in each presidential election between 1896
and 1932. The number of states usually competitive between the parties shrunk to a handful, atrophying party
organization, diminishing the stake in most political contests, and removing the inducement to bring reluctant
voters into the political arena. The vast job of mobilizing
the electorate that the nineteenth-century organizations
had performed as a matter of course no longer made sense.
As Schattschneider shrewdly remarked, "elections in one-
party areas are won not by competing with the opposition
party but by eliminating it." [4]

With parties in this generally somnambulant state, other
agencies assumed their previous functions. They lost much
of their role as entertainment media to other forms of
commercial entertainment. Many of their patronage and
welfare functions vanished as the century advanced. Most
of their positive functions in government went to the pressure groups that became the dominant form of political
organization in the twentieth century. They had already
lost the near monopoly of political information they had

enjoyed in the nineteenth century, and the erosion of this role continued throughout the century as both journalism and education gained virtual independence of party influence.[5]

Clearly some of these changes would have occurred in any case, but the complete rout of the parties as major forces in the lives of most Americans was by no means an inevitable concommitant of twentieth-century technology and social organization. Here the comparison with Europe is instructive. Such an enormous slackening of political participation appears to have no counterpart elsewhere in the world. Twentieth-century European voting totals are comparable to those of nineteenth-century America. Moreover, the groups whose voting habits atrophied most noticeably in America were—in addition to Negroes who were systematically disenfranchised—the very lower-class groups whose European counterparts were mobilized by the parties of the left. Burnham has remarked that "the large hole in voter participation which developed after 1900 roughly corresponds to the area in the electorate where a viable socialist movement 'ought' to have developed but . . . did not succeed in doing so." [6] Apparently, the development of political organization on the left, parties with one form or another of mass membership, invigorated the entire European political universe. The other parties responded in order to remain competitive. As a result, parties continued to be major sources of political information and agencies to bring voters to the polls in large numbers. What this suggests for the American situation is that the need to mobilize voters has been the chief determinant of the vitality of parties. Under the "1896 system" parties ceased performing this function to the degree they had before and lost much of their nineteenth-century vitality.

The parties' main function in the nineteenth century

had been to socialize masses of new voters. In this they were like the European leftist parties of the twentieth century. Despite differences between them in organization and ideology, both mobilized new elements to participate actively in politics. The less elaborately organized American parties were as adequate in this job as their later European counterparts. Perhaps the sad truth is that high voter participation among poor and less educated groups is a function of their newness to politics. Large-scale efforts at political education—the constantly mobilizable party membership of the European left or the partisan press and army of politically active civil servants of nineteenth-century America—may be confined to the early history of political systems or to the socialization of new elements into an older system. The zeal of the convert may apply to politics quite as much as to religion. Both the political parties and the religious denominations—the two great institutions of the nineteenth century—appear to have permanently reduced roles in modern America, and images of the old-time politics may at times stir as much nostalgia as the "old-time religion." [7]

Other parts of the system that emerged in 1896 supported the national political stasis of the age. The election of 1896 was a vote of confidence not only for the financial system of the nation, but for the courts, the existing pattern of labor-management relations, and the role of the executive in labor disturbances. Bryan had run on a platform astonishingly radical for the age, and his desire to make the election a referendum (which he repeated in 1900) was also radical. All such radicalisms were turned back with McKinley's success. The Supreme Court continued the trend it had begun in the nineties of delimiting the range of political control over the economy. The business community and the majority Republican party continued an alliance which at least partially insulated industrial management from the kind of popular pressures that had seemed so threatening previously. Most striking of all, the presidency emerged from its lengthy eclipse after Lincoln to become the new balance wheel of the political system: it not only gained positive governmental powers, but absorbed, as we shall see, many of the symbolic functions that the party system once performed.

The new politics emerging within the old forms was by no means static outside the area of party competition. Rather it expressed some of the old American preference —which Tocqueville had extensively analyzed—for the exercise of power through voluntary, essentially private, organizations. Reform movements, corporations, manufacturers' associations, labor unions, consumer groups, and the new organized middle-class professions like social work and education all vied for control of policy. Their quarrels would not threaten the majority in favor of capitalism and industrial development that Hanna had rallied in 1896. By more explicitly confining the range of politics, the 1896 system allowed more freedom within that range. It established insurgency as a major political style. There was less of a contest over constituting government, but more conflict over particular policies. The previous era had seen a politics of competition and participation addressed to the most general symbolic questions. This made it on the one hand weak in administrative performance and policy output, but also capable of decisive and radical settlement of dangerous basic questions about the organization of society. The Civil War had demonstrated this, and the nineties showed that it remained a possibility. The twentieth century would see a politics of issues and policy determination run largely as a competition among discreet and well-defined interest groups, dominating the still existent but seriously weakened participatory political system.[8] If the nineteenth century had been a general elementary education in citizenship, the new age would be a kind of high school, demanding more from the teachers and administrators and exacting standards from the students by denying admission to some and failing others. Increased policy output and decreased participation would go hand in hand. Government now had important things to do, and it did them insulated from the vagaries of a popular opinion that the nineties had suggested might no longer be discharged simply in symbolic exercises in political activity.

II

The political system that emerged in 1896 represented the triumph of an old element in American political culture largely submerged under the tide of party organization and enthusiasm that rose in the 1830s. This, of course, was the anti-party tradition in political theory and habits, so familiar in eighteenth-century America and England.[9] Eclipsed in the nineteenth century, it would dominate the twentieth. The trends which depressed party organization, tended to succeed in the new century just where they had failed previously. Malapportionment, a major issue in the colonial era, re-emerged in the twentieth century; and the under-representation of urban populations continued with little effective challenge for generations. Elitist ideologies, previously the preserve of a small educated class, began under the less threatening name of expertise, science, and bureaucracy, to capture the citadels of power. A whole array of procedural reforms made politics increasingly complicated, opening it to issue-oriented elites while limiting its popular base.[10]

The crisis of the nineties had pointed in two directions at once: to the incapacity of government to meet the needs of an industrial society as well as to the inability of the party system to shelter the new industrial empire from its many internal enemies. The 1896 system solved both problems simultaneously, by limiting popular pressure while opening the channels of government to expert opinion and continuous administration. The two concerns met in the presidency. It became the new focus for popular opinion as well as the center for the burgeoning agencies that provided the constant management the modern industrial system required. The negative aspect of 1896, the continuation of old political forms, proved crucial here. For the presidential election had performed an essential even if not always apparent function in the old system which continued and became even more important in the twentieth century. This function was to legitimize the rest of the political and governmental processes. Because the old pattern did not break in 1896, the new situation allowed this function of the presidency to continue and even to expand. The presidency became a giant umbrella, sheltering the pre-eminent private governments from the storms of popular sentiment.

The presidential contest had always been crucial for legitimizing the operations of party. Nothing fully overcame the anti-party tradition in the early republic except the contest for the presidency. Richard P. McCormick has shown how the "presidential question" forced local factions all over the country into a system of national parties. But even before this, once parties could not seriously contest the presidency, they became "factions" in the public mind (and even in the minds of their own devotees) and disappeared. As long as a party had a chance to win a presidential contest it would survive, even if, like the Democrats during the Civil War, it bore the taint of treason and secession. As soon as the public ceased believing in a party's presidential prospects, however, it died, even if, like the Whigs, it had commanded the support of almost half the nation.

This legitimizing role of the presidential contest was incorporated into the party structure that matured in the 1830s and '40s. That activity offered the mechanism whereby the parties defined their national character. It became the political process in which they literally discovered who they were, in the sense of who was a member of the party and who was not—an important function in a system of parties having no formal membership. But this identification process was also figurative or symbolic: it was a contest to define the program or—more accurately—the tendency of the party. In doing so it held up ideal character types, forms of polity, and styles of life. In this sense it served a quasi-religious function. The national convention was a secularized, protracted revival meeting. It arose in the Antimasonic party, an intensely religious movement coming out of New York's "burnt-over district" at the very time that the revivals spread from there over the land. Here was a lengthy meeting in which the faithful (the elect in a democratic age being the electorate) gathered to demonstrate that they were of the flock, to remember their saints and martyrs, revive their party spirit, enunciate their party creed, and choose from among them the man in whose name they would spread their message over the land. And they took that faith seriously: the incidence of party voting and allegiance, of single-ticket support throughout the electorate, is staggering for the half-century after the establishment of the second party system with its innovation of the new revivalistic national convention.[11]

Will Herberg in his stimulating *Protestant-Catholic-Jew* has argued that Americans have retained their religious identities as a form of labeling, a shorthand indication of who they are. It is not enough to be an American, the label contains less individual definition than being a Frenchman or an Englishman. As a result, Americans in the twentieth century have clung to their religious identities to define themselves to others. The question "What are you?" calls for the answer "WASP" or "Catholic-American" or "Jewish-American." This view of the nation's religious sociology, which seems accurate at least for the first half of the twentieth century, was not true of the nineteenth. Protestants took seriously their denominational differences; Jews were divided—and rather bitterly —into Reform and Orthodox, German and Russian; Catholics fought over their national church practices. Religion was simply too important a part of the individual American's world view to allow the flattening of distinctions necessary to a labeling device.[12]

In the nineteenth century, political party membership served this unifying function. Real differences often separated the parties as there are real differences between religions in this century, but they were not crucial to the day-to-day life of Americans much as religious differences are not today. Party politics was available as a labeling device defining who one was and offering a shorthand account of one's general attitudes and objects of hero worship. The parties served constituent rather than policy functions just as the churches do now. They placed people in a context.

The parties' most solid structures were local since people lived their lives in what Robert Wiebe has called "island communities." But the fluidity of American economic and social life and the resultant amorphousness of its institutions made these island communities not quite islands and not quite communities. The American of the nineteenth century—as Tocqueville tells us—hungered for symbols to overcome his personal isolation and the limitations of his environment. Under a rural, localist, and anti-urban ideology he let himself be conquered by urban culture more rapidly than any man in history. His need for community and for relation to a national culture was as huge as the dioramas he respected as art, and as inflated as the bombastic oratory he devoured.[13]

The political parties followed the constitutional system in providing a symbol for the nationhood the American knew he had not yet achieved. The mysticism of the Union found its reflection in an inflated nationalization of political rhetoric. The sometimes genial but often bitter struggle for power with his neighbor (who might be of a different religion, national background, or historical tradition) was best legitimized by transforming the local concerns into questions of national identity and goals. The President was each and every American writ large, a role easy or difficult in proportion to the degree to which his functions were ceremonial, as they were for much of the nineteenth century. The presidency was a charismatic *office*, requiring charismatic leaders only in times of crisis when called upon to serve more than constituent functions.

The politics of Congress could not serve this function. Its particularistic nature was quickly apparent, as was its greater weight in the constitutional system. Congress expressed the federalism under which the life of the nation actually went on, but just because of this it suffered two fatal liabilities making it incapable of serving the required symbolic role. It could not always afford to twist its more serious occupations into symbolic functions and when it did serve such purposes, they tended not to suggest the mystical bond of union as much as the ever-present conflict of sections and groups. The nationalist rhetoric of a Webster or a Clay and the limited party discipline could not overcome the institutional dynamic of Congress as an agency to air conflict. In its practical role as a compromising agent, Congress might actually serve to deal with issues in conflict; but in doing so, it verified the conflicts which it had to compromise and obscured the underlying agreements within which these conflicts took place. That role only the presidency—not even the Supreme Court as justices from Marshall to Warren have learned—could perform.

In the decline of an older more fixed deference pattern, the presidential contest provided both parties and politicians with the legitimacy they needed for their new political roles. As a member of the party of Jefferson and Jackson, or as a follower of Clay or Calhoun, one had a rationale for grasping at power. The common-man-to-the-White-House theme was a crucial underpinning for the rise of many a common man to political prominence. The parties themselves became respectable by dint of being directed toward great national values, and the one systematic expression for these values was through the contest for the presidency. Only by its ability to gain the approbation of that phantom public, the nation at large, could party rise above self-interested faction, making possible its continuity as a structure. Otherwise, the political culture of the era damned such organization as divisive.

Thus the national contest provided a touchstone for political participation. Identification with it gave politicians their legitimacy and gave voters a focus for their loyalty. Those who had worked for Jackson or for Lincoln were worthy of one's vote for Governor or even for dog catcher. This meant that men had to hold together from election to election and that voters could see them as standing for something in addition to office. The only thing that overcame the endemic distrust of party in American political culture was a *label* attached to national tendencies and values. But this label was absolutely crucial to the existence of parties: it transformed factions that one expected to be transitory and opportunistic into groups with a name and a symbolic identification, thus providing the continuity which distinguished party from faction. This labeling provided by the "presidential question" was the basis of all other continuities. As the present study indicates, no organizational mechanism held together national parties except for the common need to come together every four years to choose and then to electioneer for a presidential candidate. In that process, the century's politics of participation found its imagery.

III

Because the national party system survived the transformation of the nineties without changes in its outward form, the presidential contest continued to perform its old function. The quadrennial events still raised echoes of the past, hints that the world of mass political education and participation parties still endured. Only in presidential years did publicists voice complaints of political apathy and note the size of the non-voting public.[14] Nor was this sentiment wholly nostalgic. The presidential contest at times still served its old function. The Democratic party, in the campaigns of Al Smith and Franklin Roosevelt, brought the new immigrant communities and then the labor movement into the political universe. In 1948 the Democratic National Convention offered symbols to mobilize the emerging black vote. Eugene McCarthy in 1968 attempted without success to perform this classic function of the presidential contest for the new radicalism and youth culture. Fittingly, the indication that this gallant effort had failed was that the new elements disrupted instead of being absorbed into the curious symbolic machinery of the national convention.

More important than this continuation of the old function in regard to political participation, however, was the way that the legitimizing function carried over into the new presidency itself. The private governments, which under the aegis of political pluralism and the shelter of the presidency administered industrial America, received their ordination from the presidential election. They were installed without being judged. Twentieth-century experience showed that the President could exercise his new positive offices within the confines of the old national party system simply by removing as far as possible such concerns as regulating the economy and conducting foreign policy from the matrix of party. This was accomplished by making the regulation of business legalistic and negative (through antitrust actions) as well as independent of parties (through bipartisan and often remarkably independent regulatory agencies) [15] while conducting foreign policy through a fully bipartisan establishment of international bankers and lawyers, professional soldiers and diplomats, and broad-minded politicians not yet (like Nelson Rockefeller in the 1940s) or no longer (like Averell Harriman in the 1960s) vying for elective office.

Except in extreme crises, these functions became almost fully depoliticized. They were not the issue of presidential elections. Indeed, attempts such as Bryan's to make these contests into referenda on policy proved uniformly unsuccessful, even though the presidential contest offered the only serious control over appointments and policy. The agencies of government largely served to remove sensitive concerns from the fluctuations of politics while they aided in the self-administration of the various private governments that made up a pluralistic system. Meanwhile, the President remained the symbolic focus of politics. The presidential contest continued to define party identities and to preserve loyalties. The non-competitive political world that 1896 inaugurated enabled this great transformation to take place without coercion or violence and—as events later in the century were to suggest—without completely draining American politics of its democratic potential.

Notes

CHAPTER I

1. Maurice Duverger, *Political Parties, Their Organization and Activity in the Modern State* (London and New York, 1959), pp. 61–64; James Bryce, *The American Commonwealth* (2 vols.; New York, 1903), II, p. 3.

2. Allen Johnson and Dumas Malone, eds., *Dictionary of American Biography* (22 vols.; New York, 1928–44), III, pp. 437–39, 618, XV, pp. 4–6 (hereafter cited as *DAB*); Ruth Crandall, "American Railroad Presidents in the 1870's: Their Backgrounds and Careers," *Explorations in Entrepreneurial History*, II (July 1950), 295; Harold F. Gosnell, *Boss Platt and His New York Machine* (Chicago, 1924), pp. 55–72. Roosevelt's statement is on p. 66.

3. Comparative figures for the twentieth century show 51.7 per cent and 35.2 per cent respectively for the period from 1920–28, the low point of the century for voter turnout, and 60.3 per cent and 44.1 per cent respectively for the 1948–60 period. Walter Dean Burnham, "The Changing Shape of the American Political Universe," *American Political Science Review*, LIX (March 1965), 10 (hereafter abbreviated *APSR*).

4. *Ibid.*, p. 22.

5. Speech of James S. Clarkson delivered at Louisville, Ky., May 10, 1893, Papers of James S. Clarkson, Library of Congress (hereafter abbreviated LC); John K. Gowdy to Elijah W. Halford, Oct. 4, 1892, Papers of Benjamin Harrison, LC. See also Whitelaw Reid to Joseph Medill, Sept. 22, 1892, Reid to Alonzo B. Cornell, Nov. 11, 1892, Papers of Whitelaw Reid, LC; Levi W. Brown to Halford, Oct. 4, 1892, George W. Steele to Halford, Nov. 11, 1892, Harrison Papers; Matthew Josephson, *The Politicos, 1865–1896* (New York, 1938), p.

512; Burnham, "American Political Universe," 10–12. The politicians' impressions in 1892 are confirmed by voting statistics: see Burnham's graph, 11. The politics of the South was rather different, with voting levels always significantly lower than in the other states. However the fluctuation in turnout has remained quite similar to the rest of the nation, generally reflecting the national pattern but in an exaggerated form, as Burnham's graph strikingly illustrates.

6. Thomas C. Platt to George W. Wanmaker, Jan. 17, 1894, Papers of Lemuel E. Quigg, New York Historical Society. Survey data and election statistics demonstrate a clear link between strong party allegiance and the likelihood of voting. See Bernard R. Berelson, Paul F. Lazarsfeld, and William N. McPhee, *Voting, A Study of Opinion Formation in a Presidential Campaign* (Chicago, 1954), pp. 24–34. Close elections and participation are less directly linked. See Burnham, "American Political Universe," 17; Theodore J. Lowi, "Party, Policy, and Constitution in America," in William N. Chambers and Walter D. Burnham, eds., *The American Party Systems: Stages of Political Development* (New York, 1967), pp. 251–52. Apparently, degree of party competition is but one of a large number of variables affecting voter turnout. Its importance lies principally in its effect on party structure: "Defeat and victory and the degree of defeat and victory," Lowi writes, "are probably the most important determinants of party structure as well as party elite and interest composition." (Theodore J. Lowi, "Toward Functionalism in Political Science: The Case of Innovation in Party Systems," *APSR*, LVII [Sept. 1963], 582.) The present study supports this conclusion: the crucial question in allocating resources and assigning roles was always whether the election was "sure," "doubtful," or hopeless.

7. John G. Sproat, *"The Best Men," Liberal Reformers in the Gilded Age* (New York, 1968), pp. 139–41, 276–77; Fred I. Greenstein, *The American Party System and the American People* (Englewood Cliffs, 1963), pp. 30–36, estimates that approximately 25 per cent of the modern electorate is politically independent. On the "surge" effect in this century see Angus Campbell, "Surge and Decline: A Study of Electoral Change," *Public Opinion Quarterly*, XXIV (1960), 397–418; Charles G. Sellers, "The Equilibrium Cycle in Two-Party Politics," in William J. Crotty, Donald M. Freeman, and Douglas S. Gatlin, eds., *Political Parties and Political Behavior* (Boston, 1966), pp. 100–101.

8. Below, pp. 85–100, 125–49.

9. Burnham, "American Political Universe," 11, 22–23; William F. Zornow, *Lincoln and the Party Divided* (Norman, Okla., 1954); Earle D. Ross, *The Liberal Republican Movement* (New York, 1919).

10. The traditional view of Gilded Age politics, coming down from

Henry Adams and the reformers of the age, is elegantly expressed in Richard Hofstadter, *The American Political Tradition and the Men Who Made It* (New York, 1948), pp. 164–85. The similar estimate coming from the vantage point of the third-party orientation toward economic issues is fully stated in Josephson, *The Politicos*. For a modern estimate of the politics of the era which contrasts with the Adams-Josephson approach—as well as this writer's—see H. Wayne Morgan, *From Hayes to McKinley, National Party Politics, 1877–1896* (Syracuse, 1969). The relevant voting behavior studies are the following: Lee Benson, "Research Problems in American Political Historiography," in Mirra Komarovsky, ed., *Common Frontiers of the Social Sciences* (Glencoe, Ill., 1957), pp. 113–83; Paul John Kleppner, "The Politics of Change in the Midwest: the 1890's in Historical and Behavioral Perspective" (unpublished Ph.D. dissertation, University of Pittsburgh, 1967); Richard Joseph Jensen, "The Winning of the Midwest: A Social History of Midwestern Elections, 1888–1896" (unpublished Ph.D. dissertation, Yale University, 1967); Samuel Thompson McSeveney, "The Politics of Depression: Voting Behavior in Connecticut, New York, and New Jersey, 1893–1896" (unpublished Ph.D. dissertation, University of Iowa, 1966). For Blaine's problems as a presidential candidate, see below, pp. 59–100.

11. Distinguishing third-party movements and fusions is impossible in the presidential campaigns of the Gilded Age. Even in 1892, the Western Populists had fusion arrangements with the Democrats in most states. See below, pp. 187–88. I have therefore included the Liberal movement of 1872 among the third parties affecting presidential politics. This pattern of a falling turnout in years of strong third-party movements continues into the twentieth century. The elections of 1912, 1924, 1948, and 1968 are all marked by particularly small turnouts. See the graph in Burnham, "American Political Universe," 11; and for 1968 figures in comparison to those of the previous twelve years, see *The New York Times*, Nov. 17, 1968, p. 53.

12. Burnham, "American Political Universe," 22–28; C. Vann Woodward, *The Origins of the New South, 1877–1913* (Baton Rouge, 1951), pp. 321–49; Robert H. Wiebe, *The Search for Order, 1877–1920* (New York, 1967), pp. 104–10; Samuel P. Hays, "Political Parties and the Community-Society Continuum," in Chambers and Burnham, eds., *American Party Systems*, pp. 165–81. A sizable literature in political science stresses the stabilizing effect of a limited electorate and the generally authoritarian character of the non-voter, suggesting that those concerned with democratic values have cause to be pleased that the non-voter does not vote. See Seymour Martin Lipset, *Political Man, The Social Basis of Politics* (Garden City, 1960), passim but esp. pp. 216–19 and the items cited in the footnotes on these pages. The

nineteenth-century experience raises the question of whether non-voters do not go to the polls because of their authoritarian, anti-political attitudes, or whether in fact they have such attitudes precisely because the political system has somehow shut them out. Burnham notes, for example, the high level of political participation among rural Americans in the nineteenth century compared to their role in the twentieth. This suggests that the source of political behavior and its attendant psychology may be less in the social situation than in the structure of politics. (Burnham, 16; Lipset, pp. 110–13.) Despite the apparent political impotence of lower-class groups in nineteenth-century American politics, their remaining within the political spectrum may have offered the potential for a democratic politics of the poor that the twentieth-century American political system has lacked. Certainly the leaders of opinion of the 1890s thought this was the case.

13. Below, pp. 46, 180, 189, 190.

14. J. H. Manley to Halford, Sept. 5, 1892, Halford to Harrison, Nov. 6, 1892, Harrison Papers; Reid to A. B. Cornell, Nov. 11, 1892, Reid Papers; *Tribune Almanac, 1893*, pp. 274, 280. See also Sellers, "Equilibrium Cycle," p. 101.

15. Lewis A. Froman, Jr., "A Realistic Approach to Campaign Strategy and Tactics," in M. Kent Jennings and L. Harmon Zeigler, eds., *The Electoral Process* (Englewood Cliffs, 1966), p. 8; Paul F. Lazarsfeld, Bernard Berelson, and Hazel Gaudet, *The People's Choice* (2nd ed.; New York, 1948), p. 104. Generally, the folklore of the nineteenth-century politicians and the results of survey data square remarkably well. On the "still hunt" technique designed to keep opposition voters home, see J. H. Farley to William C. Whitney, Oct. 14, 1892, Papers of William C. Whitney, LC. Gilded Age politicians were remarkably conservative in responding to voter shifts. See below, p. 196.

16. Below, pp. 33, 96–99, 146–49. Intimidating Negro voters seems to have been especially common even outside the South. See below, p. 56.

17. Below, p. 145.

18. Sellers, "Equilibrium Cycle," pp. 100–101.

19. Berelson, et al., *Voting*, p. 22; Greenstein, *American Party System*, pp. 30–34.

20. Sproat, *"The Best Men"*, p. 121; Josephson, *The Politicos*, p. 246; Speech of John J. Ingalls, March 26, 1886, *Congressional Record*, 49th Cong., 1st Sess., p. 2786. On the masculine-feminine cultural dichotomy see George Santayana, *Character and Opinion in the United States* (Garden City, 1956), p. 27; Thomas Beer, *The Mauve Decade, American Life at the End of the Nineteenth Century* (Garden City, 1926), pp. 17–61; Larzer Ziff, *The American 1890s; Life and Times of a Lost Generation* (New York, 1966), pp. 41–45, 275–78.

21. W. Wolf to James S. Clarkson, Apr. 19, 1884, Papers of James S.

Clarkson, Iowa State Department of History and Archives (hereafter referred to as ISDHA).

22. Sellers, "Equilibrium Cycle," pp. 79–102; Lee Benson, "Research Problems in American Political Historiography," pp. 113–83; V. O. Key, "A Theory of Critical Elections," *Journal of Politics,* XVII (Feb. 1955), 3–18.

23. Leslie H. Fishel, Jr., "The Negro in Northern Politics, 1870–1900," *Mississippi Valley Historical Review,* XLII (Dec. 1955), 483–86. For a striking account of the cultural climate of the eighties, see John Higham, *Strangers in the Land, Patterns of American Nativism, 1860–1925* (New Brunswick, 1955), pp. 35–67.

24. McSeveney, "The Politics of Depression," pp. 72–76; Jensen, "Winning of the Midwest," p. 68; Kleppner, "Politics of Change," p. 201.

25. Below, pp. 190–94.

26. Arthur E. Morgan, *Edward Bellamy* (New York, 1944), pp. xi, 248. The only political work to catch the public imagination before Bellamy was Henry George's *Progress and Poverty,* published in 1879. There are no clear figures on the size of its sale or on the public it attracted. However, George's career thereafter strongly suggests that his public was principally among workingmen and especially among the Irish-Americans concerned with the land and rent problems of the old country. These were precisely the groups whose political loyalties most worried the politicians even in the era of relatively fixed political preferences. See footnote 25 and Charles Albro Barker, *Henry George* (New York, 1955). On the sale of *Progress and Poverty* see Frank Luther Mott, *Golden Multitudes: The Story of Best Sellers in the United States* (New York, 1947), pp. 167–68; James D. Hart, *The Popular Book: A History of America's Literary Taste* (New York, 1950), p. 175.

27. David A. Shannon, *The Socialist Party of America: A History* (New York, 1955), p. 3; Howard H. Quint, *The Forging of American Socialism: Origins of the Modern Movement* (Columbia, S.C., 1953), pp. vii, 72–102; below, pp. 190–94.

28. Frank Luther Mott, *History of American Magazines, 1885–1905* Cambridge, Mass., 1957), pp. 3–14; Ziff, *The American 1890s,* p. 120. *Munsey's* began in 1889; *Cosmopolitan,* which began in 1886, adopted the new format and became successful in 1889; *McClure's* followed in 1893. On religious changes, see Henry F. May, *Protestant Churches and Industrial America* (New York, 1949), pp. 170–81; Aaron I. Abell, *The Urban Impact on American Protestantism, 1865–1900* (Cambridge, Mass., 1943), pp. 68–83. On the progressivism of the 1890s see Richard Hofstadter, *The Age of Reform, From Bryan to F.D.R.* (New York, 1956), pp. 164–65; and below, pp. 202–14. Christopher Lasch's stimulating study of the confusion between culture and politics that he finds typical of "the intellectual as a social

type" presciently sets its *terminus a quo* at 1889: *The New Radical-ism in America, 1889–1913; The Intellectual as a Social Type* (New York, 1965).

29. Henry Adams, *The Education of Henry Adams, An Autobiography* (Boston, 1918), pp. 228–30, 266.

CHAPTER II

1. Andrew Wallace Crandall, *The Early History of the Republican Party, 1854–1856* (Boston, 1930), pp. 51–53, 59–61.

2. James A. Rawley, *Edward D. Morgan, 1811–1883; Merchant in Pol-itics* (New York, 1955), pp. 49–51. The quotation is on p. 51.

3. *Ibid.*, pp. 60–61, 66–70, 103, 114–16.

4. Zornow, *Lincoln and the Party Divided*, pp. 179–89; Rawley, *Morgan*, pp. 67, 111–12.

5. Charles H. Coleman, *The Election of 1868; The Democratic Effort to Regain Control* (New York, 1933), pp. 307–9; Leon Burr Rich-ardson, *William E. Chandler, Republican* (New York, 1940), pp. 90–116.

6. Richardson, *Chandler*, pp. 117–18, 125–27; Josephson, *The Politicos*, pp. 80–99.

7. Ross, *The Liberal Republican Movement* pp. 184–88; Detroit Post and Tribune, *Life of Zachariah Chandler* (Detroit, 1880), pp. 312–16. Sproat, "*The Best Men*," pp. 71–88.

8. Dorothy Ganfield Fowler, *The Cabinet Politician, The Postmaster General, 1829–1909* (New York, 1943), pp. 157–58.

9. Marshall Jewell to Zachariah Chandler, Sept. 18, 1876, Papers of Zachariah Chandler, LC; John Sherman to Richard Smith, June 14, 1880, Papers of John Sherman, LC; Benjamin Harrison to T. C. Platt, Aug. 17, 1892, Harrison Papers.

10. Fowler, *Cabinet Politician*, p. 162; James G. Blaine to Whitelaw Reid, Jan. 26, 1888, Reid Papers; Z. Chandler to R. B. Hayes, Sept. 12, 1876, Jay Gould to Z. Chandler, Nov. 30, 1876, Levi P. Morton to Z. Chandler, Jan. 20, 1877, John Murray Forbes to Z. Chandler, Mar. 7, 1877, Z. Chandler Papers.

11. Fowler, *Cabinet Politician*, pp. 162, 171–72; F. T. Bickford to Reid, Aug., 1879, Reid Papers; Richard C. McCormick to Edward McPher-son, Nov. 29, 1879, Papers of Edward McPherson, LC; W. B. Shattue to William E. Chandler, Mar. 4, 1880, Samuel H. Drew to Chandler, Mar. 6, 1880, W. B. Shattue to Chandler, Mar. 6, 1880, Papers of William E. Chandler, LC (hereafter cited as Chandler Papers).

12. *The Nation*, XXX (Jan. 8, 1880), 20.

13. Detroit Post and Tribune, *Zachariah Chandler*, p. 388.

14. Chicago *Tribune*, Jan. 9, 1879, cited in Ernest L. Bogart and Charles M. Thompson, *The Industrial State, 1870–1893* (Springfield, Ill., 1920), p. 129; Charles A. Church, *History of the Republican Party*

in Illinois, 1854–1912 (Rockford, Ill., 1912), pp. 135–39; F. W. Palmer to John A. Logan, Feb. 26, 1880, L. Joslyn to Logan, Feb. 26, 1880, Jesse Spaulding to Logan, Apr. 6, 1880, Logan to J. Donald Cameron, telegram, May 10, 1880, Papers of John A. Logan, LC; Isaac E. Adams, *Life of Emery A. Storrs* (Chicago, 1886), pp. 660–82; Republican Party, *Official Proceedings of the National Conventions of 1868, 1872, 1876, and 1880* (Minneapolis, 1903), pp. 467–97 (hereafter cited as *Proceedings, 1880*); John Sherman to Richard Smith, June 14, 1880, Sherman Papers. On Logan see *DAB*, VI, pp. 363–65; Mary S. Logan, *Reminiscences of a Soldier's Wife* (New York, 1916).

15. Donald Barr Chidsey, *The Gentleman from New York, A Life of Roscoe Conkling* (New Haven, 1935); and *DAB*, IV, pp. 346–47.

16. DeAlva Stanwood Alexander, *A Political History of the State of New York* (4 vols.; New York, 1906-23), III, pp. 390–92, 407-17; *Harper's Weekly*, XXIII (Feb. 8, 1879), 102.

17. New York *Sun*, Sept. 8, 1879, quoted in Alexander, *Political History*, III, p. 416; *Harper's Weekly*, XXIII (Sept. 20, 1879), 742–43, (Sept. 27, 1879), 762, (Oct. 11, 1879), 802–3, (Nov. 1, 1879), 862.

18. Reid to Garfield, Jan. 16, 1881, Apr. 11, 1881, Reid to Isaac Bromley, Jan. 27, 1881, Reid Papers; Alexander, *Political History*, III, pp. 464–68; Chauncey M. Depew, *My Memoirs of Eighty Years* (New York, 1924), p. 112. There are dozens of letters from Platt written between 1877 and 1881 in the Reid Papers: see esp. Platt to Reid, Feb. 16, 1880.

19. Alexander, *Political History*, III, pp. 428-37.

20. Rudolph Blankenburg, "Forty Years in the Wilderness; Or, Masters and Rulers of 'The Freemen' of Pennsylvania," *The Arena*, XXXIII (Feb. 1905), 113–27; Herbert Welsh, "The Degradation of Pennsylvania Politics," *The Forum*, XII (Nov. 1891), 330–45; Thomas V. Cooper and Hector T. Fenton, *American Politics, Non-Partisan, From the Beginning to Date* (Philadelphia, 1883), passim.

21. *The Nation*, XXX (Feb. 12, 1880), 111–12; W. E. Chandler to McPherson, Jan. 30, 1880, Luther G. Sherman to McPherson, Feb. 9, 1880, McPherson Papers; A. M. Gibson to Chandler, Feb. 3, 1880, Chandler to Garfield, June 14, 1880, Chandler Papers.

22. D. Wagotoff to Chandler, Mar. 8, 1880, Chandler Papers; James F. Wilson to James S. Clarkson, Apr. 2, 1880, Clarkson Papers, ISDHA.

23. Richardson, *Chandler*, pp. 249–55; Sarah Forbes Hughes, *Letters and Recollections of John Murray Forbes* (2 vols.; Boston, 1899), IV, pp. 192–93; George Frisbie Hoar, *Autobiography of Seventy Years* (2 vols.; New York, 1903), I, pp. 390–93.

24. Thomas Collier Platt, *Autobiography* (New York, 1910), p. 119; John Sherman to Richard Smith, June 14, 1880, Sherman Papers; *The Statesman*, June 17, 1880.

25. Henry L. Stoddard, *As I Knew Them, Presidents and Politics from*

Grant to Coolidge (New York, 1927), p. 52. For Blaine's life see David Saville Muzzey, *James G. Blaine, A Political Idol of Other Days* (New York, 1935).

26. Muzzey, *Blaine,* pp. 100–113, 158; Richardson, *Chandler,* pp. 173–76; Joseph H. Manley to Chandler, Mar. 11, 1880, Chandler Papers.
27. H. Wayne Morgan, *William McKinley and His America* (Syracuse, 1963), p. 93; Jeannette P. Nichols, "John Sherman: A Study in Inflation," *Mississippi Valley Historical Review,* XXI (Sept. 1934), 181–94.
28. John Sherman to Richard Smith, June 14, 1880, Sherman Papers; Chandler to McPherson, Jan. 30, 1880, Blaine to McPherson, Feb. 6, 1880, Luther G. Sherman to McPherson, Feb. 9, 1880, McPherson Papers; A. M. Gibson to Chandler, Feb. 3, 1880, William H. Kemble to Chandler, Feb. 28, 1880, Chandler Papers.
29. Blaine to Murat Halstead, May 3, 1880, Papers of Murat Halstead, Historical and Philosophical Society of Ohio; Claude Moore Fuess, *Carl Schurz, Reformer, 1829–1906* (New York, 1932), p. 271; *The New York Times,* May 7, 1880.
30. Blaine to Reid, Mar. 15, Apr. 25, 1880, Reid Papers; Charles Foster to James A. Garfield, Feb. 13, 23, Mar. 22, Apr. 17, 1880, Papers of James A. Garfield, LC; Chandler to McPherson, Jan. 30, 1880, McPherson Papers; *The Nation,* XXX (Feb. 12, 1880), 112.
31. Richardson, *Chandler,* pp. 257–58; Fowler, *Cabinet Politician,* p. 173; W. C. Cooper to Garfield, June 9, 1880, W. C. Cooper to Charles Foster, June 26, 1880, Garfield Papers.
32. Chandler to Garfield, June 14, 1880, Chandler Papers; [John M. Forbes] to Chandler, June 20, 1880, Foster to Garfield, June 23, 1880, Garfield to Foster, June 29, 1880, Garfield Papers.
33. E. D. Bickham to Garfield, June 30, 1880, Foster to Garfield, June 23, 1880, Forbes to Garfield, June 27, 1880, Garfield Papers; Chandler to Garfield, June 14, 1880, W. C. Cooper to Chandler, June 29, 1880, Chandler Papers; Richardson, *Chandler,* p. 258; Hughes, *John Murray Forbes,* II, p. 196.
34. Chandler to Garfield, June 14, 1880, Forbes to Chandler, June 25, 1880, Chandler Papers; Reid to Blaine, telegram, [July 1, 1880], Blaine to Reid, telegram, July 2, 1880, Reid Papers; Reid to Garfield, July 3, 1880, Garfield Papers, AcDR 64–55, items 12 and 13, LC. For Elkins, see Oscar Doane Lambert, *Stephen Benton Elkins* (Pittsburgh, 1955).
35. Theodore Clarke Smith, *The Life and Letters of James Abram Garfield* (2 vols.; New Haven, 1925), II, p. 999; Chandler to Garfield, Feb. 17, 1881, Garfield to Foster, June 29, 30, 1880, Garfield Papers; W. C. Cooper to Chandler, June 29, 1880, Chandler Papers; Richardson, *Chandler,* pp. 258–59; Hughes, *John Murray Forbes,* II, pp. 196–98.
36. Jewell to Garfield, July 24, 27, Oct. 1, 15, 1880, R. C. McCormick to

Garfield, Oct. 15, 1880, Garfield Papers; R. C. McCormick to Chandler, Aug. 13, Oct. 5, 1880, Chandler Papers.

37. Forbes to Garfield, July 7, 1880, Thomas M. Nichol to Garfield, July 25, 1880, McCormick to Garfield, Aug. 21, 1880, Jewell to Garfield, Oct. 18, 1880, Garfield Papers; Reid to Garfield, July 30, Aug. 3, 1880, Garfield Papers, AcDR 64–55, items 12 and 13.

38. New York *Tribune,* Feb. 12, 1881; George Frederick Howe, *Chester A. Arthur* (New York, 1934), pp. 129–30.

39. Garfield Journal, Feb. 17, 1881, Blaine to Garfield, Feb. 23, 1881, Garfield Papers; Chandler to Garfield, Feb. 17, 1881: in Richardson, *Chandler,* pp. 266–67.

40. Josephson, *The Politicos,* pp. 299–301.

41. McCormick to Garfield, Aug. 16, 21, Oct. 5, 1880, Dorsey to Garfield, July 16, Sept. 17, 1880, A. P. Miller to Garfield, Aug. 14, 1880, Jewell to Garfield, Oct. 5, 1880, Garfield Papers; Reid to Garfield, Aug. 13, 1880, Garfield Papers, AcDR 64–55, items 12 and 13; McCormick to Chandler, Aug. 13, Oct. 5, 1880, Chandler Papers.

42. Arthur to Preston B. Plumb, June 30, 1880, Plumb to Garfield, June 30, 1880, Garfield to Dorsey, July 9, 1880, McCormick to Garfield, July 14, 1880, Frank Hiscock to Garfield, July 25, 1880, T. M. Nichol to Garfield, July 25, 1880, Garfield to Chandler, July 26, 1880, Garfield to Dorsey, July 28, 1880, Garfield Papers; Reid to Garfield, July 3, 1880, Garfield to Dorsey, July 3, 1880, Garfield Papers, AcDR 64–55, items 12 and 13; Jewell to Chandler, July 21, 1880, Chandler Papers.

43. Dorsey to Garfield, July 25, 1880, Jewell to Garfield, July 27, 29, 1880, Garfield to Dorsey, July 28, 1880, Garfield Papers.

44. Platt, *Autobiography,* pp. 124–37; Smith, *Garfield,* II, pp. 1013–17; Richardson, *Chandler,* pp. 259–61; Howe, *Arthur,* pp. 116–20; Josephson, *The Politicos,* pp. 295–99; Alexander, *Political History,* III, p. 363.

45. Platt, *Autobiography,* pp. 503, 509, and passim. For a view of the relationship of organization and rhetoric directly contradictory of mine, see David J. Rothman, *Politics and Power, the United States Senate, 1869–1901,* (Cambridge, Mass., 1966), p. 222.

46. Platt, *Autobiography,* pp. 125–26; Howe, *Arthur,* pp. 108–9, 115; Jewell to Garfield, July 24, 1880, Hiscock to Garfield, Dorsey to Garfield, T. M. Nichol to Garfield, July 25, 1880, Garfield Papers.

47. Platt, *Autobiography,* pp. 126–27; Reid to Garfield, Aug. 13, 31, 1880, Garfield Papers, AcDR 64–55, items 12 and 13.

48. Reid to Garfield, July 30, 1880, Garfield Papers, AcDR 64–55, items 12 and 13; Garfield to Blaine, July 30, 1880, Garfield Papers.

49. Garfield Journal, Aug. 5, 1880, Garfield Papers.

50. Robert McNutt McElroy, *Levi P. Morton, Banker, Diplomat, and Statesman* (New York, 1930), pp. 109–11; McCormick to Chandler,

July 23, 1880, Chandler Papers; Forbes to Garfield, July 7, 1880, Garfield Papers; Reid to Garfield, Aug. 31, 1880, Garfield Papers, AcDR 64-55, items 12 and 13; Reid to Garfield, Dec. 21, 1880, Reid Papers.

51. Garfield to Reid, Aug. 30, 1880, Garfield to S. B. Elkins, Sept. 3, 1880, Garfield Papers; *Harper's Weekly*, XXVII (Nov. 15, 1884), 748; Reid to Blaine, Sept. 1, 1880, L. P. Morton to Reid, Sept. 2, 1880, Reid to Garfield, Sept. 2, 1880, Reid Papers.

52. Jewell to Garfield, Sept. 1, 14, 18, 23, Oct. 1, 5, 1880, McCormick to Garfield, Oct. 26, 1880, Garfield Papers.

53. Fowler, *Cabinet Politician*, pp. 171-72; Cornelius P. Cotter and Bernard C. Hennessy, *Politics Without Power: National Party Committees* (New York, 1964), p. 175; Jay A. Hubbell to Garfield, June 25, Aug. 23, 1880, Garfield to Hubbell, Aug. 22, 1880, J. N. Tyner to Garfield, July 15, 1880, Garfield Papers; Jewell to Logan, Sept. 29, 1880, Logan Papers.

54. Foster to Garfield, Aug. 17, 1880, M. H. McKay to Garfield, Oct. 27, 1880, Wharton Barker to Garfield, Oct. 7, 16, 1880, Garfield Papers; Blaine to Elkins, Sept. 12, 1880, Papers of Stephen B. Elkins, West Virginia University Library.

55. Reid to Garfield, Aug. 31, 1880, Garfield Papers, AcDR 64-55, items 12 and 13; Jewell to Garfield, Aug. 30, 1880, Garfield Papers; Reid to Garfield, Dec. 21, 1880, Reid Papers.

56. *The "Granger Cases,"* 94 U.S. 113-87; *The "Sinking Fund Cases,"* 99 U.S. 700-769; Benjamin R. Twiss, *Lawyers and the Constitution: How Laissez-Faire Came to the Supreme Court* (Princeton, 1942), pp. 63-92; Arnold M. Paul, *Conservative Crisis and the Rule of Law: Attitudes of Bar and Bench, 1887-1895* (Ithaca, 1960), pp. 8-10, 68-74; Carl Brent Swisher, *Stephen J. Field, Craftsman of the Law* (Washington, D.C., 1930), pp. 246-49. See Walter Nugent's characterization of the late seventies as "The Period of Stress," in *Money and American Society, 1865-1900* (New York, 1968), p. 5.

57. The quotation from Waite is in 94 U.S. 134 (1876), from Field in 94 U.S. 184 (1876). His dissent in the Sinking-Fund cases is in 99 U.S. 759-67 (1878). Paul, *Conservative Crisis and the Rule of Law*, p. 235; Robert G. McCloskey, *American Conservatism in the Age of Enterprise: A Study of William Graham Summer, Stephen J. Field and Andrew Carnegie* (Cambridge, Mass., 1951), pp. 114-16; Sidney Fine, *Laissez-Faire and the General-Welfare State: A Study of Conflict in American Thought, 1865-1901* (Ann Arbor, 1951), pp. 146-47.

58. Jewell to Garfield, Aug. 30, 1880, Garfield Papers; Reid to Garfield, Aug. 31, 1880, Garfield Papers, AcDR 64-55, items 12 and 13.

59. Garfield to Reid, Sept. 2, 1880, Reid to Garfield, Sept. 6, 1880, Garfield Papers, AcDR 64-55, items 12 and 13.

60. Foster to Preston B. Plumb, Sept. 6, 1880, Garfield Papers.

61. Garfield to Reid, Sept. 15, 1880, Garfield Papers. Strong's dissent is in 99 U.S. 731–44 (1878).
62. Garfield to Reid, Sept. 23, 1880, Garfield Papers. Smith, *Garfield*, II, p. 1029, quotes some of this correspondence, but totally misses its import.
63. Jewell to Garfield, Sept. 29, Oct. 5, 1880, Garfield Papers; McCormick to Chandler, Oct. 5, 1880, Chandler Papers.
64. Jewell to Garfield, Sept. 1, Oct. 5, 1880, John C. New to Garfield, Sept. 4, 1880, W. W. Dudley to Garfield, Sept. 9, 1880, Garfield to Reid, Sept. 15, 1880, Dorsey to Garfield, Sept. 17, 1880, McCormick to Garfield, Oct. 5, 26, 1880, McPherson to Garfield, Oct. 9, 1880, Garfield Papers; McCormick to Chandler, Oct. 5, 1880, Chandler Papers; Indianapolis *Journal*, Oct. 7, 11, 1880.
65. McCormick to Chandler, Sept. 27, Oct. 5, 1880, Chandler Papers; New to Garfield, Sept. 4, 1880, McCormick to Garfield, Sept. 28, 1880, Jewell to Garfield, Oct. 5, 1880, Garfield Papers; Jewell to Allison, Sept. 18, 1880, Papers of William Boyd Allison, ISDHA.
66. Jewell to Garfield, Oct. 5, 1880, Garfield Papers; Harry Barnard, *Rutherford B. Hayes and His America* (Indianapolis, 1954), pp. 450–51. Testimony to Dudley's commanding role in all phases of the Indiana campaign comes from James N. Tyner to Garfield, July 15, 1880, Garfield Papers, and newspaper reports of the campaign. See Indianapolis *Journal*, Sept. 29 through Oct. 13, 1880. For biographical information on Dudley see *National Cyclopedia of American Biography* (49 vols.; New York, 1892–1966), II, p. 222.
67. W. W. Dudley to Garfield, Aug. 10, 1880, Amos Townsend to Garfield, Sept. 3, 1880, Garfield to Amos Townsend, Sept. 7, 1880, Garfield Papers; Allan Nevins, *Study in Power: John D. Rockefeller, Industrialist and Philanthropist* (2 vols.; New York, 1953), II, p. 468.
68. Josephson, *The Politicos*, p. 291; Dudley to Garfield, Aug. 10, 1880, J. N. Tyner to Garfield, July 15, 1880, Garfield Papers; Nevins, *Study in Power*, II, pp. 469–70.
69. Dorsey to Garfield, Sept. 20, 1880, A. P. Miller to Garfield, Aug. 14, 1880, New to Garfield, Sept. 4, 1880, Dudley to Garfield, Sept. 9, 1880, Jewell to Garfield, Oct. 5, 8, 1880, McCormick to Garfield, Oct. 26, 1880, Garfield Papers; Indianapolis *Journal*, Oct. 5, 11, 1880.
70. Dorsey to Garfield, Sept. 20, 1880, Garfield Papers; Indianapolis *Journal*, Sept. 29 through Oct. 13, 1880; J. N. Tyner to Z. Chandler, Nov. 1, 1876, Z. Chandler Papers; Dudley to "Dear Sir," Oct. 24, 1888, Papers of Grover Cleveland, Series 2, LC. (Hereafter cited as Cleveland Papers.)
71. Dorsey to Garfield, Sept. 27, 1880, Garfield Papers; Howe, *Arthur*, pp. 129–30. The meticulous accounts of Chester A. Arthur for the New York state committee offer a reasonable comparison, for if New York was less venal than Indiana (which is questionable) it was larger

and as hotly contested. Arthur's disbursements for election-day expenses amounted to precisely $40,446: Account Book, "Campaign of 1880, Deposit Book and Cheques Special a/c, Closed Oct. 3, 1881, Second National Bank of the City of N.Y. in Account with C.A. Arthur, 1880," Papers of Chester A. Arthur, LC.

72. McCormick to Chandler, Oct. 5, 1880, Chandler Papers.
73. G. W. Hooker to Chandler, July 23, 1880, Chandler Papers.

CHAPTER III

1. Richard C. Bain, *Convention Decisions and Voting Records* (Washington, D.C., 1960), Appendix D. Conkling's remark is quoted in Julia Bundy Foraker, *I Would Live It Again, Memoirs of a Vivid Life* (New York, 1932), p. 228. This is one of the most charming memoirs of the era.

2. Howe, *Arthur*, pp. 20–34, 51, and passim: Stoddard, *As I Knew Them*, p. 117; Warner M. Bateman to Chandler, Dec. 10, 1881, Chandler Papers; Blaine to Reid, Dec. 21, 1881, Reid Papers; Vincent P. DeSantis, *The Republican Party Faces the Southern Question—The New Departure Years, 1877–1897* (Baltimore, 1959), pp. 150–56, and passim; Stanley P. Hirshson, *Farewell to the Bloody Shirt, Northern Republicans and the Southern Negro, 1877–1893* (Bloomington, Ind., 1962), pp. 99–122.

3. Blaine to Garfield, Dec. 10, 1880, Garfield to Blaine, Dec. 19, 1880, in Mary Abigail Dodge [Gail Hamilton], *Biography of James G. Blaine* (Norwich, 1895) pp. 490–94; Blaine to Reid, Dec. 21, 1881, Apr. 22, Sept. 26, Dec. 18, 1882, Feb. 13, May 20, 1883, Reid Papers; J. Donald Cameron to Simon Cameron, Nov. 1, 1883, Papers of Simon Cameron, LC; Chicago *Tribune*, Sept. 19, 1882; Philadelphia *Press*, Nov. 29, 1883; New York *Tribune*, Nov. 29, 1883; Muzzey, *Blaine*, p. 220; Dodge, *Blaine*, pp. 624–27; Howe, *Arthur*, pp. 220, 255–56. The material in the Reid Papers shows that Howe is too harsh on Arthur in blaming him for deteriorating relations with Blaine (Howe, *Arthur*, pp. 194–95).

4. David M. Pletcher, *The Awkward Years, American Foreign Relations Under Garfield and Arthur* (Columbia, Mo., 1962), pp. 59–86, 257.

5. Speech of James S. Clarkson delivered at Louisville, Kentucky, May 10, 1893, Clarkson Papers, LC: Sherman to Elkins, Sept. 1, 1884, Sherman Papers; Republican Party, *Official Proceedings of the Republican National Conventions, 1884–1888* (Minneapolis, 1903), 1884 convention, p. 5 (hereafter cited as *Proceedings, 1884*); William Henry Smith to Henry Watterson, Oct. 10, 1882, Papers of William Henry Smith, Ohio State Historical Society; James A. Barnes, *John G. Carlisle, Financial Statesman* (New York, 1931), pp. 64–67.

6. Blaine to Reid, Dec. 10, 1879: in Royal Cortissoz, *The Life of Whitelaw Reid* (2 vols.; New York, 1921), II, p. 17; Chauncey M. Depew to

Reid, July 22, 1883, Reid to Warner Miller, Apr. 21, 1884, W. H. Robertson to Reid, May 13, 1884, Reid to Robertson, May 15, 1884, Reid Papers. Because "half-breed" was strictly a pejorative label having currency only among Blaine's opponents, its use is avoided in the text. "Stalwart," on the other hand, was unambiguously used by both sides to refer to the men who supported Grant up through 1880, and carried very positive connotations to the men who so identified themselves. See Detroit Post and Tribune, *Zachariah Chandler*, p. 388, as well as numerous passages in Thomas Platt's *Autobiography*.

7. Cyrenus Cole, *Iowa Through the Years* (Iowa City, 1940), p. 397; William P. Wolfe to Clarkson, Apr. 19, 1884, [illegible] to Clarkson, Apr. 9, 1884, James Peck to Clarkson, May 8, 1884, Clarkson Papers, ISDHA.

8. Clarkson to Reid, May 16, 1884, Clarkson to W. W. Phelps, May 16, 1884, Notation, Phelps to Reid on Clarkson to Phelps, May 16, 1884, Reid Papers.

9. Reid to Judge W. H. West, May 15, 17, 1884, Reid Papers.

10. Reid to Phelps, May 20, 1884, Reid to Clarkson, May 21, 1884, Reid Papers.

11. Lambert, *Elkins*, pp. 31, 45–51, 91, 93, and passim; Elmer Ellis, *Henry Moore Teller, Defender of the West* (Caldwell, Idaho, 1941), p. 112; Muzzey, *Blaine*, p. 233; Blaine to Elkins, Apr. 10, 1875, Nov. 17, 1879, Feb. 10, Apr. 11, May 18, Nov. 18, 1881, Jan. 23, 1882, Logan to Elkins, July 4, 1883, Elkins Papers.

12. Blaine to Elkins, Jan. 15, Sept. 2, 11, 1882, Jan. 16, 1883, Elkins Papers; Howe, *Arthur*, pp. 183–84; Lambert, *Elkins*, p. 90.

13. Lambert, *Elkins*, p. 54; Blaine to Elkins, April, 1881, May 18, 1881, Elkins Papers.

14. Blaine to Elkins, May 22, 1884, Elkins Papers.

15. Hamlin Garland, *Ulysses S. Grant* (New York, 1898), pp. 486–503; Lambert, *Elkins*, pp. 89, 91, 93; Philadelphia *Press*, Jan. 31, 1884; Adam Badeau, *Grant in Peace* (Hartford, 1877), pp. 527–28; Logan, *Reminiscences of a Soldier's Wife*, pp. 327–29; Blaine to Elkins, Feb. 10, Apr. 11, Nov. [?], 18, Aug. 4, 10, 1882, Logan to Elkins, July 4, 1883, Elkins Papers.

16. New York *Herald*, Oct. 30, 1882; Washington, D.C. *Evening Star*, Oct. 30, 1882; Howe, *Arthur*, pp. 162–63, 167, 213, 215; Blaine to Reid, n.d., Reid Papers: internal evidence dates the letter in the fall of 1882; Dodge, *Blaine*, pp. 564, 616, 624.

17. Chaffee to Logan, June 3, 1883, Logan Papers; Philadelphia *Press*, Dec. 12, 13, 18, 1883; Washington, D.C. *National Republican*, Dec. 18, 1883.

18. Philadelphia *Press*, Dec. 13, 1883.

19. Philadelphia *Press*, Mar. 18, 24, 1884.

20. L[ogan] U[riah] Reavis to Logan, May 11, 1884, Logan Papers.

21. Chaffee to Logan, May 19, 1884, Elkins to Logan, May 24, 25, 1884, Logan Papers.

22. In the states of the old Confederacy, Arthur had 169 delegates to Blaine's 39 on the first ballot. In the normally Republican and doubtful states excluding the four largest, Blaine led 168 votes to 31 (*Proceedings, 1884*, pp. 141–42).

23. Benjamin Harrison Brewster to Simon Cameron, Apr. 1, 1882, Cameron Papers; Philadelphia *Press*, Jan. 19, 1882; Cooper and Fenton, *American Politics*, pp. 307–13.

24. Brewster to Simon Cameron, Nov. 28, 1882, Cameron Papers; Blaine to Reid, Oct. 25, 1882, Reid Papers.

25. Brewster to J. D. Cameron, Nov. 28, 1882, enclosed in J. D. Cameron to Simon Cameron, May 21, 1882, Brewster to Simon Cameron, Dec. 11, 1883, Cameron Papers; Matthew S. Quay to Arthur, July 10, 19, 1883, J. D. Cameron to Arthur, May 18, 1883, Arthur Papers.

26. Philadelphia *Press*, Oct. 12, 27, Nov. 22, 1883; J. D. Cameron to Simon Cameron, Nov. 1, 1883, Cameron Papers.

27. Brewster to Simon Cameron, Nov. 28, 1882, Dec. 11, 1883, Cameron Papers; Philadelphia *Press*, Feb. 12, 1884.

28. Philadelphia *Press*, Jan. 3, Mar. 15–22, 27, 1884; Wharton Barker to Benjamin Harrison, Mar. 26, 1884, Papers of Wharton Barker, LC.

29. Philadelphia *Press*, Mar. 12, 13, 1884; Pittsburgh *Dispatch*, Apr. 3, 4, 1884.

30. There is no biography of this remarkable and complicated man. D. J. Stackpole, *Behind the Scenes with A Newspaper Man, Fifty Years in the Life of an Editor* (Philadelphia, 1927), pp. 92–109 is a positive assessment. Walter Davenport, *Power and Glory, The Life of Boies Penrose* (New York, 1931), pp. 55–90, and passim, treats Quay as "a political racketeer" (p. 73), a harsh judgment, but not necessarily incorrect. The author could not get permission to use Quay's papers which are in the possession of Dean James A. Kehl, University of Pittsburgh.

31. Philadelphia *Press*, Apr. 15, 1884.

32. Philadelphia *Press*, Apr. 15, 16, 17, 19, 1884; Pittsburgh *Dispatch*, Apr. 16, 17, 18, 1884.

33. Reid to Garfield, Feb. 3, 1881, Reid Papers; George E. Spencer to Chandler, Feb. 19, 1881, Elkins to Chandler, Feb. 20, 1881, Chandler Papers.

34. Reid to Garfield, Apr. 11, 1881, Reid Papers; Alexander, *Political History*, III, p. 363.

35. Alexander, *Political History*, III, p. 485; Howe, *Arthur*, p. 199.

36. Alexander, *Political History*, III, pp. 492–99; Howe, *Arthur*, pp. 198–203; Blaine to Reid, Apr. 1, 1882, Reid Papers.

37. Richardson, *Chandler*, p. 313; A. E. Daggett to Chandler, Apr. 26,

1882, Platt to Chandler, Nov. 27, Dec. 5, 1883, Chandler Papers; Platt, *Autobiography*, pp. 178–83.

38. Platt, *Autobiography*, pp. 178, 181; Matilda M. Gresham, *Life of Walter Quintin Gresham* (2 vols.; Chicago, 1919), II, p. 501; Lambert, *Elkins*, pp. 98–99; Phelps to Blaine, June 9, 1884: in Dodge, *Blaine*, p. 627.

39. New York *Tribune*, Apr. 21, 22, 23, 25, 1884; New York *Evening Post*, Apr. 22, 1884; Reid to Warner Miller, Apr. 21, 1884, Reid Papers.

40. Elkins to Blaine, Apr. 23, 1884, Papers of James G. Blaine, LC; Theodore Roosevelt to Henry Cabot Lodge, May 5, 1884, in Elting Morison, ed., *The Letters of Theodore Roosevelt* (8 vols.; Cambridge, Mass., 1951–54), I, p. 68.

41. Sherman to Willard Warner, May 5, 1884, "Memorandum for Judge Foraker," n.d., Letterbook 7, pp. 417–23, C. W. Moulton to Sherman, Feb. 18, 1884, J. C. F. Beylan to Sherman, Feb. 29, 1884, Warner Bateman to Sherman, Mar. 11, 1884, Sherman to Henry C. Hedges, May 17, 1884, J. B. Foraker to Sherman, May 21, 1884, Sherman Papers.

42. W. M. Bateman to Sherman, Jan. 12, Mar. 15, May 4, 1884, Sherman to W. M. Bateman, Jan. 15, 1884, Richard Smith to Sherman, Feb. 1, 1884, E. F. Wood to Sherman, Mar. 8, 1884, C. L. Kurtz, [?] Johnson, and "D" [J. C. Donaldson?] to Sherman, Apr. 22, 1884, Sherman Papers; Blaine to Reid, Apr. 21, 1884, Elkins to Reid, May 25, 1884, Reid to West, May 26, 1884, Reid Papers; Harvey S. Ford, ed., "The Diary of John Beatty, January–June, 1884: Part III," *Ohio State Archaeological and Historical Quarterly*, LIX (Jan. 1950), 80–81; Cincinnati *Commercial Gazette*, Apr. 25, 1884.

43. Of Blaine's 334½ votes on the first ballot, 268 came from Republican and doubtful states. Arthur commanded only 45 votes from doubtful states (31 from his home state) to Blaine's 106, and but 29 of 322 votes from clearly Republican states. If Logan's 40 votes from Illinois are added to the Blaine total, the disparity is even more striking. *Proceedings, 1884*, pp. 141–42.

44. West to E. G. Johnson, May 24, 1884, enclosed in E. G. Johnson to Sherman, May 24, 1884, Sherman Papers; C. A. Boutelle to Clarkson, May [?], 1884, Clarkson Papers, ISDHA.

45. *Proceedings, 1884*, pp. 6–23.

46. Of the 334½ votes for Blaine on the first ballot, apparently only 12 votes were cast for Lynch with 4 abstentions. Of the 485½ votes cast for candidates other than Blaine, approximately 412 were cast for Lynch and 65½ for Clayton with 8 abstentions. These figures are approximate: the balloting for presidential candidates was by states, while that for chairman was by individual delegates since the convention had not yet adopted rules. Where the votes can be checked ex-

actly because of roll calls on the presidential vote, out of a total of 44 votes, only one of 16 Blaine delegates voted for Lynch, while 5 of 28 delegates who voted for candidates other than Blaine voted for Clayton. Of these, two who supported Logan perhaps ought to be counted as in the Blaine camp. *Proceedings, 1884,* pp. 10–13, 17–22, 139–42; Cincinnati *Commercial Gazette,* June 4, 1884.

47. *Proceedings, 1884,* pp. 37–39, 43; Muzzey, *Blaine,* pp. 281–83; Cincinnati *Commercial Gazette,* June 4, 5, 1884.

48. C. L. Kurtz to Sherman, May 29, 30, 1884, Byron D. West to Sherman, June 5, 1884, Sherman Papers; Howe, *Arthur,* p. 261; Richardson, *Chandler,* p. 349; Wharton Barker to Harrison, June 9, 1884, Harrison Papers. Indiana gave Blaine 18 of 30 votes on the first ballot: *Proceedings, 1884,* pp. 141–42.

49. W. M. Bateman to Sherman, Apr. 26, 1884, R. C. Parsons to Sherman, Apr. 22, 1884, S. T. Everett to Sherman, Apr. 23, 1884, Henry S. Sherman to Sherman, May 1, 1884, Sherman Papers.

50. C. L. Kurtz to Sherman, June 1, 1884, J. C. Donaldson to Sherman, June 6, 1884, E. E. Wood to Sherman, June 13, 1884, Sherman to Hanna, June 12, 1884, Sherman Papers.

51. Theodore Roosevelt to Anna Roosevelt, June 8, 1884, in Morison, *Letters,* I, pp. 70–72; Hanna to Sherman, June 10, 1884, J. L. Robinson to Sherman, telegram, June 6, 1884, C. L. Kurtz to Sherman, June 8, 1884, Sherman Papers.

52. Elkins to Logan, May 25, 1884, Logan Papers.

53. *Proceedings, 1884,* p. 151.

54. *Ibid.,* pp. 155, 157: the voting totals given above are the sum of the columns, p. 155. Arithmetic errors are common in the printed proceedings.

55. Blaine to Elkins, June 13, 1884, Elkins Papers.

56. Blaine to Elkins, June 24, 1884, Elkins Papers; John P. Montgomery to Clarkson, June 10, 1884, Clarkson Papers, ISDHA; Elkins to Logan, June 15, 1884, Logan Papers; New York *Tribune,* June 26, 27, 1884.

57. Adelbert Bower Sagaser, *The First Two Decades of the Pendleton Act, A Study of Civil Service Reform,* the University Studies of the University of Nebraska (Lincoln, Neb., 1934–35), XXXIV–XXXV, pp. 48–54, 71; Paul P. Van Riper, *History of the United States Civil Service* (Evanston and New York, 1958), pp. 90–94; Ari A. Hoogenboom, *Outlawing the Spoils, A History of the Civil Service Reform Movement 1865–1883* (Urbana, 1961), pp. 226–29, 236–52. Blaine, after the campaign, was convinced that the administration had worked to defeat him. See Blaine to Reid, Dec. 6, 13, 16, 1884, with enclosures, Reid Papers, Box 104, 1884 folder.

58. Fowler, *Cabinet Politician,* p. 186; New York *Tribune,* July 24, 1884. For the legal status of enforced assessments see *Ex Parte Curtis,* 106 U.S. 371 (1882).

59. B. F. Jones to McPherson, July 21, 1884, J. P. D. West to McPherson, Sept. 19, 1884, Samuel Fessenden to McPherson, Sept. 20, 1884, Clarkson to McPherson, Sept. 23, 1884, J. R. Hawley to McPherson, Oct. 19, 1884, McPherson Papers.

60. Blaine to Elkins, Aug. 5, 1884, Elkins Papers; Preston B. Plumb to Harrison, July 3, 1888, Harrison Papers.

61. Muzzey, *Blaine*, pp. 306–7; Elkins to Logan, June 15, 1884, Logan Papers.

62. Chaffee to Logan, Aug. 8, 1884, B. F. Jones to David T. Littler, Aug. 21, 1884, Logan Papers.

63. New York *Tribune*, Oct. 11, 22, Nov. 17, 1884; Elkins to McPherson, Oct. 11, 1884, McPherson Papers. While there is no direct evidence on St. John's relation to the Democrats in 1884, in the next presidential campaign he was in the pay of the Democratic National Committee. See William L. Scott to Daniel Lamont, Sept. 14, 1888, Cleveland Papers; J. R. Burton to Harrison, Aug. 6, 1888, Harrison Papers.

64. Blaine to Elkins, July 27, 1884, Elkins Papers; Hans Louis Trefousse, *Ben Butler: The South Called Him BEAST!* (New York, 1957), pp. 250–51; Richard S. West, Jr., *Lincoln's Scapegoat General, A Life of Benjamin Butler, 1818–1893* (Boston, 1965), pp. 383, 399–401; Richardson, *Chandler*, pp. 350–53; New York *Tribune*, Aug. 9, 19, 31, 1884.

65. Quoted in Muzzey, *Blaine*, pp. 296–97.

66. Blaine to Reid, June 28, July 27, Sept. 17, 1884, Reid Papers; Harrison C. Thomas, *The Return of the Democratic Party to Power in 1884* (New York, 1919), p. 204. For a discriminating portrait of the Mugwumps see Geoffrey Blodgett, *The Gentle Reformers; Massachusetts Democrats in the Cleveland Era* (Cambridge, Mass., 1966), esp. chapter 2. See also John G. Sproat, *"The Best Men."*

67. Hirshson, *Farewell to the Bloody Shirt*, pp. 124–26; New York *Tribune*, Oct. 2, 1884; G. F. Dawson to Logan, Oct. 8, 1884, M. Woodhull to Logan, Oct. 17, 1884, Logan Papers; M. Woodhull to Chandler, Sept. 30, 1884, Reid to Chandler, Sept. 27, 1884, Reid Papers.

68. John J. Cavanaugh to Harrison, Oct. 10, 1888, Harrison Papers.

69. Thomas N. Brown, *Irish-American Nationalism, 1870–1890* (Philadelphia, 1966) is an excellent study. See especially chapter VIII.

70. Muzzey, *Blaine*, p. 309; G. F. Dawson to Logan, Oct. 8, 1884, Logan Papers.

71. Sherman to Reid, Sept. 9, 1884, Blaine to Reid, June 13, 1884, Reid to Blaine, June 25, 1884, Blaine to Phelps, Aug. 2, 1884, Reid Papers; Muzzey, *Blaine*, pp. 310, 313; New York *Tribune*, Oct. 27, 1884. For Reid and the unions in 1892 see Lemuel E. Quigg to Reid, May 24, 1892, Reid Papers; Reid to Harrison, June 29, 1892, Harrison Papers.

72. Muzzey, *Blaine*, p. 313; Howe, *Arthur*, p. 123.

73. Thomas, *Return of the Democratic Party*, pp. 121–24; Shelby M. Cullom to Logan, July 31, 1884, B. F. Jones to Logan, Sept. 2, 1884,

G. F. Dawson to Logan, Oct. 8, 1884, Logan Papers; John Hay to Reid, Aug. 31, 1884, Clarkson to Jay Gould, Oct. 6, 1884, Elkins to Reid, Oct. 6, 8, 1884, B. F. Jones to Reid, Oct. 9, 1884, Reid Papers; Clarkson to Harrison, Apr. 23, 1892, Harrison Papers.

74. Sherman to Reid, Sept. 9, 1884, Clarkson to Gould, Oct. 6, 1884, Reid Papers; Blaine to Elkins, Aug. 5, 1884, Elkins Papers; Sherman to Elkins, Sept. 1, 1884, Sherman Papers; Dudley to Harrison, Aug. 14, 24, 1884, Harrison Papers; Allan Nevins, *Grover Cleveland, A Study in Courage* (New York, 1933), p. 172.

75. Blaine to Elkins, Aug. 5, 1884, Elkins Papers; Elkins to Reid, Oct. 4, 6, 8, 1884, Reid to Elkins, Oct. 8, 1884, Clarkson to Gould and notation Gould to Reid, Oct. 6, 1884, B. F. Jones to Reid, Oct. 8, 1884, Reid Papers; D. McConville to W. C. Whitney, Aug. 4, 1892, Whitney Papers. On Blaine's personal contributions see Clarkson to William Loeb, Jr., Aug. 19, 1906, Papers of Theodore Roosevelt, LC; Blaine to Reid, Jan. 26, 1888, Reid Papers.

76. Harrison to Wharton Barker, Oct. 25, Nov. 1, 25, 1884, Barker to Harrison, Oct. 30, 1884, Barker Papers; Clarkson to Harrison, Oct. 15, 1888, Harrison Papers.

77. Jones to Logan, Oct. 19, 1884, Logan Papers.

78. Muzzey, *Blaine*, pp. 314–16; J. C. Reed to Frederick J. Phillips, July 9, 1884, Arthur Papers; John B. Harrilton to Logan, Aug. 26, 1884, Logan Papers; Reid to Blaine, Oct. 18, 1884, Reid to M. H. DeYoung, n.d., Blaine to Reid, Dec. 19, 1884, Reid Papers; R. H. Guinness to Daniel Lamont, Dec. 21, 1887, Cleveland Papers.

79. Blaine to Reid, telegram, Oct. 18, 1884, Reid to Blaine, Oct. 18, 1884, Reid Papers; Blaine to Elkins, Oct. 19, 1884, Elkins Papers; Nevins, *Cleveland*, pp. 182–83.

80. Reid to Blaine, Oct. 18, 1884, Reid Papers; Nevins, *Cleveland*, pp. 184–85; William Gorham Rice and Francis Lynde Stetson, "Was New York's Vote Stolen?" *North American Review*, CXCIX (Jan. 1914), 92; McCormick to Major Bickham, Nov. 5, 1884, "W——— of Fordham" to Logan, Nov. 10, 1884, Logan Papers. Brown, *Irish-American Nationalism*, pp. 141–43 doubts that the Burchard incident had very much impact. Undoubtedly this is true, weighted against the statistics of New York State voting. It was no more responsible than numerous other accidental factors. Republican politicians attributed the loss of only a few thousand votes to it, but that was enough in 1884. See Reid to John Hay, Dec. 1, 1884, Reid Papers.

81. Muzzey, *Blaine*, pp. 318–20.

82. Benson, "Research Problems in American Political Historiography," pp. 123–46, is a perceptive discussion of the pitfalls of interpreting this election in terms of particular incidents and issues.

83. Clarkson to Elkins, Feb. 2, 1887, Elkins Papers.

CHAPTER IV

1. Clarkson to Elkins, Feb. 2, 1887, B. F. Jones to Elkins, Mar. 1, 1887, Jan. 24, Apr. 25, 1888, Elkins Papers; Jones to Clarkson, Apr. 8, 1888, Clarkson Papers, ISDHA.

2. Blaine to Elkins, June 30, 1887, R. C. Kerens to Elkins, June 2, 1887, Jones to Elkins, Aug. 25, 1887, Elkins Papers; Nathaniel M. Hubbard to Allison, Aug. 6, 1887, Allison Papers.

3. Republican Party, *Official Proceedings of the Republican National Conventions, 1884–1888* (Minneapolis, 1903), 1888 convention, pp. 8–9 (hereafter cited as *Proceedings, 1888*).

4. Philadelphia *Press*, editorial, Dec. 11, 1887; George F. Spinney to Daniel Lamont, Dec. 17, 1887, Cleveland Papers; Reid to John Hay, June 9, 1886, Blaine to Reid, Oct. 11, 1887, Reid to Blaine, Jan. 2, 1888, Reid Papers; Muzzey, *Blaine*, pp. 356–57.

5. Blaine to B. F. Jones, Jan. 25, 1888, Blaine to Patrick Ford, Jan. [ ], 1888: in Dodge, *Blaine*, pp. 603–4; Blaine to Reid, Jan. 12, 1888, Reid Papers; Mabel Abigail Dodge to Elkins, Jan. 24, 1888, Elkins Papers.

6. Blaine to Elkins, Mar. 1, 1888, Elkins Papers; Blaine to Harrison, July 19, 1888, Harrison Papers. For informed estimates of the party's chances in these states see Reid to Blaine, Dec. 23, 1887, Blaine to Reid, Jan. 26, 1888, Reid Papers; S. B. Benson to Harrison, Nov. 9, 1887, D. S. Alexander to Harrison, Nov. 13, 1887, Harrison Papers; Clarkson to Jacob Rich, Nov. 16, 1887, Clarkson to Allison, Apr. 25, 1888, Allison Papers.

7. Reid to Blaine, Dec. 23, 1887, Reid to John Hay, Mar. 16, 20, 1888, Phelps to Reid, June 10, 1888, Reid Papers; Roswell P. Flower to Cleveland, Apr. 17, 1888, Cleveland Papers; Elkins to Harrison, Feb. 27, 1888, Harrison Papers. For the responses of the other candidates and their managers see Louis T. Michener to Elkins, Mar. 9, Apr. 20, 1888, Clarkson to Elkins, May 18, 1888, Elkins Papers; Reid to Phelps, May 22, 1888, Reid Papers; Elkins to Harrison, Feb. 27, 1888, Sherman to Harrison, June 30, 1888, Harrison Papers.

8. Harry J. Sievers, *Benjamin Harrison, Hoosier Statesman* (New York, 1959), passim. For Harrison's availability see pp. 316–28; Wharton Barker to Harrison, Nov. 21, 1884, Preston B. Plumb to Harrison, Nov. 10, 1886, Dudley to Harrison, Dec. 19, 1887, Harrison Papers.

9. Sievers, *Hoosier Statesman*, pp. 294–98; D. S. Alexander to Russell B. Harrison, July 26, 1883, James M. Johnson to R. B. Harrison, telegrams, June 2, July 11, 13, 1885, Benjamin Harrison to R. B. Harrison, May 28, June 6, Aug. 9, 11, 12, 20, 1886, Elkins to R. B. Harrison, July 4, 11, 22, 26, 29, Aug. 3, 11, 30, Sept. 15, 27, 1886, Feb. 28, Mar. 24, Sept. 4, Oct. 12, 14, 20, Nov. 14, 1891, Apr. 1, 15, 17, 1892, Tom Moore, Jr. to R. B. Harrison, Dec. 2, 1886, W. H. H. Miller to R. B. Harrison, July 14, 1886, R. C. Kerens to R. B. Harrison, Nov. 6, 1891, R. B.

Harrison to B. Harrison, Dec. 1891 (In Dec. 25–31 file), R. B. Harrison to Elkins, Sept. 18, Dec. 14, 1895, Papers of Russell B. Harrison, Lilly Library (Bloomington, Ind.); R. B. Harrison to Elkins, Jan. 25, 1887, July 30, 1888, June 28, July 2, 1891, Judge Cyrus C. Hines to Elkins, Jan. 26, Feb. 1, 1887, B. Harrison to Elkins, June 30, July 18, 1887, Elkins to H. G. Davis, Sept. 29, 1889, Elkins Papers; Elkins to Harrison, Aug. 11, Oct. 9, Nov. 13, 1886, Harrison to C. C. Hines, June 28, 1886, Harrison Papers.

10. Sievers, *Hoosier Statesman*, pp. 309–11; Elkins to Harrison, Feb. 11, 14, Mar. 31, 1888, Harrison Papers.

11. Elkins to Michener, Mar. 21, 1888, Papers of Louis T. Michener, LC; Harrison to Elkins, Jan. 7, 1888, Michener to Elkins, Apr. 20, 1888, Elkins Papers; Dudley to Harrison, Dec. 19, 1887, Elkins to Harrison, Feb. 27, May 7, 1888, Harrison Papers; Gresham, *Gresham*, II, pp. 567–68.

12. Elkins to Harrison, Feb. 14, 27, 1888, Harrison Papers.

13. M. A. Dodge to Elkins, Apr. 13, 1888, Clarkson to Elkins, May 18, 1888, Elkins Papers; Elkins to Reid, Apr. 23, 1888, W. A. Hamill and C. M. Donaldson to Elkins, May 15, 1888, J. T. Robeson and T. C. Muse to Elkins, May 16, 1888, Reid to Phelps, May 22, 1888, Reid Papers.

14. Clarkson to Jacob Rich, Nov. 16, 1887, Clarkson to Allison, Apr. 25, 26, 27, May 6, 9, 25, 29, 1888, Clarkson to D. B. Henderson, telegram, May 30, 1888, Allison Papers; Clarkson to Elkins, May 18, 1888, Elkins Papers; Hanna to J. B. Foraker, Mar. 27, 1888, in Joseph Benson Foraker, *Notes of a Busy Life* (2 vols.; Cincinnati, 1916), I, p. 326.

15. Herbert Croly, *Marcus Alonzo Hanna* (New York, 1912), pp. 131, 138; Gresham, *Gresham*, II, p. 574; Harrison to Michener, Feb. 22, 1887, Harrison Papers; Hiscock to Reid, Feb. 25, 1888, John Hay to Reid, Mar. 16, 1888, Blaine to Reid, July 6, 1888, Reid Papers; Thomas Nichols to W. H. Smith, May 23, 1888, Sherman to Smith, May 25, 1888, William Henry Smith Papers.

16. Muzzey, *Blaine*, p. 375; Harriet S. B. Beale, ed., *The Letters of Mrs. James G. Blaine* (2 vols.; New York, 1908), II, pp. 185–86; Elkins to Harrison, Feb. 14, 1888, Elkins to Michener, June 10, 1888, Harrison Papers; Reid to Murat Halstead, Feb. 16, 1888, C. A. Boutelle to Reid, Feb. 24, 1888, Hiscock to Reid, Feb. 25, 1888, Reid Papers; Alexander, *Political History*, IV, pp. 116–17, 129–30.

17. Foraker, *Notes*, I, pp. 240–65; Foraker's expression is on p. 254, Sherman's is quoted on p. 264. See also Clarkson to Jacob Rich, Nov. 16, 1887, Allison Papers.

18. Foraker, *Notes*, I, p. 253, Thomas E. Felt, "The Rise of Mark Hanna" (unpublished Ph.D. dissertation, Michigan State University, 1960), p. 157.

19. Barker to Sherman, Dec. 24, 1887, Feb. 5, 1888, Sherman to Barker,

Dec. 27, 1887, Jan. 20, 1888, Barker Papers; Charles A. Sinn to Cleveland, June 12, 1888, Cleveland Papers; Foraker, *Notes,* I, pp. 323–35; Blaine to Reid, July 6, 1888, Reid Papers; *The New York Times,* June 19, 1888.

20. Hiscock to Reid, Feb. 25, 1888, Reid Papers.

21. Edward A. White, "The Republican Party in National Politics, 1888–1891" (unpublished Ph.D. dissertation, University of Wisconsin, 1941), p. 81; Phelps to Reid, Mar. 20, 1888, Platt to Reid, Apr. 10, 1888, Reid Papers; Alexander, *Political History,* IV, pp. 116–17; Platt, *Autobiography,* p. 205.

22. Alexander, *Political History,* IV, p. 116; Elkins to Reid, May 15, 1888, Reid to Phelps, May 22, 1888, Phelps to Reid, May 25, 1888, Reid to Depew, May 26, 1888, Reid Papers; B. F. Jones to Elkins, May 21, 1888, Elkins Papers; Elkins to Harrison, May 7, 1888, Harrison Papers; Elkins to Michener, May 8, 1888, Michener Papers; Elkins to Clarkson, May 6, 1888: in Sievers, *Hoosier Statesman,* p. 327.

23. Elkins to Reid, May 12, 1888, Reid Papers; Sherman to Barker, May 21, 1888, Sherman to Hanna, telegram, June 19, 1888, Sherman Papers.

24. Indianapolis *News,* May 22, 1888; Reid to Phelps, May 22, 1888, Blaine to Reid, May 17, 1888, Reid Papers. The letter was written on the fourteenth, and for some unknown reason dated the seventeenth; see the covering letter, Blaine to Reid, May 14, 1888 and telegram, May 14, 1888, Reid Papers.

25. Platt to Reid, May 29, 1888, Reid to Phelps, May 22, 1888, E. Lambert to Reid, May 28, 1888, Phelps to Reid, May 29, 1888, Reid to Elkins, June 1, 1888, Reid to M. H. DeYoung, June 2, 1888, Phelps to Reid, June 10, 1888, Reid Papers; Barker to Harrison, June 4, 1888, Elkins to Michener, June 10, 1888, Harrison Papers; Michener to Barker, June 5, 1888, Barker Papers.

26. Platt and Hiscock to Sherman, telegram, June 24, 1888, Sherman Papers; Gresham, *Gresham,* II, pp. 577–82; Phelps to Reid, June 10, 13, 1888, Reid Papers; Alexander, *Political History,* IV, p. 119.

27. Sievers, *Hoosier Statesman,* p. 326; Elkins to Reid, June 8, 1888, Reid Papers; Elkins to Michener, June 10, 1888, Elkins to Harrison, June 13, 1888, W. H. H. Miller to Michener, June 15, 1888, Harrison Papers; Dodge, *Blaine,* p. 607.

28. Clarkson to Elkins, May 18, 1888, Elkins Papers; Dodge, *Blaine,* p. 607; *Proceedings, 1888,* pp. 11–14, 41, 159–60.

29. Reid to Phelps, May 22, 1888, Elkins to Reid, May 15, 1888, Reid Papers; Indianapolis *News,* June 19, 22, 1888; Chicago *Tribune,* June 21–25, 1888.

30. *The New York Times,* June 19, 22, 23, 1888; Indianapolis *News,* June 22, 1888; Sherman to Hanna, telegram, June 19, 1888, Sherman Papers; James W. Husted to Harrison, June 22, 1888, Harrison Papers.

31. *Proceedings, 1888,* pp. 152–71.

32. *The New York Times,* June 22, 23, 24, 1888, Indianapolis *News,* June 23, 1888, Chicago *Tribune,* June 24, 1888; Hanna to Sherman, June 15, 1888, telegram, June 22, 1888, Sherman Papers; Muzzey, *Blaine,* pp. 376–79.

33. *Proceedings, 1888,* pp. 173–82; Indianapolis *News,* June 23, 1888; *The New York Times,* June 24, 25, 1888; W. H. Smith to Reid, telegram, June 23, 1888, Reid Papers; W. H. Smith to Sherman, June 25, 1888, W. H. Smith Papers; Foraker, *Notes,* I, pp. 366–67.

34. *The New York Times,* June 24, 1888; Platt, *Autobiography,* p. 205. W. H. Smith to Reid, telegram, June 23, 1888, Reid Papers; Smith to Reid, June 24, 1888, Smith to Sherman, June 25, 1888, William Henry Smith Papers.

35. *The New York Times,* June 24, 25, 1888. Root's dispatches were signed "F.D.R."

36. Halstead to Sherman, telegram, June 23, 1888, Hanna to Sherman, telegram, June 23, 1888, Sherman Papers; Indianapolis *News,* June 23, 1888; Foraker, *Notes,* I, pp. 342–44.

37. Sherman to Hanna, telegram, June 23, 1888, Sherman Papers. Cf. Sherman to Harrison, June 30, 1888, Harrison Papers; Foraker to R. McCurdy, Aug. 27, 1888: in Morgan, *McKinley,* p. 101.

38. *The New York Times,* June 25, 1888; White, "Republican Party," p. 81; Hanna to Sherman, telegram, June 22, 1888, Sherman Papers; Morgan, *McKinley,* p. 543, n. 27; Gresham, *Gresham,* II, pp. 572–99: the quotation is on p. 599.

39. Gresham, *Gresham,* II, pp. 572–99; White, "Republican Party," pp. 12, 19; Quay to Sherman, June 12, 1888, Sherman to Hanna, June 19, 1888, Hanna to Sherman, June 15, 22, 25, 1888, Cameron to Quay, telegrams, June 25, 1888, Sherman Papers; John B. Elam and Michener to Harrison, June 17, 1888, Michener Papers; Harry H. Smith to Harrison, July 9, 1888, [unsigned] to William M. Bayne, June 23, 1888, Harrison Papers. This last was a pledge letter which Harrison was asked to sign. On the envelope of the letter he wrote "I said 'no.' "

40. White, "Republican Party," p. 143; Reid to Depew, June 24, 1888, Reid Papers; Platt and Hiscock to Sherman, telegram, June 24, 1888, Sherman Papers; Alexander, *Political History,* IV, pp. 120–21; J. H. Woodard to Harrison, Nov. 9, 1888, Harrison Papers.

41. *Proceedings, 1888,* p. 175; Gresham, *Gresham,* II, pp. 598–600; *The New York Times,* June 24, 25, 1888. For knowledge of Harrison's connection with Elkins, see Chicago *Tribune,* June 22, 1888.

42. Muzzey, *Blaine,* p. 379; Andrew Carnegie to Reid, telegram, June 25, 1888, Blaine to Reid, July 6, 1888, Reid Papers.

43. Since the publication of Nathaniel W. Stephenson, *Nelson W. Aldrich, A Leader in American Politics* (New York, 1930) some accounts have mentioned the sending of a secret envoy to Harrison in Indianapolis by the anti-Blaine group. See Josephson, *The Politicos,* p. 418; and

Leland L. Sage, *William Boyd Allison: A Study in Practical Politics* (Iowa City, Iowa, 1956), pp. 224–25.

This story (in Stephenson, *Aldrich*, pp. 71–72, 434) is almost certainly false. There is no contemporary evidence for it. Elkins went to great lengths to keep his earlier meeting with Harrison secret, yet the Indianapolis newspapers knew about it. See Indianapolis *News*, June 18, 1888. A conference with five men at the climactic moment of the convention could hardly escape detection. The whole story is based on a recollection of almost forty years later by Nicholas Murray Butler, who admitted to Stephenson that "I have gotten to the point where I hesitate to make any statement relative to my past experiences without checking up my memory by the record" (Butler to N. W. Stephenson, Feb. 10, 1927, Papers of Nelson W. Aldrich, LC, Box 52).

Butler first said that the envoy was "to make certain that Harrison would accept." When his interviewer, Jeanette P. Nichols, discovered that this reason was absurd, she queried him and he changed the story. The men had to find out "if they could feel that they understood him and he them" (J. Nichols, Notes, 1888, Aldrich Papers, Box 46). Butler's confused recollection is not difficult to explain. Aldrich *was* an emissary of the anti-Blaine group in negotiations having to do with Harrison's nomination. But these negotiations were with the New York delegation in Chicago—a much more sensible place to inquire about Harrison's chances than in Indianapolis. See the Chicago *Tribune*, June 24, 25, 1888 for detailed reports on the various conferences.

44. Gresham, *Gresham*, II, pp. 599–600; Sage, *Allison*, pp. 226–27; Phelps to Harrison, telegram, June 25, 1888, Harrison Papers; W. H. Smith to Sherman, June 25, 1888, W. H. Smith Papers.

45. Harrison to Blaine, June 30, 1888, Sherman to Harrison, June 30, 1888, Harrison Papers; Sage, *Allison*, p. 226; Gresham, *Gresham*, II, pp. 577, 585–86, 598; Indianapolis *News*, June 26, 1888; Indianapolis *Journal*, June 26, 1888 (italics supplied).

46. Clarkson to Harrison, June 30, July 3, Oct. 1, 15, 1888, Harry H. Smith to Harrison, July 9, 1888, Harrison Papers; Elkins to Michener, July 6, 1888, Michener Papers; Indianapolis *News*, June 19, 27, 1888; *The New York Times*, July 13, 1888; Sievers, *Hoosier Statesman*, p. 366.

47. Clarkson to Harrison, June 30, 1888, Sherman to Harrison, July 13, 1888, Harrison Papers; Harrison to Sherman, July 14, 1888, Sherman Papers; *The New York Times*, July 11, 12, 1888.

48. Clarkson to Jacob Rich, Nov. 16, 1887, Allison Papers; New York *Tribune*, June 21, 1888; Indianapolis *News*, June 22, 1888; Hirshson, *Farewell to the Bloody Shirt*, pp. 158–65; Rayford W. Logan, *The Betrayal of the Negro, from Rutherford B. Hayes to Woodrow Wilson*

(New York, 1965), p. 218; Sievers, *Hoosier Statesman,* p. 361; Clarkson to Harrison, July 25, 1888, Reid to Harrison, Sept. 25, 1888, Harrison to Reid, Sept. 27, 1888, Reid to Harrison, Oct. 6, 1888, Harrison Papers; J. Sloat Fassett to Reid, Sept. 26, 1888, Reid Papers. On midwestern hostility to the tariff emphasis see Joseph Medill to Harrison, Sept. 16, 1888, Eugene G. Hay to Harrison, Aug. 10, 1888, Harrison Papers; Medill to Allison, Sept. 23, 1888, Allison Papers.

49. Reid to Hiscock, July 23, 1888, Chandler to Reid, July 25, 1888, Hiscock to Reid, July 26, 1888, Reid to Phelps, Sept. 24, 1888, Reid Papers; W. E. Barrett to Harrison, July 25, 1888, Medill to Harrison, Aug. 2, Sept. 16, 1888, Sherman to Harrison, Aug. 4, 17, Sept. 12, 1888, Allison to Harrison, Oct. 13, 1888, Harrison Papers; Nevins, *Cleveland,* p. 432; Sage, *Allison,* pp. 231–32; *Harper's Weekly,* XXXII (Oct. 13, 1888), 769.

50. Hiscock to Reid, July 19, 26, 1888, Reid Papers; Sage, *Allison,* p. 232; Rothman, *Politics and Power,* pp. 90–92. Rothman argues (p. 90) that the Republican Senator's binding caucus was not the result of "national declarations," but of the "new role of the Senate party organization," and that the Senate tariff bill "proved" that Republican Senators were "willing and able to formulate a tariff and compromise their differences" (p. 92). He quotes from Hiscock's letter to Reid of July 26, but overlooks the passage in which Hiscock specifies that the bill is not designed to become a tariff law. See also the letter cited in footnote 51 for John Sherman's similar understanding of the bill.

51. Sherman to Harrison, Oct. 1, 1888, Allison to Harrison, Oct. 13, 1888, Harrison Papers; Medill to Allison, Oct. 12, 1888, Allison Papers.

52. Blaine to Reid, Jan. 26, 1888, Reid Papers; Clarkson to William Loeb, Jr., Aug. 19, 1906, Theodore Roosevelt Papers; Josephson, *The Politicos,* pp. 424–25; *The Nation,* XLVII (July 26, 1888), 64.

53. *The New York Times,* July 13, 1888; Josephson, *The Politicos,* p. 422; Sievers, *Hoosier Statesman,* p. 357, n. 26; Ida M. Tarbell, *The Tariff In Our Times* (New York, 1911), pp. 173–75.

54. J. M. Swank to Hanna, Feb. 28, 1896, Papers of William McKinley, LC.

55. Quoted in A. T. Volwiler, "Tariff Strategy and Propaganda, 1887–1888," *American Historical Review,* XXXVI (Oct. 1930), 96. (This journal hereafter cited as *AHR.*) Rothman, *Politics and Power,* p. 187, interprets this letter very differently. I think the disclaimer of "improper means" far less important than that Swank got precisely the rate he demanded.

56. U.S. Congress, *Senate Reports,* 50th Cong., 1st Sess., 1887–88, IX, Rept. 2332, p. 930.

57. Nevins, *Cleveland,* pp. 418–19; Volwiler, "Tariff Strategy," 81–88. For the size of the leaflets, see Swank's "Confidential Circular," n.d., Harrison Papers, v. 42, folio 9310.

58. Volwiler, "Tariff Strategy," 92–94; Barker to Harrison, June 30, 1888, Barker Papers. For the tariff schedules, see U.S. Congress, *Congressional Record*, 50th Cong., 1st Sess., 1887–88, XIX, part 10, p. 9580. The estimate of the size of the fund is based on Swank's report to Allison. Late in September he had collected $37,000 after having tapped the entire membership of the Association. He promised another $35,000 to $40,000 by soliciting them for a duplication of their previous checks: Volwiler, "Tariff Strategy," 94–96.

59. Herbert A. Gibbons, *John Wanamaker*, (2 vols.; New York, 1926), I, pp. 253–54; *The Nation*, XLVII (July 5, 1888), 1; James H. Coyle to Harrison, July 26, 1888, Harrison Papers; C. E. Smith to Michener, June 29, Aug. 2, 1888, Michener Papers. The letter of August 2 uses a code for the names of the principals. By context and comparison with other sources I assign the following identifications: "Mary"—Wanamaker, "Frances"—Dolan, "Atlantic"—Quay, "Charter"—cabinet position (promised to Pennsylvania, but whether or not definitely to Wanamaker is uncertain), "Mexico"—John C. New, "Sunrise"—Harrison. I have been unable to identify "Union." On Dolan see *DAB*, III, pp. 355–56.

60. C. E. Smith to Michener, Aug. 2, 1888 (the various letters in the text are quoted *verbatim* in this letter), Smith to Michener, Nov. 10, 1888, Michener Papers.

61. Gibbons, *Wanamaker*, I, pp. 257–59; *The New York Times*, Oct. 5, 1888, *The Nation*, XLVII (Nov. 22, 1888), 404, (Nov. 29, 1888), 428; White, "Republican Party," pp. 185–86; William Foyle to Daniel Lamont, Oct. 6, 1888, Cleveand Papers; Barker to Harrison, Oct. 9, 1888, Barker Papers.

62. Felt, "Rise of Mark Hanna," pp. 148–49; R. B. Harrison to Benjamin Harrison, July 28, 1888, Harrison Papers.

63. W. H. Marston to George C. Bliss, June 26, 1888, Horace K. Thurber to Morton, July 6, 19, 1888, Papers of Levi P. Morton, New York Public Library; Cornelius N. Bliss to Reid, Sept. 13, 1888, Reid Papers; B. F. Jones to Elkins, Aug. 31, 1888, Elkins Papers; *The Nation*, XLVII (Nov. 29, 1888), 425, (Dec. 6, 1888), 433. The quotation about the political "market" is in *The Nation*, XLVII (Nov. 22, 1888), 406.

64. A. E. Bateman to Reid, July 20, 1888, Reid Papers; C. L. Kurtz to Sherman, May 25, 1884, C. D. Firestone to Sherman, May 28, 1884, Sherman Papers; Allan Nevins, *Abram S. Hewitt, with Some Account of Peter Cooper* (New York, 1935), p. 521; Croly, *Hanna*, pp. 51–52, 108–114; Josephson, *The Politicos*, pp. 83, 101–2.

65. Speech of James S. Clarkson delivered at Louisville, Ky. May 10, 1893, Clarkson Papers, LC.

66. Moisei Ostrogorski, *Democracy and the Party System* (New York, 1910), pp. 167–68; Philadelphia *Press*, Dec. 16, 1887; George F. Spinney

to Daniel Lamont, Dec. 17, 1887, Silas W. Burt to Lamont, Dec. 20, 1887, Cleveland Papers; *The New York Times,* July 12, 13, 1888; Volwiler, "Tariff Strategy," 81–88; *The Nation,* XLVII (Sept. 20, 1888), 222.

67. B. F. Jones to Logan, Sept. 2, 1884, Logan Papers; T. A. Fulton to Lamont, June 15, 1888, Cleveland Papers; Barker to Harrison, Aug. 6, 1888, Barker Papers; *The Nation,* XLVII (Aug. 16, 1888), 121, (Aug. 23, 1888), 142.

68. Josephson. *The Politicos,* pp. 71–76 and passim; *The Nation,* XLVII (Nov. 29, 1888), 428.

69. Calvin S. Brice to Lamont, Sept. 11, 1888, Cleveland Papers; *Harper's Weekly,* XXXII (Oct. 6, 1888), 761–68. The Republicans had 182 electoral votes from states that required little or no outside help, while the Democrats had only 153 from the safe Southern and border states. The Republicans needed an additional 19 votes from doubtful states to the Democrats' 48. New York had 26 electoral votes, Indiana 15, New Jersey 9, and Connecticut 6.

70. Warner Miller to Harrison, Nov. 10, 1888, Blaine to Harrison, Nov. 9, 1888, Harrison Papers; S. P. Sheerin to Lamont, Sept. 12, 1888, Cleveland Papers.

71. Platt to Harrison, July 7, 1888, Clarkson to Harrison, Nov. 2, 1888, Harrison Papers; Platt to Reid, Sept. 21, 1888, Reid Papers.

72. R. B. Harrison to Benjamin Harrison, G. D. Meiklejohn to T. Butterfield, Aug. 8, 1888, Eugene G. Hay to Harrison, Aug. 10, 1888, Harrison Papers; Charles Beardsley to Clarkson, Sept. 21, 1888, Clarkson Papers, ISDHA; Beardsley to Allison, Sept. 11, 20, 22, 1888, Clarkson to Allison, Sept. 15, 1888, Allison Papers.

73. Reid to A. E. Bateman, July 18, 1888, Reid Papers; Basil B. Gordon to Cleveland, Sept. 9, 1892, Cleveland Papers; Anthony Higgins to Barker, Oct. 5, Nov. 1, 1888, H. C. Parsons to Barker, Oct. 26, 1888, Levi P. Morton to Barker, Oct. 30, 1888, Barker Papers; Gerald Wayne Smith, *Nathan Goff, Jr., A Biography* (Charleston, W. Va., 1959), p. 165; Nelson Blake, *William Mahone of Virginia* (Richmond, Va., 1935), pp. 238–43; DeSantis, *Republicans Face the Southern Question,* pp. 191–92.

74. N. H. Stewart to Cleveland, Dec. 6, 1887, John A. Mason to Lamont, Dec. 7, 1887, John H. Reagan to Cleveland, July 7, 1888, Cleveland Papers; Eugene G. Hay to Harrison, Aug. 10, 1888, Harrison Papers; William E. Chandler, *The Growth of the Use of Money in Politics and of the Railroad Power in New Hampshire* (Concord, N.H., 1899), pp. 6–9.

75. J. N. Huston to Elkins, Oct. 15, 1888, Elkins Papers; Wm. H. English to Cleveland, July 8, 1888, Cleveland Papers.

76. Blaine to Harrison, Oct. 7, 1888, Clarkson to Harrison, Oct. 1, 15, 1888, Murat Halstead to Harrison, Oct. 16, 1888, Harrison Papers; Sievers, *Hoosier Statesman,* p. 404.

77. Reid to Harrison, Sept. 25, Oct. 6, 16, 1888, Harrison to Reid, Sept. 27, Oct. 9, 1888, Clarkson to Harrison, Oct. 15, 1888, Harrison Papers.

78. Halstead to Harrison, Oct. 23, 1888, Blaine to Harrison, Oct. 25, 1888, Harrison Papers.

79. Clarkson to Harrison, Oct. 15, 1888, Harrison Papers; Dudley to "Dear Sir," Oct. 24, 1888, Cleveland Papers; "The Battle in the State in 1888," Memorandum, Michener Papers; Indianapolis *News*, Nov. 1, 2, 3, 4, 5, 1888; Sievers, *Hoosier Statesman*, p. 419; Gresham, *Gresham*, II, p. 605.

80. Indianapolis *News*, Oct. 31, 1888; Gresham, *Gresham*, II, p. 605; Reid to Harrison, Nov. 3, 1888, Harrison Papers; Nevins, *Cleveland*, pp. 438–39; Bloomington *Saturday Courier*, Nov. 3, 10, 17, 1888; Bloomington *Telephone*, Dec. 11, 1888; Josephson, *The Politicos*, p. 433. For similar Democratic circulars see Harrison to Reid, Oct. 9, 1888, Reid Papers.

81. Platt to Harrison, July 7, 1888, C. E. Smith to Michener, Aug. 3, 1888, F. E. Coe to Harrison, Sept. 8, 1888, Clarkson to Harrison, Nov. 2, 1888, J. N. Knapp to Harrison, Nov. 10, 1888, Harrison Papers; Barker to Platt, Oct. 16, 1888, Barker Papers; Alexander, *Political History*, IV, p. 122.

82. Clarkson to Harrison, Nov. 2, 1888, Harrison Papers; John Devoy to Barker, Oct. 30, 1888, Barker Papers; Edward T. Wood to Cleveland, Sept. 17, 1888, Edward Cooper to Lamont, Nov. 5, 1888, C. Augustus Haviland to Cleveland, Nov. 11, 1888, Cleveland Papers; Nevins, *Cleveland*, p. 427; Nevins, *Hewitt*, pp. 523–26.

83. Nevins, *Hewitt*, pp. 468–69, 521–27; John B. Riley to Lamont, Oct. 4, 1888, Thomas Duffy to Lamont, Oct. 14, 1888, Cleveland Papers; John Devoy to Barker, Oct. 30, 1888, Barker Papers.

84. Herbert J. Bass, *"I am a Democrat," The Political Career of David Bennett Hill* (Syracuse, 1961), pp. 81–92; Cleveland to W. S. Bissell, Jan. 3, 1888, Cleveland Papers; Platt to Reid, Sept. 21, 1888, Reid Papers. Both Bass, *David Bennett Hill*, p. 110, and Nevins, *Cleveland*, p. 424, maintain that Cleveland—as he continually asserted at the time—simply kept his hands off the New York gubernatorial situation. But a number of letters make clear that he actively stifled Hill's opposition. He apparently believed that he needed Hill on the ticket to win in New York, even though he refused to give Hill his public endorsement out of fear of losing the independent vote. See Cleveland to W. R. Grace, July 14, 1888, W. R. Grace to Cleveland, July 16, 1888, Cleveland to W. S. Bissell, July 17, 1888, Cleveland Papers.

85. Platt to Reid, Sept. 21, 1888, Reid Papers; W. M. Ivins to Lamont, Aug. 11, 1888, G. W. Green to Lamont, Sept. 28, 1888, Daniel W. McCauley to Cleveland, Oct. 1, 1888, A. C. McGlachlin to Lamont, Oct. 15, 1888, Cleveland Papers; W. Scott O'Connor to Harrison, Oct. 24, 1888, Harrison Papers; Alexander, *Political History*, IV, pp.

113, 129. Charles Foster to E. W. Halford, May 25, 1892, Harrison Papers, describes a visit by "Wm. Grace of NY" asking to be "recognized" with a place as shipping commissioner. Given Grace's interests in South American trade, this was almost certainly either Grace himself or his son William Russell Grace, Jr. It is hard to imagine anything other than the 1888 election for which he could seek to be recognized by the Harrison administration. In 1892 Grace was cooperating with Platt in New York: see James R. O'Barne [?] to Harrison, Apr. 22, 1892, Harrison Papers.

86. Nevins, *Hewitt*, p. 526.

87. W. L. Scott to Lamont, Sept. 14, 1888, Cleveland Papers; J. R. Burton to Harrison, Aug. 6, 1888, Harrison Papers; *The New York Times*, July 7, 1888.

88. Warner Miller to Harrison, Oct. 1, Nov. 10, 1888, Harrison Papers; John E. Cady to Lamont, Oct. 1, 1888, Cleveland Papers; John Devoy to William Carroll, Oct. 19, 1888, Devoy to Barker, Oct. 25, 1888, Barker Papers; Alexander, *Political History*, IV, pp. 124, 130.

89. C. Augustus Haviland to Cleveland, Nov. 11, 1888, Lamont to D. B. Hill, Nov. 7, 1888, John B. Thacher to Cleveland, Nov. 7, 1888, Francis Lynde Stetson to Cleveland, Nov. 9, 1888, Cleveland Papers; Bass, *David Bennett Hill*, pp. 121–25.

90. Edward Murphy, Jr. to Lamont, Sept. 5, 1888, Cleveland Papers; *The Nation*, XLVII (Nov. 29, 1888), 425–26; Clarkson to Harrison, Nov. 2, 1888, Harrison Papers; Harrison to L. P. Morton, Oct. 29, 1888, Levi P. Morton Papers.

Chapter V

1. Hirshson, *Farewell to the Bloody Shirt*, pp. 166–67, stresses that Harrison "received more Southern ballots than any other Republican presidential candidate since the end of Reconstruction." DeSantis, *Republicans Face the Southern Question*, pp. 190–91, on the other hand, shows that in *percentage* of total votes cast, 1888 marks a disastrous Republican decline. If anything, this suggests the uncertainty of Republican prospects in the South. Of course, party managers would not be concerned with overall figures, but with their chances in particular states such as Virginia and North Carolina.

2. Hirshson, *Farewell to the Bloody Shirt*, pp. 185–89; Blake, *Mahone*, p. 249; A. E. Bateman to Harrison, Nov. 14, 1892, Harrison Papers.

3. Alexander, *Political History*, IV, p. 137; Calvin S. Brice to Cleveland, Nov. 8, 1889, Cleveland Papers.

4. Jensen, "The Winning of the Midwest," p. 68; Kleppner, "The Politics of Change in the Midwest," pp. 201–3, 219–21; McSeveney, "The Politics of Depression," pp. 72–76; Horace S. Merrill, *Bourbon Democracy of the Middle West, 1865–1896* (Baton Rouge, 1953), pp. 203–5.

5. Speech of James S. Clarkson delivered at Louisville, Ky., May 10, 1893,

Clarkson Papers, LC; H. C. Chapin, "The Local Committee and Its Works," in Republican Party, *Proceedings of the Tenth Republican National Convention* (Minneapolis, 1892), pp. 4–7 (hereafter cited as *Proceedings, 1892*); W. J. Arkell to Harrison, Feb. 10, 1892, Harrison Papers.

6. Harrison to George Shiras, Jr., Aug. 11, 1892, Harrison Papers; Morgan, *McKinley*, p. 478; Samuel W. McCall, *The Life of Thomas Brackett Reid* (Boston, 1941), p. 171; McSeveney, "Politics of Depression," pp. 242–44. While McSeveney never makes the point specifically, at many points his work suggests that the electorate that he studied conceived of its cultural conflicts in state and local terms, but turned to Washington to assuage its economic fears. See his discussion of the Wilson tariff bill ("Politics of Depression," pp. 228 ff.), of Republican tariff arguments (pp. 242–44), of Democratic state-oriented campaigning on cultural issues versus Republican nationally oriented campaigning on economic ones (pp. 254 ff.), of the centrality of the tariff issue in national politics (p. 475). The midwestern pattern seems to be similar. See Merrill, *Bourbon Democracy*, passim, esp. pp. 207–9, 225–27.

7. Josephson, *The Politicos*, pp. 434, 450–63; John Sherman to W. H. Smith, Sept. 26, 1890, W. H. Smith Papers; Mary R. Dearing, *Veterans in Politics, The Story of the G.A.R.* (Baton Rouge, 1952), pp. 392–401; Fowler, *Cabinet Politician*, pp. 212–20.

8. Harrison to Elkins, Jan. 18, 1889, Harrison Papers.

9. A. T. Volwiler, ed., *The Correspondence Between Benjamin Harrison and James G. Blaine, 1882–1893* (Philadelphia, 1940), p. 300; Platt, *Autobiography*, pp. 206–8; A. B. Cornell to Reid, Jan. 6, 1889, Lemuel E. Quigg to Reid, June 15, 1892, Reid Papers.

10. Fowler, *Cabinet Politician*, pp. 210–12; Barker to Harrison, Jan. 28, 1889, W. Carwell to Barker, Jan. 31, 1889, Barker to David Turpie, June 13, 1892, Barker Papers; Clarkson to Allison, Feb. 26, 1892, Allison Papers; *The Nation*, L (Feb. 27, 1890), 168, (May 22, 1890), 404.

11. Blaine to Reid, Nov. 27, 1888, John Hay to Reid, Feb. 20, 1889, Reid Papers; Elkins to Harrison, Feb. 19, 1889, Elkins to H. G. Davis, Oct. 28, 1889, Elkins Papers.

12. Clarkson to Allison, Nov. 13, 1888, Allison Papers; Elkins to Reid, Mar. 28, Sept. 30, 1889, Nov. 14, 1890, Reid Papers; Reid to Harrison, Aug. 6, 1892, Harrison Papers; *The Nation*, L (Apr. 17, 1890), 305, (May 1, 1890), 345, LIII (Aug. 20, 1891), 133; Sievers, *Hoosier Statesman*, pp. 420–21; Fowler, *Cabinet Politician*, pp. 220–21.

13. Clarkson to Sherman, Oct. 20, 1890, Sherman Papers; Elkins to Reid, Nov. 14, 1890, L. E. Quigg to Reid, May 24, 1892, Reid Papers; White, "Republican Party," pp. 432–33; *The Nation*, LI (Nov. 6, 1890), 350; Alexander, *Political History*, IV, p. 85; Louis A. Dent to T. H. Carter, Jan. 27, 1891, R. B. Harrison Papers; Clarkson to Allison, Sept. 11, 20, 1890, Allison Papers.

14. New York *World,* Nov. 7, 1890; *The Nation,* LI (Nov. 13, 1890), 371; McSeveney, "Politics of Depression," pp. 72–80; White, "Republican Party," p. 498; Hirshson, *Farewell to the Bloody Shirt,* pp. 228–33; Richard E. Welch, Jr., "The Federal Elections Bill of 1890: Postscripts and Prelude," *Journal of American History,* LII (Dec. 1965), 511–26; Muzzey, *Blaine,* pp. 461–69; A. L. Conger to Elkins, Mar. 31, May 22, 1891, Elkins Papers, file 1954 Jan. 21; Elkins to Reid, Nov. 14, 1890, John Hay to Reid, Apr. 12, 1891, Quigg to Reid, May 24, 1892, Reid Papers.

15. Alexander, *Political History,* IV, p. 147; Muzzey, *Blaine,* pp. 469–71; *Proceedings, 1892,* p. 5; Jesse Taylor to James McMillan, June 17, 1891, Papers of James McMillan, Detroit Public Library; Lewis Baker to Johnson Newlon Camden, Nov. 30, 1891, Papers of Johnson Newlon Camden, West Virginia University Library.

16. W. T. Durbin to Halford, Jan. 18, 1892, John Hamilton to Halford, Mar. 16, 1892, Harrison Papers; Reid to John Hay, Aug. 3, 1891, Reid Papers; A. L. Conger to Elkins, May 22, 1891, Elkins Papers, file 1954 Jan. 21; *The Nation,* LIII (Dec. 3, 1891), 417, LIV (Jan. 21, 1892), 220; Gresham, *Gresham,* II, p. 660; Sage, *Allison,* pp. 249–50; Ellis, *Teller,* p. 205; Muzzey, *Blaine,* p. 469.

17. *The Nation,* LII (Mar. 26, 1891), 249; Reid to John Hay, Aug. 3, 1891, Depew to Reid, Aug. 30, 1891, Reid Papers; Muzzey, *Blaine,* pp. 471–74.

18. A. L. Conger to Elkins, May 22, 1891, Elkins Papers file 1954 Jan. 21; Elkins to R. B. Harrison, Feb. 21, 1891, R. B. Harrison Papers; Fowler, *Cabinet Politician,* p. 220; *The Nation,* LIII (July 16, 1891), 37, (July 23, 1891), 60, (Aug. 6, 1891), 93, (Aug. 27, 1891), 152; Platt, *Autobiography,* pp. 215–16; Alexander, *Political History,* IV, pp. 149–50; Clarkson to G. M. Dodge, July 23, 1891, Harrison Papers.

19. Elkins to R. B. Harrison, Feb. 21, 28, Sept. 4, Oct. 12, 20, 1891, B. F. Hobart to R. B. Harrison, Feb. 10, 11, 1891, R. F. Kerens to R. B. Harrison, Feb. 12, 1891, W. J. Arkell to R. B. Harrison, May 11, 1891, R. B. Harrison Papers; Blaine to Elkins, Aug. 15, 1889, Elkins to H. G. Davis, Aug. 29, Sept. 19, 1889, Harrison to Elkins, Feb. 23, 1891, Platt to Elkins, July 9, 1891, R. B. Harrison to Elkins, Aug. 15, 1891, Blaine to Elkins, Aug. 30, 1891, Elkins Papers; Muzzey, *Blaine,* p. 461.

20. Charles Foster to Elkins, July 25, 1891, John W. Mason to Elkins, Aug. 26, 1891, Garret A. Hobart to Elkins, Nov. 14, 1891, R. B. Harrison to Elkins, Nov. 17, 1891, Elkins Papers; Elkins to R. B. Harrison, Oct. 30, Nov. 5, 1891, R. B. Harrison to Benjamin Harrison, n.d. [Dec., 1891], (Nov.–Dec. 1891 box, Dec. 25–31 file), Elkins to R. B. Harrison, Sept. 4, Nov. 14, 20, 1891, R. C. Kerens to R. B. Harrison, Nov. 6, 1891, R. B. Harrison Papers; Blaine to D. Nicholson, Jan. 13, 1892, Reid Papers.

21. Stanton J. Peele to Halford, Jan. 23, Feb. 10, 1892, Church Howe to

Harrison, Apr. 28, 1892, Harrison Papers; Quigg to Reid, May 21, 1892, Reid Papers; Gresham, *Gresham,* II, pp. 660–62; Sage, *Allison,* p. 250; Donald M. Dozer, "Benjamin Harrison and the Presidential Campaign of 1892," *AHR,* LIV (Oct. 1948), 57; Alger to McMillan, Feb. 25, Apr. 15, 1892, McMillan Papers.

22. Morgan, *McKinley,* pp. 156–57, 164; Croly, *Hanna,* p. 165; E. A. Rathbone to Halford, Mar. 7, 1892, D. S. Alexander to Harrison, May 4, 1892, Harrison Papers; Hanna to Sherman, Apr. 7, 1892, Sherman Papers; Quigg to Reid, May 21, 31, 1892, Reid Papers; Dozer, "Benj. Harrison," 57; Herman H. Kohlsaat, *From McKinley to Harding* (New York, 1923), pp. 8–9; Felt, "Rise of Mark Hanna," p. 243.

23. Sherman to A. E. Bateman, June 1892, quoted in Dozer, "Benj. Harrison," 57–58; Hanna to Sherman, Apr. 7, 1892, Sherman Papers; R. B. Gelatt to James McMillan, Feb. 25, 1892, R. A. Alger to McMillan, Feb. 27, Mar. 7, 1892, W. A. Gavett to McMillan, Apr. 15, 1892, McMillan Papers; John H. Gear to Jacob Rich, Feb. 13, 1892, Gear to Allison, Feb. 22, 26, 1892, Allison Papers.

24. D. S. Alexander to Halford, Apr. 29, 1892, J. B. Elam to Halford, Jan. 10, 1892, R. R. Shiel to Halford, Jan. 16, 1892, J. R. Hallowell to Halford, Feb. 15, 1892, J. W. Fifer to Harrison, Mar. 14, 1892, E. H. Conger to Halford, Mar. 18, 1892, T. V. Cooper to Halford, Apr. 2, 1892, J. H. Gould to Halford, Apr. 21, 1892, J. T. Foster to Halford, Apr. 29, 1892, J. T. McNeely to Harrison, May 1, 1892, Harrison Papers; Elkins to Reid, June 9, 1892, Reid Papers; Muzzey, *Blaine,* p. 471; Volwiler, *Correspondence,* pp. 245, 248–51, 273–79, 291–94.

25. T. V. Cooper to Halford, Jan. 2, Apr. 2, May 3, 20, 1892, Michener to Halford, Mar. 10, 1892, A. V. Dockery to Halford, May 5, 1892, W. T. Durbin to Halford, May 28, 1892, Harrison to J. W. Fifer, Mar. 16, 1892, Harrison Papers.

26. Quigg to Reid, May 23, 1892, Reid Papers.

27. Sage, *Allison,* pp. 251–53; Clarkson to Allison, Feb. 26, 1892, Allison Papers; Elkins to Harrison, Mar. 12, 1892, Harrison to James A. Beaver, Mar. 9, 1892, T. V. Cooper to Halford, May 3, 1892, D. S. Alexander to Harrison, May 4, 1892, Harrison to D. S. Alexander, May 7, 1892, Harrison Papers.

28. Hiscock to Harrison, Aug. 13, 1892, Harrison Papers; Quigg to Reid, May 21, 23, 31, 1892, Reid Papers.

29. Quigg to Reid, May 24, 1892, Reid Papers.

30. *Ibid.,* Reid to Elkins, May 26, 1892, Quigg to Reid, May 30, 1892, Reid Papers; Muzzey, *Blaine,* pp. 472–73.

31. Quigg to Reid, May 31, 1892, Reid Papers.

32. Quigg to Reid, May 24, 31, 1892, Elkins to Reid, June 9, 1892, Reid Papers; G. W. Steele to Harrison, C. H. T. Collis to Halford, June 4, 1892, Harrison Papers; Muzzey, *Blaine,* pp. 473–75. For Blaine's

uncertainty about the propriety of remaining in the cabinet while being a candidate see Blaine to D. Nicholson, Jan. 13, 1892, Reid Papers.

33. Memorandum, "The Minneapolis Convention of June 7th to 10th, 1892," Harrison to Michener, June 10, 1892, Michener Papers; Quigg to Reid, May 23, June 15, 1892, Reid Papers; R. B. Harrison to W. J. Merrill, Halford to R. B. Harrison, May 28, 1892, J. B. Collins to R. B. Harrison, June 4, 1892, R. B. Harrison Papers; Michener to Halford, telegram, June 8, 1892, M. M. Estee to Halford, June 11, 1892, Harrison Papers; W. H. Smith to Foraker, June 15, 1892, W. H. Smith Papers; Indianapolis *News*, May 30, June 3, 1892; Dozer, "Benj. Harrison," 60–61.

34. *The New York Times*, June 2, 3, 7, 1892; W. J. Arkell to Halford, June 6, 1892, C. H. T. Collis to Halford, June 7, 1892, Michener to Halford, telegram, June 7, 1892, Harrison Papers. The Harrison managers' poll on the eve of the convention showed 511 of 906 delegates for the President. A *New York Times* poll gave him 488 votes on the first ballot.

35. Michener to Halford, telegrams, June 8, 9, 1892, R. R. Shiel to Halford, telegram, June 8, 1892, Harrison Papers; Memorandum, "The Minneapolis Convention," Michener Papers; *The New York Times*, June 10, 1892; *Proceedings, 1892*, p. 81.

36. W. J. Arkell to Halford, June 6, 1892, Michener to Halford, June 7, 1892, Percy A. Heath to Halford, June 9, 1892, John A. Gear to W. B. Allison, June 14, 1892, Harrison Papers; John A. Garraty, ed., *The Barber and the Historian: the Correspondence of George A. Myers and James Ford Rhodes, 1910–1923* (Columbus, Ohio, 1956), p. 103; Morgan, *McKinley*, pp. 165–67; Hanna to Sherman, telegram, June 9, 14, 1892, Sherman Papers.

37. E. G. Rathbone to Halford, telegram, June 10, 1892, Harrison Papers; Hanna to Sherman, June 14, 1892, Charles G. Baird to Sherman, June 11, 1892, T. M. King to Sherman, June 7, 1892, Sherman Papers; John Hay to Reid, June 26, 1892, Reid Papers. McKinley polled 182 votes, Blaine 182½: *Proceedings, 1892*, p. 141.

38. Hanna to Sherman, June 14, 1892, Sherman Papers; *The New York Times*, May 30, 1892; R. R. Shiel to Harrison, July 12, 1892, Shiel to Halford, July 20, 1892, Harrison Papers; Indianapolis *News*, June 8, 1892.

39. Clarkson to Dodge, Oct. 7, 1892, Dodge Papers; J. K. Gowdy to Halford, Oct. 13, 1892, T. H. Carter to Halford, Oct. 15, 1892, W. O. Bradley to Halford, Oct. 22, Nov. 1, 1892, J. H. Manley to Halford, Oct. 20, 22, Nov. 2, 1892, W. M. Hahn to Halford, Oct. 25, 1892, W. T. Durbin to Harrison, Nov. 2, 1892, Harrison Papers; George H. Knoles, *The Presidential Campaign and Election of 1892* (Stanford University, 1942), pp. 233–34; Douglas Serrein to George Harvey, Sept.

25, 1892, W. C. Whitney Papers; Reid to A. B. Cornell, Nov. 11, 1892, Reid Papers.

40. Harrison to C. N. Bliss, June 3, 1892, Clarkson to Harrison, telegram, June 11, 1892, A. E. Bateman to Harrison, June [?], 22, 1892, J. H. Gould to Halford, June 16, 1892, Nathaniel McKay to Halford, June 21, 1892, Hamilton Disston to Harrison, June 26, 1892, Harrison to G. M. Dodge, June 13, 1892, Michener to Halford, June 27, July 2, 1892, Harrison to Depew, June 27, 1892, Hamilton Disston to Halford, July 1, 1892, A. W. Tourgee to Harrison, June 24, 1892, C. W. Wooley to Harrison, June 24, 1892, G. M. Dodge to Harrison, June 28, 1892, Harrison Papers; Quigg to Reid, June 15, 18, 1892, Reid Papers; G. A. Hobart to Michener, June 13, 1892, Michener Papers; *The New York Times*, June 26, 1892.

41. Church, *Republican Party in Illinois*, pp. 139, 147, 150, 155; *The New York Times*, June 29, July 6, 1892; Quigg to Reid, June 18, 1892, Elkins to Reid, June 25, 1892, Reid Papers; T. H. Carter to Mrs. Carter, June 27, 30, 1892, Papers of Thomas Henry Carter, LC.

42. *The New York Times*, June 6, 26, July 6, 17, 1892; Clarkson to Harrison, June 25, 1892, Michener to Halford, July 1, 1892, "Statement dictated by T. H. Carter," July 5, 1892, Philetus Sawyer to H. C. Payne, telegram, July 13, 1892, Halford to Spooner, telegram, July 13, 1892 (both written in Harrison's hand), Spooner to Halford, July 14, 1892, R. B. Harrison to Benj. Harrison, July 16, 1892, Harrison Papers; Carter to Mrs. Carter, July 15, 21, 1892, Carter Papers; G. A. Hobart to Michener, June 13, 1892, Michener Papers.

43. A. E. Bateman to Harrison, Aug. 19, 1892, Harrison to Bateman, Aug. 24, 1892, Carter to Halford, Aug. 23, 1892, Michener to Halford, Sept. 6, 1892, Thomas H. McKee to Edward McPherson, telegram, Nov. 10, 1892, Harrison Papers; Carter to Mrs. Carter, n.d. [late October], Carter Papers; Reid to Carter, Oct. 1, 1892, Reid to Milholland, Oct. 11, 1892, Reid Papers; George F. Parker to Cleveland, Sept. 22, 1892, Cleveland Papers; *The New York Times*, June 29, July 17, 1892.

44. Another politician close to Harrison suggested that the administration look for "the best Hebrew that could be named" to raise funds in the Jewish community: D. S. Alexander to Halford, June 18, 1892, Harrison Papers.

45. C. N. Bliss to Harrison, June 22, 1892, Clarkson to Halford, Aug. 18, 1892, A. E. Bateman to Harrison, Aug. 19, 1892, John Wanamaker to Harrison, Aug. 2, 1892, Redfield Proctor to Harrison, Aug. 22, 1892, Harrison to Wanamaker, Aug. 25, 1892, Carter to Harrison, Aug. 26, 1892, Bliss to Harrison, Nov. 10, 1892, W. H. Hahn to Halford, Sept. 17, 1892, Harrison Papers; Clarkson to William Loeb, Jr., Aug. 19, 1906, Theodore Roosevelt Papers; Knoles, *Election of 1892*, p. 128.

46. Clarkson to Halford, Apr. 23, 1892, C. H. Grosvenor to Halford, Aug.

29, 1892, Harrison Papers. On the Commission see Leonard D. White, *The Republican Era: 1869–1901, A Study in Administrative History* (New York, 1958), pp. 323–24. On the welfare functions of patronage and pensions see John Livingston to Cleveland, Sept. 4, 1892, Cleveland Papers.

47. C. H. Grosvenor to Halford, Aug. 29, 1892, J. H. Manley to Halford, Sept. 5, 1892, Harrison Papers; Knoles, *Election of 1892*, pp. 145–46, 203–4. Of modern studies in voting behavior, see Lazarfeld, et al. *The People's Choice* pp. xvii, 73–74, 94–95, 104; Froman, "A Realistic Approach to Campaign Strategy and Tactics," p. 8.

48. Knoles, *Election of 1892*, p. 203; W. S. McAllister to W. C. Whitney, Aug. 6, 1892, Basil B. Gordon to Whitney, Oct. 7, 1892, W. C. Whitney Papers; Cleveland to W. F. Vilas, Aug. 9, 1892, Cleveland Papers; J. W. Vrooman to Halford, July 30, 1892, W. M. Hahn to Halford, Oct. 25, 1892, J. H. Manley to Halford, Oct. 26, 1892, Harrison Papers; Elkins to R. B. Harrison, Oct. 7, telegrams Oct. 17, 22, 1892, R. B. Harrison Papers; DeSantis, *Republicans Face the Southern Question*, pp. 229–46.

49. Alexander, *Political History*, IV, pp. 132–34, 154–57; A. B. Cornell to Reid, June 6, 1889, Depew to Reid, Aug. 30, 1891, John E. Milholland to Reid, Feb. 12, 1892, Quigg to Reid, June 15, 18, 1892, Reid Papers; John T. Foster to Halford, May 23, 1892, W. J. Arkell to Harrison, Feb. 10, 1892, A. B. Cornell to Harrison, June 3, 1892, G. M. Dodge to Elkins, May 3, 1892, Dodge to Harrison, June 28, 1892, E. L. Adams to Harrison, June 10, 1892, Harrison Papers.

50. Quigg to Reid, June 15, 1892, Reid Papers.

51. Reid to J. C. New, Aug. 5, 1892, Quigg to Reid, June 15, 18, 1892, Platt to Reid, Aug. 4, 1892, Reid Papers; Hiscock to Harrison, Aug. 3, 1892, Harrison Papers.

52. Reid to Harrison, Aug. 6, 1892, Harrison Papers.

53. Hiscock to Harrison, Aug. 13, 1892, Harrison Papers.

54. Harrison to Platt, Aug. 17, 1892, Harrison Papers. See also Harrison to Reid, Aug. 15, 1892, Harrison Papers.

55. Platt to Harrison, Aug. 22, 1892, Carter to Harrison, Aug. 26, 1892, Platt to Harrison, Oct. 7, 1892, George Adee to Harrison, Nov. 11, 1892, Carter to Harrison, Aug. 26, 1892, C. H. T. Collis to Harrison, Nov. 6, 1892, C. N. Bliss to Harrison, Nov. 10, 1892, Harrison Papers; Reid to Medill, Aug. 26, Sept. 22, 1892, Reid to William P. Tomlinson, Aug. 30, 1892, Reid to C. N. Bliss, Sept. 2, 1892, Reid to Charles W. Hackett, Sept. 8, 1892, Reid Papers. On the indifference of the electorate see J. K. Gowdy to Halford, Sept. 29, 1892, Levi W. Brown to Halford, Oct. 4, 1892, Harrison Papers; Reid to Medill, Sept. 22, 1892, Reid Papers; Josephson, *The Politicos*, p. 512.

56. Hanna to Sherman, June 14, 1892, Sherman Papers; C. W. Wooley to Harrison, July 22, 1892, Levi W. Brown to Halford, Oct. 4, 1892,

Benjamin Butterworth to Halford, Nov. 4, 1892, Harrison Papers; A. C. Carlisle to Cleveland, Oct. 25, 1892, Cleveland Papers; Felt, "Rise of Mark Hanna," pp. 251–52.

57. J. H. Farley to Whitney, Oct. 14, 1892, W. C. Whitney Papers; Levi W. Brown to Halford, Oct. 4, 1892, Harrison Papers; W. W. Lawrence to A. B. Upshaw, Sept. 26, 1892, Papers of Don M. Dickinson, LC.

58. Merrill, *Bourbon Democracy*, pp. 225–36; R. R. Shiel to Halford, July 20, 1892, Harrison Papers; W. C. Goudy to Cleveland, Sept. 14, 1892, C. H. Jones to Cleveland, Sept. 15, 1892, Cleveland Papers; Delos P. Phelps to Whitney, Aug. 1, 1892, W. C. Whitney Papers.

59. Bass, *David Bennett Hill*, p. 229; Nevins, *Cleveland*, pp. 467–68; Knoles, *Election of 1892*, pp. 133, 180–87; A. B. McKinley to Whitney, Sept. 3, 1892, James E. Boyd to Whitney, Sept. 16, 1892, George L. Miller to Whitney, Oct. 7, 1892, W. C. Whitney Papers; Harrison to Michener, Aug. 24, 1892, Michener Papers.

60. Joseph M. Carey to Halford, Oct. 21, 1892, W. M. Hahn to Halford, Oct. 25, 1892, Harrison Papers.

61. Paolo E. Coletta, *William Jennings Bryan* (Lincoln, Neb., 1964), pp. 70–78; James E. Boyd to Whitney, Sept. 6, 1892, George L. Miller to Whitney, Oct. 7, 1892, W. C. Whitney Papers; Percy S. Heath to Halford, Oct. 20, 1892, J. H. Manley to Halford, Oct. 26, 1892, Harrison Papers.

62. Gresham, *Gresham*, II, pp. 609, 668; John Hay to Reid, June 26, 1892, Reid Papers; John K. Gowdy to W. H. H. Miller, July 19, 1892, R. R. Shiel to Halford, July 12, 1892, Smiley N. Chambers to Halford, July 12, 1892, Harrison Papers.

63. Michener to Gowdy, Sept. 16, 1892, Michener to Halford, Oct. 11, 1892, W. M. Marine to Halford, Oct. 17, 1892, Frank M. Millikan to Halford, Oct. 24, 1892, J. K. Gowdy to Halford, Aug. 30, Sept. 29, Oct. 13, 1892, Harrison to Foraker, Oct. 7, 1892, Carter to Halford, Oct. 15, Nov. 1, 1892, D. M. Ransdell to Harrison, Oct. 18, 1892, J. N. Huston to Halford, Oct. 20, 1892, Halford to Harrison, Nov. 6, 1892, Harrison Papers; Halford to Depew, Oct. 1, 1892, Papers of Chauncey M. Depew, LC.

64. D. M. Ransdell to Harrison, Oct. 18, Nov. 9, 1892, R. R. Shiel to Halford, Oct. 18, 1892, Carter to Halford, Nov. 1, 1892, J. H. Manley to Halford, Nov. 2, 1892, W. T. Durbin to Harrison, Nov. 2, 1892, Halford to Harrison, Nov. 6, 1892, Harrison Papers.

65. Knoles, *Election of 1892*, pp. 237–47; McSeveney, "Politics of Depression," pp. 72–92; Albert H. Horton to Halford, Nov. 10, 1892, G. W. E. Dorsey to Halford, Nov. 15, 1892, Albert H. Horton to Harrison, Nov. 21, 1892, clipping, Baltimore *Herald*, Nov. 10, 1892, Charles H. T. Collis to Harrison, Nov. 18, 1892, Harrison to Gilbert A. Pierce, Nov. 16, 1892, Harrison Papers; D. S. Alexander to R. B. Harrison, Nov. 14, 1892, R. B. Harrison Papers; M. M. Estee to Halford, June 11, 1892,

Reid to Harrison, June 29, 1892, Harrison Papers; Reid to H. C. Frick, July 29, 1892, Reid to A. B. Cornell, Nov. 11, 1892, Reid Papers.

66. Carl N. Degler, "American Political Parties and the Rise of the City: An Interpretation," *Journal of American History*, LI (June 1964), 41–59, esp. 46; J. H. Manley to Harrison, Nov. 9, 1892, Elliott F. Shepard to Harrison, Nov. 14, 1892, S. N. Chambers to Harrison, Nov. 15, 1892, S. M. Cullom to Harrison, n.d. (v. 151), Harrison Papers.

67. Orville H. Platt to Barker, Nov. 15, 1892, Barker Papers. On the theme of impending revolution see Frederic Cople Jaher, *Doubters and Dissenters: Cataclysmic Thought in America, 1885–1918* (London, 1964).

68. C. H. Jones to Cleveland, Sept. 15, 1892, Cleveland to W. S. Bissell, Nov. 8, 1892, Cleveland to Francis C. Barlow, Nov. 10, 1892, C. S. Cary to Cleveland, Nov. 13, 1892, Thomas Moonlight to Cleveland, Nov. 27, 1892, printed invitation of "The Committee of One Hundred," Terre Haute, Indiana, Apr. 5, 1892, Cleveland Papers; Harrison to Michener, Aug. 24, 1893, Michener Papers; S. W. Fordyce to Whitney, July 13, 1892, W. C. Whitney Papers; Gresham, *Gresham*, II, p. 675; Barker, *Henry George*, pp. 602–3.

CHAPTER VI

1. Orville H. Platt to Barker, Nov. 15, 1892, Barker Papers; Milton Friedman and Anna Jacobson Schwartz, *A Monetary History of the United States, 1867–1960* (Princeton, 1963), pp. 106–8; Charles Hoffman, "The Depression of the Nineties," *Journal of Economic History*, CVI (June 1956), 137–64.

2. Neither the long-term causes nor the long-range effects of the Democratic decline—which affected the politics of an entire political generation—are subjects for this study, which concentrates only on the short-term effects of this major political change on the calculations of the opposing party's national leaders. On the political revolution of the 1890s and the Democratic party see the following: Hays, "The Social Analysis of American Political History," 385–86; Benson, "Research Problems in American Political Historiography," pp. 113–83; Key, "Critical Elections," 3–17; Carl N. Degler, "American Political Parties and the Rise of the City: An Interpretation," 41–59; Hollingsworth, *Whirligig of Politics*, chapters 1 and 2; Jensen, "Winning of the Midwest"; Kleppner, "Politics of Change"; McSeveney, "Politics of Depression"; Blodgett, *The Gentle Reformers*.

3. Platt to George W. Wanmaker, Jan. 17, 1894, Quigg Papers; *Tribune Almanac 1893*, 308; *Tribune Almanac 1895*, 329. McSeveney, "Politics of Depression," pp. 152–56, discusses changes in voting in New York from 1893 to 1894.

4. McSeveney, "Politics of Depression," pp. 232–34; *Tribune Almanac 1895*, 327–29.
5. Quigg to Reid, Dec. 3, 1894, Reid Papers; McSeveney, "Politics of Depression," pp. 297–303, 325–26.
6. Reid to Elkins, Feb. 28, 1896, Reid Papers; W. R. Holloway to Allison, Feb. 14, 1896, Allison Papers.
7. Morgan, *McKinley*, p. 152; Felt, "Rise of Mark Hanna," p. 277; McKinley to H. H. Kohlsaat, May 23, 1895, McKinley to J. F. Laning, May 27, 1895, McKinley Papers; Hamilton Disston to M. S. Quay, Apr. 1, 1895, Papers of Matthew Stanley Quay, LC.
8. Elkins to Reid, Mar. 10, 1896, Reid to D. Nicholson, May 16, 1896, Reid Papers; Josephson, *The Politicos*, chapter 18: "The Rise of a National Boss: Mark Hanna."
9. The most recent and most complete account is Stanley L. Jones, *The Presidential Election of 1896* (Madison, 1964); Paul W. Glad, *McKinley, Bryan, and the People* (Philadelphia, 1964), is the most perceptive; recent biographical studies of McKinley, Hanna, and Bryan by H. Wayne Morgan, Thomas E. Felt, and Paolo J. Coletta respectively have been cited above; Hollingsworth, *Whirligig of Politics* is detailed and perceptive on the Democrats; Robert F. Durden, *The Climax of Populism: the Election of 1896* (Lexington, Ky., 1965) gives a careful account of the Populists in 1896; Friedman and Schwartz, *Monetary History*, chapter 3, throws important light on the central issue of the campaign; so does Gilbert C. Fite, "Republican Strategy and the Farm Vote in the Presidential Campaign of 1896," *AHR*, LXV (July 1960), 787–806. The works of Blodgett, Jensen, Kleppner, and McSeveney previously cited give local details which throw valuable light on the campaign nationally.
10. Croly, *Hanna*, pp. 110–19. The quotation is from p. 110.
11. *DAB*, III, pp. 544–45; Allen O. Myers, *Bosses and Boodles in Ohio Politics* (Cincinnati, 1895), pp. 86–88. On Myers see Everett Walters, *Joseph Benson Foraker, An Uncompromising Republican* (Columbus, Ohio, 1948), p. 34; Croly, *Hanna*, pp. 250–51.
12. C. Vann Woodward, *Reunion and Reaction, The Compromise of 1877 and the End of Reconstruction* (Boston, 1951), p. 116; Harry Barnard, *Rutherford B. Hayes and His America* (Indianapolis, 1954), p. 363.
13. Croly, *Hanna*, pp. 118, 135, 165; Reid to Murat Halstead, July 12, 1880, Murat Halstead Papers. Croly's statement (*Hanna*, p. 116), strictly on hearsay evidence, that Hanna "originated the idea of a Business Man's Republican Campaign Club" in 1880, which spread from Cleveland to other cities, is certainly false. Thomas M. Nichol, a friend of Garfield's and "chief man of the 'Honest Money League' of the North-West" was traveling under the auspices of the Republican National Committee organizing such groups. See Garfield to Reid,

July 24, 1880, Reid Papers; Thomas M. Nichol to W. H. Smith, July 11, 1880, W. H. Smith Papers.
14. Croly, *Hanna*, pp. 177–79; Jones, *Election of 1896*, pp. 100–105; Morgan, *McKinley*, pp. 187–89; Glad, *McKinley, Bryan and the People*, pp. 97–103; Kohlsaat, *From McKinley to Harding*, pp. 30–31; Thomas Bentley Mott, *Myron T. Herrick, Friend of France, An Autobiographical Biography* (New York, 1929), pp. 59–61.
15. See, for example, M. S. Quay to McKinley, May 21, 1900, Quay Papers.
16. On New York and Pennsylvania state battles and the role of McKinley's candidacy in them, see below, pp. 207–14.
17. A. B. Cummins to Allison, Apr. 5, 1894, Clarkson to Allison, Oct. 15, 1894, Allison Papers; Jones, *Election of 1896*, pp. 101–2. On Clarkson see the biographical sketch in *National Cyclopedia of American Biography*, II, pp. 118–19; Anna H. Clarkson to G. M. Dodge, Sept. 29, 1896, Clarkson to Dodge, Oct. 4, 1896, Papers of Grenville M. Dodge, ISDHA.
18. *DAB*, XII, pp. 236–37; Jones, *Election of 1896*, p. 101; William A. Robinson, *Thomas B. Reed, Parliamentarian* (New York, 1930), chapter 16; Richardson, *Chandler*, pp. 490, 633.
19. Elkins to Reid, Mar. 5, 1896, Reid Papers; Clarkson to Allison, June 4, 1895, Allison Papers; Harrison to Elkins, Feb. 3, 1896, Elkins Papers; Lambert, *Elkins*, pp. 191–95; Rothman, *Power and Politics*, pp. 49–50.
20. Powell Clayton to Elkins, Jan. 17, 1896, Elkins Papers; Reid to McKinley, Feb. 24, 1896, Reid to Nicholson, Mar. 19, 1896, Reid Papers; McKinley to Elkins, Apr. 7, 1896, McKinley to Charles H. Hart, Apr. 22, 1896, McKinley Papers; Clarkson to Allison, Sept. 16, 1895, Allison Papers.
21. Elkins to Reid, Feb. 18, Mar. 10, 1896, Reid to McKinley, Feb. 24, 1896, Reid Papers; Clifford Arrick to Elkins, Apr. 24, 1896, Elkins Papers; Lambert, *Elkins*, pp. 201–3.
22. McKinley to Reid, Feb. 19, 1896, Reid to Depew, Mar. 13, 1896, Reid to McKinley, May 12, 1896, Reid Papers; D. F. Sprager to Chandler, Mar. 17, 1896, Chandler Papers; M. S. Quay to McKinley, May 15, 1895, McKinley Papers.
23. Clarkson to Allison, July 7, 1895, Allison Papers; Blankenburg, "Forty Years in the Wilderness," 225–39; *The New York Times*, Sept. 4, 1895.
24. Jones, *Election of 1896*, p. 149; Quay to McKinley, May 15, 1895, Hanna to McKinley, Feb. 28, 1896, Hanna to Philander C. Knox, Feb. 28, 1896, McKinley Papers.
25. William Osborne to McKinley, Jan. 16, 1896, C. H. Grosvenor to McKinley, Feb. 19, 1896, J. H. Taylor to McKinley, Feb. 19, 1896, McKinley to W. A. Clark, Mar. 2, 1896, Hanna to McKinley, July 8, 1896, McKinley Papers.
26. Jones, *Election of 1896*, pp. 154–55; Republican Party, *Official Pro-*

ceedings of the Eleventh Republican National Convention (Minneapolis, 1896), p. 123 (hereafter cited as *Proceedings, 1896*); Hanna to McKinley, July 8, 1896, McKinley Papers.

27. Alexander, *Political History*, IV, pp. 204–46; Platt, *Autobiography*, p. 267; Quigg to Reid, Dec. 3, 1894, Reid Papers.

28. Alexander, *Political History*, IV, pp. 234–35, 249; Platt, *Autobiography*, pp. 308–9; "Letter to the Editor of the *Tribune*" written by Reid and signed "Wall Street," Dec. 8, 1895 (in Letterbook, v. 150), Reid to Nicholson, Dec. 9, 1895, Reid to Milholland, Jan. 2, 1896, Reid Papers; Clarkson to Allison, Sept. 16, 1895, Allison Papers; Perry Belmont to Manton Marble, Jan. 31, 1896, Papers of Manton Marble, LC.

29. W. M. Osborne to McKinley, Jan. 16, 1896, Hanna to P. C. Knox, Feb. 28, 1896, J. M. Swank to Hanna, Feb. 28, 1896, McKinley Papers; Clarkson to Allison, Nov. 28, Dec. 14, 1895, Allison Papers; Clarkson to Dodge, Mar. 6, 1896, Dodge Papers; Jones, *Election of 1896*, pp. 140–42, 373.

30. Jones, *Election of 1896*, p. 134; Sage, *Allison*, pp. 263–64; Clarkson to Allison, Dec. 14, 23, 1895, Jan. 5, Feb. 25, 1896, Allison Papers; E. P. Ripley to Dodge, Jan. 16, 30, 1896, Clarkson to Dodge, Feb. 18, Mar. 6, May 28, 1896, Dodge Papers. Platt's comment is quoted in Reid to Elkins, Feb. 28, 1896, copy in McKinley Papers.

31. Clarkson to Allison, Dec. 14, 23, 1895, Feb. 25, Mar. 10, Apr. 9, 1896, J. W. Gates to Allison, Feb. 17, 1896, Allison Papers; Clarkson to Dodge, May 28, 1896, Dodge Papers.

32. J. M. Swank to Hanna, Feb. 28, 1896, McKinley Papers.

33. John Hay to Reid, Feb. 15, 1896, Reid Papers; Jones, *Election of 1896*, pp. 151–52.

34. Platt to Morton, Dec. 11, 1895, W. Youngblood to Morton, Feb. 28, 1896, Morton Papers; C. H. Grosvenor to McKinley, Feb. 19, 1896, McKinley Papers; H. C. Warmouth to Chandler, Feb. 4, 1896, Chandler to Warmouth, Feb. 17, 1896, T. L. Case to Chandler, Mar. 19, 1896, Chandler Papers; Depew to Reid, Dec. 27, 1895, Jan. 25, 1896, Reid to Depew, Mar. 13, 1896, Reid to Nicholson, Mar. 19, 1896, Reid Papers; Platt to Barker, June 7, 1895, Barker Papers; McElroy, *Morton*, pp. 287, 289.

35. Alexander, *Political History*, IV, pp. 249–50; Reid to Milholland, Apr. 1, 1896, Reid to McKinley, Apr. 2, 1896, Reid Papers.

36. Platt to Quigg, May 1, 1896, Quigg Papers; Reid to Nicholson, May 6, 16, 1896, Reid to McKinley, May 12, 1896, Reid Papers; Platt to Morton, Aug. 4, 1896, Morton Papers; Alexander, *Political History*, IV, pp. 250–52; Jones, *Election of 1896*, pp. 153–56.

37. Morgan, *McKinley*, pp. 92–104; Jones, *Election of 1896*, p. 110; Foraker, *Notes*, I, p. 440; Harold Zink, *City Bosses in the United States* (Durham, N.C., 1930), p. 261.

38. Foraker, *Notes*, I, pp. 452–53; Felt, "Rise of Mark Hanna," pp. 284–86; Croly, *Hanna*, p. 177; Joseph P. Smith to Charles Dick, June 9, 1895, Papers of Charles Dick, Ohio Historical Society.

39. Margaret Leech, *In the Days of McKinley* (New York, 1959), pp. 64–65; Clarkson to Allison, July 7, 1895, Allison Papers; Joseph P. Smith to Charles Dick, June 9, 1895, Charles Dick Papers; Hanna to McKinley, Feb. 28, 1896, McKinley Papers.

40. Felt, "Rise of Mark Hanna," p. 302; W. G. Silbey to McKinley, Jan. 13, 1896, McKinley to Foraker, Jan. 29, Apr. 7, 1896, Charles Kinney to Joseph Smith, Apr. 10, 1896, James Boyle to M. M. Boothman, Apr. 11, 1896, McKinley Papers; Hanna to Charles Dick, Feb. 25, 1896, Charles Dick Papers.

41. Jere Brown to George Myers, Apr. 18, 22, 1896, Charles Cottrill to George Myers, Apr. 3, May 1, 1896, Papers of George F. Myers, Ohio Historical Society.

42. Foraker, *Notes*, I, pp. 496–506; Croly, *Hanna*, pp. 239–41.

43. Jones, *Election of 1896*, chapters 8–11, passim.

44. Joel A. Tarr, "William Lorimer of Illinois: A Study in Boss Politics" (unpublished Ph.D. dissertation, Northwestern University, 1963), pp. 69–71.

45. Austin Ranney, *The Doctrine of Responsible Party Government; its Origins and Present State* (Urbana, 1962), pp. 3–5 and passim. Robinson, *Thomas B. Reed*, pp. 195–234. The import of the Reed rules, and the tensions, pressures, and interests that produced them, have not been adequately studied. Rothman, *Politics and Power,* on the other hand, by generally neglecting the seventies and eighties and underestimating the degree of party control of congressional voting behavior in the Reconstruction era and earlier, heavily overestimates the changes of the nineties. Joel H. Silbey, *The Shrine of Party, Congressional Voting Behavior, 1841–1852* (Pittsburgh, 1967); and David Donald, *The Politics of Reconstruction, 1863–1867* (Baton Rouge, 1965) suggest that party counted for a great deal more in the earlier period than Rothman assumed. Ari Hoogenboom, "Industrialism and Political Leadership: A Case Study of the United States Senate," in Frederick C. Jaher, ed., *The Age of Industrialism in America, Essays in Social Structure and Cultural Values* (New York and London, 1968), pp. 49–78, esp. 69–72 argues persuasively that the Senate, especially since 1860, has changed amazingly little in organization, function, or leadership.

46. Jones, *Election of 1896,* pp. 119–25: the quotation is on p. 124; Tarr, "William Lorimer," pp. 40–84.

47. Bascom N. Timmons, ed., *A Journal of the McKinley Years* (Chicago, 1950), pp. 66, 68 (hereafter cited as Dawes, *Journal*); Jones, *Election of 1896,* p. 121; Tarr, "William Lorimer," pp. 64, 72–73; Dawes to General C. W. Pavey, Jan. 21, Mar. 9, 31, 1896, Dawes to W. F. Cal-

houn, Feb. 26, Mar. 18, 1896, Dawes to Hanna, Mar. 9, 1896, Dawes to Eldon C. Dewitt, Mar. 3, Apr. 4, 1896, Dawes to W. M. Osborne, Apr. 17, May 4, 1896, C. W. Pavey to Dawes, Jan. 1, Mar. 7, 10, 31, Apr. 1, 1896, Joseph P. Smith to Dawes, Nov. 8, 1895, Jan. 29, Mar. 4, 29, 1896, Papers of Charles G. Dawes, Northwestern University Library.

48. Tarr, "William Lorimer," pp. 79, 84; Dawes to McKinley, Mar. 13, 1896, John McNulta to McKinley, Apr. 9, 1896, McKinley Papers; Dawes, *Journal*, pp. 76–81: see pp. 78, 80 for Dawes's comments on McNulta.

49. Dawes, *Journal*, pp. 77–81; Tarr, "William Lorimer," pp. 80–89; Dawes to W. M. Osborne, May 4, 1896, Dawes Papers. Another notable example of this heightened organization on the state level was the arrangement which Michigan Senator James McMillan effected with D. E. Alward, secretary of the Michigan state committee, for Alward to remain at his post and receive a salary between campaigns, an arrangement begun, significantly, with the 1894 campaign. See D. E. Alward to McMillan, Apr. 4, 1895, Alward to G. M. Black, Apr. 29, 1896, G. M. Black to Alward, Apr. 30, 1896, McMillan to William C. McMillan, Apr. 4, 1896, McMillan to Mr. Scripps, Apr. 4, 1896, McMillan Papers.

50. For examples of voluntary aid to McKinley's cause see McKinley to S. M. Fordyce, Jan. 8, 9, 1896, Bernard Kelly to McKinley, Jan. 13, 1896, W. L. Bates to McKinley, Feb. 13, 1896, John Boyle to E. L. Gilmore, Mar. 5, 1896, James A. Gary to McKinley, Apr. 13, 1896, Hanna to W. F. Harn, Apr. 20, 1896, McKinley Papers; Joseph P. Smith to Dawes, Nov. 8, 1895, Jan. 29, 1896, Dawes Papers.

51. Jere Brown to George F. Myers, Apr. 18, 1896, George F. Myers Papers; Felt, "Rise of Mark Hanna," pp. 282–84.

52. W. Youngblood to L. P. Morton, Feb. 28, 1896, Morton Papers; R. A. Moseley to Chandler, Mar. 10, May 15, June 2, 1896, Chandler to R. A. Moseley, June 3, 1896, Chandler Papers. Platt, *Autobiography*, p. 331; Hanna to Myers, Apr. 14, 1896, George F. Myers Papers.

53. Jere Brown to Hanna, Apr. 11, 1896, Jere Brown to Myers, June 4, 1896, George F. Myers Papers.

54. Chandler to A. L. Conger, Mar., 1896, A. L. Conger to Chandler, Mar. 21, 1896, "Special Dispatch," Mar. 22, 1896, J. M. Swank to Quay, Mar. 24, 1896 (extract copied in Chandler's handwriting), Chandler to C. E. Smith, July 2, 1896, Chandler Papers; Jones, *Election of 1896*, p. 145; Dawes, *Journal*, p. 66; Croly, *Hanna*, pp. 183–84.

55. Jones, *Election of 1896*, p. 151; Clarkson to Dodge, Mar. 6, 1896, Dodge Papers.

56. *Proceedings, 1896*, p. 123; Elkins to Reid, Mar. 10, 1896, Reid to Elkins, Mar. 17, 1896, Reid Papers; Clarkson to Allison, Mar. 10, 1896, Allison Papers; Clarkson to Dodge, May 28, 1896, Dodge Papers.

57. Edward O. Wolcott to Moreton Frewen, Apr. 25, 1896, Papers of

Moreton Frewen, LC. See Paul Glad's astute discussion of this: *McKinley, Bryan and the People,* pp. 102–3.

CHAPTER VII

1. Thomas H. McKee to Barker, Jan. 7, 1895, Barker Papers; Warner P. Sutton to Chandler, June 25, 1896, Chandler Papers; Jones, *Election of 1896,* pp. 93, 101.
2. McKinley to C. A. Boutelle, Aug. 1, 1896, McKinley to H. H. Kohlsaat, Aug. 5, 1896, W. N. Osborne to McKinley, Sept. 1, 1896, McKinley Papers. For pressure on McKinley to modify his stand see Aaron A. Ferris to McKinley, July 28, 1896, Washington Hesing to McKinley, July 25, 1896, David Baillie to McKinley, July 13, 1896, McKinley Papers.
3. McSeveney, "Politics of Depression," pp. 228–31, 242–43, 303; Glad, *McKinley, Bryan and the People,* pp. 182–83; Degler, "Political Parties and the Rise of the City," 44–45.
4. Osborne to McKinley, Sept. 1, 1896, McKinley Papers; O. H. Platt to Chandler, June 26, 1896, Chandler Papers.
5. Chandler to C. H. Grosvenor, June 24, 1896, Chandler to C. E. Smith, July 2, 1896, Frank W. Clancy to Chandler, July 9, 1896, Chandler to McKinley, July 25, 1896, D. B. Hill to Chandler, Aug. 1, 1896, Chandler Papers.
6. Francis Amasa Walker to Chandler, Sept. 12, 1896, F. A. Blade to Chandler, Nov. 13, 1896, Chandler Papers; George F. Hoar to Moreton Frewen, June 23, 1896, Moreton Frewen Papers; Philadelphia *Press,* July 1, 1896.
7. Reid to G. A. Hobart, July 2, 1896, Reid to Mr. Lyman, Aug. 17, 1896, Reid Papers.
8. Reid to John Hay, June 19, 1896, Reid Papers; Chandler to J. H. Manley, Aug. 4, 1896, Chandler Papers; Clarkson to Samuel Fessenden, July 21, 1896, Clarkson Papers, LC; Felt, "Rise of Mark Hanna," p. 344.
9. Dawes to Hanna, July 1, 1896, Dawes Papers; McKinley to Quay, June 26, 1896, Dawes to McKinley, July 3, 1896, McKinley to Hanna, July 7, 1896, Hanna to McKinley, July 8, 1896, McKinley Papers; Manley to Chandler, Aug. 7, 1896, Chandler Papers; Reid to Hanna, July 4, 1896, Hanna to Reid, July 6, 1896, Reid to Hobart, July 8, 1896, Reid Papers; Felt, "Rise of Mark Hanna," p. 324.
10. Hanna to Reid, July 6, 1896, Reid Papers; Dawes to Hanna, July 30, 1896, McKinley Papers; Felt, "Rise of Mark Hanna," pp. 330–32; Dawes, *Journal,* pp. 89–94; Jones, *Election of 1896,* pp. 160–61.
11. Clarkson to Samuel Fessenden, July 21, 1896, Clarkson Papers, LC.
12. G. B. Pray to Dodge, Aug. 12, 1896, Dodge Papers.
13. H. G. McMillan to Clarkson, Sept. 5, 1896, Clarkson Papers, LC; I. M. Treynor to Dodge, Sept. 17, 1896, Dodge Papers.

14. H. G. McMillan to Clarkson, Sept. 5, 1896, Clarkson Papers, LC; Allison to Dodge, Sept. 5, 1896, Dodge Papers; Dawes to Hanna, July 30, 1896, McKinley Papers.
15. Dawes to Hanna, July 30, 1896, Dawes to McKinley, Aug. 1, 1896, McKinley Papers; H. G. McMillan to Clarkson, Sept. 5, 1896, Clarkson to McMillan, Oct. 9, 1896, Clarkson Papers, LC.
16. Nelson Dingley, Jr. to McKinley, July 26, 1896, W. P. Frye to McKinley, July 27, 1896, McKinley Papers; Chandler to J. H. Manley, Aug. 4, 1896, Manley to Chandler, Aug. 7, 1896, Chandler Papers; Josiah Crosby to W. J. Bryan, Sept. 9, 1896, Papers of William Jennings Bryan, LC.
17. John Hay to Reid, Nov. 7, Aug. 31, 1896, Reid Papers; Justin Morrill to M. M. Parker, Oct. 22, 1896, Papers of Justin Morrill, LC.
18. H. C. Lodge to Chandler, Sept. 3, 1896, Chandler Papers; see above, Chapter VI, footnote 2.
19. Friedman and Schwartz, *Monetary History*, pp. 112–13. Curtis's statement is quoted in Barnes, "Gold Standard Democrats," pp. 440–41. On the silver scare in New York see Reid to Hanna, July 4, 1896, Reid Papers; A. H. Lewis to Bryan, July 29, 1896, Bryan Papers; W. M. Osborne to McKinley, Aug. 11, 1896, McKinley Papers.
20. List of "Gentlemen invited by Warner Miller, or Mr. Milholland and expected at 451 Madison Avenue on the evening of Thursday, June 25th, 1896," John Milholland File, Reid Papers; Reid to Hanna, June 26, July 4, 1896, Hanna to Reid, July 2, 1896, Reid to Hobart, July 8, 1896, Warner Miller to Reid, July 16, 1896, Reid Papers; David Baillie to McKinley, July 13, 1896, McKinley Papers; Platt to Quigg, Dec. 21, 1896, Quigg Papers.
21. Reid to Mr. Lyman, Aug. 19, 1896, Hanna to Reid, Aug. 22, 1896, Reid to John Milholland, Sept. 3, 1896, Reid to Mr. Tuttle, Oct. 14, 1896, Reid Papers; Platt to Morton, Aug. 4, 1896, Morton Papers; Felt, "Rise of Mark Hanna," p. 291, n. 12; Fowler, *Cabinet Politician*, pp. 253–54.
22. Clarkson to Samuel Fessenden, Oct. 15, 1896, Clarkson to H. G. McMillan, Oct. 9, 1896, Clarkson Papers, LC; Felt, "Rise of Mark Hanna," p. 333.
23. Alexander, *Political History*, IV, pp. 284–85; F. L. Stedman to Bryan, Oct. 29, 1896, George W. Batten to Bryan, Oct. 30, 1896, Bryan Papers; McSeveney, "Politics of Depression," pp. 399–463.
24. See, for example, Clarkson to Samuel Fessenden, Oct. 15, 1896, Clarkson Papers, LC.
25. Reid to McKinley, June 11, 1896, Reid to Hanna, July 23, 27, 28, 1896, Hanna to Reid, July 24, 1896, Reid Papers; Felt, "Rise of Mark Hanna," p. 325.
26. W. M. Osborne to McKinley, Aug. 11, 1896, McKinley Papers; Hanna to Reid, Aug. 22, 1896, Reid Papers; W. M. Hahn to Clarkson, Sept.

30, 1896, Clarkson to H. G. McMillan, Oct. 9, 1896, Clarkson Papers, LC; Dawes, *Journal*, pp. 95–96; Dawes to Hanna, Aug. 29, 31, 1896, Dawes Papers.

27. Glad, *McKinley, Bryan, and the People*, p. 168; Croly, *Hanna*, pp. 219–20; Josephson, *The Politicos*, pp. 697–98; Reid to John Hay, June 19, 1896, Reid Papers; Nevins, *Study in Power*, II, pp. 469–70; Thomas Beer, *Hanna* (New York, 1929), p. 162.

28. Felt, "Rise of Mark Hanna," pp. 343–44; Nevins, *Hewitt*, pp. 563–67; McKinley to Hewitt, July 30, 1896, McKinley to R. P. Flower, Aug. 4, 1896, McKinley Papers; Merrill, *Bourbon Democracy*, p. 142 and passim for Hill's political activities.

29. Nevins, *Study in Power*, II, pp. 277–79, 333, 469–70; Ralph and Muriel Hidy, *Pioneering in Big Business, 1882–1911* (New York, 1955), p. 664; Felt, "Rise of Mark Hanna," pp. 161–62.

30. The evolution of political attitudes and organizations in the large life insurance companies is very similar to that of the Standard. See Morton Keller, *The Life Insurance Enterprise* (Cambridge, Mass., 1963), pp. 214–22 and especially the statement of the President of the Mutual Life Insurance Company quoted on p. 228. Records of campaign contributions scattered through such collections as the Whitney, Cleveland, Reid, Harrison, Clarkson, Barker, and Z. Chandler Papers rarely show corporate contributions.

31. Chandler to Reid, Oct. 4, 1900, Reid Papers.

32. Andrew Carnegie to Wayne MacVeagh, Oct. 26, 1896, Papers of Wayne MacVeagh, Historical Society of Pennsylvania; Keller, *Life Insurance Enterprise*, pp. 229–30; *DAB*, XI, p. 562 on McCall; Croly, *Hanna*, p. 220; Beer, *Hanna*, p. 161, gives a striking example of enormous direct campaign services. The Republicans certainly did not win the election through fraud and intimidation, but the evidence for this political practice is extensive. With regard to 1896, by far the best discussion of the problem is in McSeveney, "Politics of Depression," pp. 435–38.

33. Reid to McKinley, Nov. 6, 1896, Reid Papers; McKinley to William D. Bynum, Nov. 7, 1896, McKinley to Francis T. Homer, Nov. 7, 1896, McKinley Papers; Nevins, *Hewitt*, pp. 563–67.

34. Clarkson to Halford, Apr. 23, 1892, Harrison Papers.

35. Croly, *Hanna*, pp. 465–79. The quotation is from p. 465.

CHAPTER VIII

1. Beer, *Hanna*, p. 134.

2. Cotter and Hennessy, *Politics Without Power*, passim; Alexander Heard, *The Costs of Democracy* (Chapel Hill, 1960), p. 289 and passim; V. O. Key, *Politics, Parties, and Pressure Groups* (5th ed.; New York, 1964), p. 342; Theodore J. Lowi, "Party, Policy, and Constitution in America," pp. 268–74.

Notes

3. Burnham, "The Changing Shape of the American Political Universe," 7–28.
4. Elmer E. Schattschneider, *The Semi-Sovereign People: A Realist's View of Democracy in America* (New York, 1960), pp. 78–85. The quotation is on p. 85.
5. For an excellent extended analysis of American parties in a comparative perspective see Leon D. Epstein, *Political Parties in Western Democracies* (New York, 1967).
6. Burnham, "Party Systems and the Political Process," in Burnham and Chambers, eds., *American Party Systems*, p. 301.
7. Recent declines in party membership in the most advanced European nations suggest that there too the effects of the extension of the suffrage—which came so much later than in the United States—are beginning to wane. If this is in fact the motive force behind high voting totals, the diminution of party memberships ought to be followed by a decline in the number of people voting and the regularity with which their voting expresses a party orientation, although naturally this result will vary according to constitutional arrangements and other factors in the different political cultures. The decline, if it comes, is not likely to be as abrupt or as extensive as in the United States. The next great turn of the American political wheel, the realignment of the thirties, regained some of the ground lost under the 1896 system. Voting totals rose and the competition between the parties re-emerged in much of the nation, as the new immigrant groups and labor organizations were grafted onto the political system. Yet even the New Deal re-adjustment did not return American politics to the levels of participation of the nineteenth century, nor do observers of American politics see this as at all likely in the future. Mobilization and participation probably cease to be primary political values in the absence of overt efforts to socialize new voters. Over the long run, mass politics may well be a more lethargic process than nineteenth-century American experience suggested, even if not quite so dead as it appeared in the era after 1896. See Epstein, *Political Parties*, pp. 250–56; Burnham, "Changing Shape of the American Political Universe."
8. Grant McConnell, *Private Power and American Democracy* (New York, 1967), passim.
9. Caroline Robbins, *The Eighteenth-Century Commonwealthsman: Studies in the Transmission, Development and Circumstance of English Liberal Thought from the Restoration of Charles II until the War with the Thirteen Colonies* (Cambridge, Mass., 1959); Robbins, " 'Discordant Parties,' A Study in the Acceptance of Party by Englishmen," *Political Science Quarterly*, LXXIII (Dec. 1958), 505–29; Bernard Bailyn, *The Ideological Origins of the American Revolution* (Cambridge, Mass., 1967).

10. See Robert H. Wiebe's careful discussion of this: *The Search for Order*, pp. 145–63.

11. There had been national conventions of a sort before the Antimasonic party, but they lacked the revival character that national conventions have maintained since. See David Hackett Fischer, *The Revolution of American Conservatism: The Federalist Party in the Era of Jeffersonian Democracy* (New York, 1965), pp. 84–90. On the Antimasonic party, see Charles McCarthy, "The Antimasonic Party," in American Historical Association, *Annual Report of the American Historical Association for the Year 1902* (2 vols.; Washington, D.C., 1903), I, pp. 365–574, esp. 398, 540–44.

12. Will Herberg, *Protestant, Catholic, Jew: An Essay in American Religious Sociology* (Garden City, 1955).

13. Wiebe, *The Search for Order*, pp. 2–10, 44; Alexis de Tocqueville, *Democracy in America*, II, 2nd Book, chapter II: "Of Individualism in Democratic Countries."

14. This is particularly suggestive since approximately one-third *more* people vote in presidential years than in any other election: Burnham, "Changing Shape of the American Political Universe," 9.

15. Independent of party, that is, not of the groups being regulated.

Index